1000 SONGS that ROCK YOUR WORLD

DAVE THOMPSON

Published by

Krause Publications, a division of F+W Media, Inc.
700 East State Street • Iola, WI 54990-0001
715-445-2214 • 888-457-2873
www.krausebooks.com

To order books or other products call toll-free 1-800-258-0929
or visit us online at www.krausebooks.com or www.Shop.Collect.com

ISBN-13: 978-1-4402-1422-6
ISBN-10: 1-4402-1422-0

Designed by Rachael L. Wolter
Edited by Dan Brownell

Printed in China

CONTENTS

INTRODUCTION

Reaching the Thousand

Compiling the top 1,000 songs in rock'n'roll history was the work of fifty-five years. That's how long rock'n'roll has been around and, in chronological terms, that's where this book begins—with Bill Haley's "Rock Around the Clock," the 1955 hit record that set the western world rocking. The song itself ranks no higher than a berth in the mid-200s here, but in terms of historical impact and importance, it was, and it remains, one of the most significant records ever made. In fact, it might be *the* most significant. Others may have changed the world or rewritten the rulebook, but "Rock Around the Clock" is what actually started the whole thing off. Everything that came afterwards was simply following in its footsteps.

So, one down, 999 to go.

The songs that make up this book were selected for a variety of reasons. Some, again, can be said to have "started" something… early huge hits for Elvis, the Beatles, the Rolling Stones, igniting careers that are still held in awe today. Others are part of the furniture… all-time radio and critical favorites by Bruce Springsteen, U2, REM, the Who, Led Zeppelin. And others are simply too huge to ignore—classics by Queen, the Blue Oyster Cult, Fleetwood Mac, Alice Cooper.

But success is only one of the criteria involved. The book delves into weekly Top 40 charts, but it also studies the record review pages in a mountain of magazines. It listens to both new and oldies radio, but it also scratches beneath the surface to see what the listeners would prefer to be hearing. It talks to friends, colleagues, associates, and music fans in and outside the music industry, to discover what they would consider the most important songs written and recorded in the past half-century-plus, but it also draws on that most intangible of qualities, the simple feeling that a record *belongs* here.

It will probably be argued, and we—the author, the editor, the publishing team in general—would agree, that not every song fits the precise definition of rock, because nobody has yet come up with one that everybody can agree with. For a time, we considered restricting the book's contents only to artists who appeared in the "Rock" section in the local music megastore—which was great until they reorganized all the categories, and Dylan turned up in the Folk section, and Yoko Ono was shifted to World Music. She has only one song on this list, but that's not the point.

Other conundrums. Nobody who contemplates the history of rock can do so without giving equal consideration to soul, funk, R&B, country, jazz, blues, disco, experimental… so many genres, so many definitions…. All have contributed much to the field, whether it's Rod Stewart or the Vanilla Fudge rewiring an old Motown classic, the Stones and

Yardbirds cutting their teeth on Robert Johnson, or Public Image Ltd wearing out their early Parliament LPs, before feeding them through some John Cage. And the borders blurred further, every time we took receipt of another list of suggested songs.

So a handful of covers crept in, songs that would never be considered rock'n'rollers in their original form, but which, in hands that were not their makers, were transformed into rock classics regardless: Vanilla Fudge's take on "You Keep Me Hanging On" (the Supremes), Elvis Presley's "Hound Dog" (Big Mama Thornton), and any number of rocking revisions of old country, blues, and soul hits. We stand by their inclusion, however, and here's why. A great song knows no borders or restrictions; it's just that sometimes, we need to hear it in a different context to realize how great it is. You're probably still not going to agree with, or even understand, the inclusion of every song on the list. But somewhere out there, there's an argument in favor of every single one of them.

And on the subject of covers... it will escape nobody's attention that, even among the rockers, a lot of the songs included here are not performed by the original artist: the Jimi Hendrix Experience taking on Dylan's "All Along the Watchtower," David Bowie's resurrection of Jacques Brel's "My Death," Depeche Mode riding Bobby Troup's "Route 66," the Carpenters' shimmering interpretation of Leon Russell's "Superstar" and—hang on a moment, the Carpenters? What do they have to do with rock'n'roll?

Aside from an unsung influence on everyone from ABBA to Sonic Youth (witness the Scott Thurston-curated Carpenters tribute); a taste in covers that ranged from Herman's Hermits to Klaatu; and a solid grip on precisely the same kind of pop beauty that made heroes of the Shangri-Las, the Beach Boys, and the rest of the early 1960s. Aside from all that. Well, we return to the definition of rock'n'roll, and the arguments you're already formulating out there. Before you write in, remember, without pop, there'd be no rock, and until the advent of the "serious" LP in 1966 (*Revolver*, *Aftermath*, and *Blonde On Blonde*), pop was almost all there was. So we celebrate it where it's wonderful, and we hope that you will as well.

The story, and the struggles, does not end there. We could fill an entire book with every argument that this volume will incite, but we will leave that for another time. For now, looking at the indexes will tell you what we have determined what the 1,000 greatest rock songs are. The rest of the book will tell you what they were *about*, in the form of a series of unique lists that range from cars, girls, and the joy of sex, to some of the most imaginative and unlikely themes and notions ever set to music.

ACKNOWLEDGMENTS

Thanks to everybody who had a hand in this book, beginning with everyone at F+W who conspired to make it such a beauty to behold, as well as Heritage Auctions for allowing us access to their photo archives.

Then to the army of friends, acquaintances and passing strangers who threw in their own suggestions as to what does and doesn't constitute a great rock song—and to all the musicians and composers who then sat down to tell me the story behind their song.

And finally—Amy Hanson,who sat and listened to the thousand with me, and helped me reject another thousand at least. Jo-Ann Greene, who debated the meaning of "rock" in the first place. Oliver, Toby and Trevor, all of whom discovered new and fascinating ways of demonstrating their own personal love or hatred of individual songs; Bateerz,who made certain there was plenty of soda… and, of course, everybody who made these songs and performances a reality in the first place. Because, without them… well, there's always Volume Two to think about, isn't there?

TOP 1000 BY RANKING

001 Bus Stop *Hollies* (20)
002 Season of the Witch *Donovan* (21)
003 Jungleland *Bruce Springsteen* (21)
004 Won't Get Fooled Again *Who* (22)
005 Rock and Roll *Gary Glitter* (22)
006 Desolation Row *Bob Dylan* (266)
007 While My Guitar Gently Weeps *Beatles* (158)
008 Year of the Cat *Al Stewart* (142)
009 Famous Blue Raincoat *Leonard Cohen* (128)
010 Gimme Shelter *Rolling Stones* (293)
011 Rhiannon *Fleetwood Mac* (41)
012 Stairway to Heaven *Led Zeppelin* (231)
013 Hey Jude *Beatles* (88)
014 Like a Hurricane *Neil Young* (73)
015 Like a Rolling Stone *Bob Dylan* (75, 88)
016 A Day in the Life *Beatles* (51)
017 Elemental Child *T Rex* (158)
018 Born To Run *Bruce Springsteen* (82)
019 I Walk on Gilded Splinters *Dr John* (274)
020 Shake Some Action *Flaming Groovies* (87)
021 Smoke on the Water *Deep Purple* (164)
022 Be Bop a Lula *Gene Vincent & His Blue Caps* (181)
023 Wish You Were Here *Pink Floyd* (91)
024 Life on Mars *David Bowie* (108)
025 Trampled Underfoot *Led Zeppelin* (82)
026 Musical Box *Genesis* (56)
027 Number One Crush *Garbage* (56)
028 I'm Not in Love *10CC* (28)
029 Lily, Rosemary, & The Jack of Hearts *Bob Dylan* (88)
030 Bridge Over Troubled Water *Simon & Garfunkel* (236)
031 She's Not There *Zombies* (100)
032 School's Out *Alice Cooper* (174)
033 Sympathy for the Devil *Rolling Stones* (291)
034 Past, Present, Future *Shangri-Las* (56)
035 Waterloo Sunset *Kinks* (196)
036 Everyday is Like Sunday *Morrissey* (171)
037 America *Simon & Garfunkel* (226)
038 Layla *Derek & The Dominos* (158)
039 Heroes and Villains *Beach Boys* (108)
040 Bad Moon Rising *Creedence Clearwater Revival* (165)
041 I'm Eighteen *Alice Cooper* (270)
042 All Along the Watchtower *Jimi Hendrix Experience* (65)
043 American Pie *Don McLean* (194)
044 Celluloid Heroes *Kinks* (108)
045 Bored Teenagers *Adverts* (270)
046 See Emily Play *Pink Floyd* (288)
047 All the Young Dudes *Mott the Hoople* (270)
048 Baba O'Riley *Who* (270)
049 Low Spark of High Heeled Boys *Traffic* (66)
050 My Generation *Who* (271)
051 The Boys Are Back in Town *Thin Lizzy* (66)
052 The Next Time *Cliff Richard* (47)
053 Bohemian Rhapsody *Queen* (201)
054 In a Broken Dream *Python Lee Jackson* (284)
055 Changing of the Guard *Bob Dylan* (137)
056 Instant Karma *Plastic Ono Band* (153)
057 Suite: Judy Blue Eyes *Crosby Stills & Nash* (296)
058 Hocus Pocus *Focus* (169)
059 Rosalita (Come Out Tonight) *Bruce Springsteen* (261)
060 Midnight Rambler *Rolling Stones* (184)
061 A Man Needs A Maid *Neil Young* (108)
062 A Groovy Kind of Love *Mindbenders* (100)
063 Dream On *Aerosmith* (239)
064 New York Mining Disaster 1941 *Bee Gees* (165)
065 Can't Find My Way Home *Blind Faith* (243)
066 Superstar *Carpenters* (113)
067 Caroline Says II *Lou Reed* (51)
068 God Only Knows *Beach Boys* (30)
069 I Feel Fine *Beatles* (156)
070 Alright Now *Free* (29)
071 D'yer Maker *Led Zeppelin* (91)
072 Let It Be *Beatles* (236)
073 Don't Fear the Reaper *Blue Oyster Cult* (51)
074 Satisfaction *Rolling Stones* (142)
075 4th of July, Asbury Park (Sandy) *Bruce Springsteen* (187)
076 Statesboro Blues *Allman Brothers* (226)
077 Silver Springs *Fleetwood Mac* (129)
078 Octopus *Syd Barrett* (198)
079 She's Gone *Hall & Oates* (47)
080 Refugees *Van Der Graaf Generator* (293)
081 Tupelo Honey *Van Morrison* (226)
082 Roadrunner *Modern Lovers* (71)
083 Reason to Believe *Rod Stewart* (120)
084 Diamonds and Rust *Joan Baez* (204)
085 You Really Got Me *Kinks* (100)
086 I'm Waiting for the Man *Velvet Underground* (144)
087 Cowgirl in the Sand *Neil Young* (159)
088 Imagine *John Lennon* (241)
089 Kashmir *Led Zeppelin* (91)
090 Bad to the Bone *George Thorogood & The Destroyers* (57)
091 Sultans of Swing *Dire Straits* (151)
092 New Rose *Damned* (296)
093 Loser *Beck* (268)
094 Ballad of a Thin Man *Bob Dylan* (284)
095 London Calling *Clash* (266)
096 Who Do You Love *Juicy Lucy* (233)
097 Across the Universe *Beatles* (243)
098 Autumn Almanac *Kinks* (231)
099 Roadhouse Blues *Doors* (82)
100 Hotel California *Eagles* (162)
101 House of the Rising Sun *Animals* (258)
102 Ball and Chain *Big Brother & The Holding Company* (253)
103 Do Ya Think I'm Sexy *Rod Stewart* (76)
104 Dust in the Wind *Kansas* (73)
105 Sunshine of Your Love *Cream* (296)
106 Come Out and Play *Offspring* (271)
107 The Boxer *Simon & Garfunkel* (272)
108 Highway to Hell *AC/DC* (83)
109 Solsbury Hill *Peter Gabriel* (92)
110 Violet *Hole* (117)
111 Funeral for a Friend Love Lies Bleeding *Elton John* (52)
112 Smells Like Teen Spirit *Nirvana* (131)
113 Take Me Out *Franz Ferdinand* (284)
114 Sweet Jane *Velvet Underground* (261)
115 God *John Lennon* (30)
116 Dead Babies *Alice Cooper* (52)
117 What Have They Done to My Song, Ma *Melanie* (201)

118 Stagger Lee *Nick Cave & The Bad Seeds* (184)
119 Another Day *Paul McCartney* (155)
120 Privilege *Patti Smith Group* (236)
121 Mother's Little Helper *Rolling Stones* (144)
122 More Than a Feeling *Boston* (176)
123 Brown Eyed Girl *Van Morrison* (129)
124 Daydream Believer *Monkees* (239)
125 Beautiful Day *U2* (291)
126 Heroes *David Bowie* (92)
127 Don't Let Me Be Misunderstood *Animals* (202)
128 Helter Skelter *Beatles* (213)
129 Wild Horses *Rolling Stones* (198)
130 Ballad of Dwight Frye *Alice Cooper* (109)
131 All Day and All of the Night *Kinks* (155)
132 White Rabbit *Jefferson Airplane* (198)
133 Eloise *Barry Ryan* (261)
134 Sara *Fleetwood Mac* (261)
135 Up on Cripple Creek *Band* (226)
136 Let It Bleed *Rolling Stones* (71)
137 Supper's Ready *Genesis* (133)
138 Abandoned Love *Bob Dylan* (204)
139 I Love Rock'n'Roll *Arrows* (71)
140 White Man in Hammersmith Palais *Clash* (196)
141 25 or 6 to 4 *Chicago* (189)
142 Summertime Blues *Eddie Cochran* (75)
143 Someone Saved My Life Tonight *Elton John* (268)
144 Sweet Baby James *James Taylor* (98)
145 Maybelline *Chuck Berry* (261)
146 These Days *Jackson Browne* (243)
147 Freight Train *Chas McDevitt Skiffle Group (Featuring Nancy Whiskey)* (172)
148 A Night Like This *Cure* (157)
149 Don't Think Twice, It's Alright *Bob Dylan* (57)
150 You Keep Me Hanging On *Vanilla Fudge* (217)
151 That'll Be the Day *Buddy Holly* (191)
152 Hurdy Gurdy Man *Donovan* (159)
153 American Woman *Guess Who* (153)
154 On the Road Again *Canned Heat* (244)
155 Walk This Way *Aerosmith* (244)
156 You Can't Always Get What You Want *Rolling Stones* (144)
157 Daniel *Bat for Lashes* (98)
158 Strawberry Fields Forever *Beatles* (78)
159 Magic Bus *Who* (244)
160 Good Vibrations *Beach Boys* (296)
161 Help *Beatles* (269)
162 Dancing in the Dark *Bruce Springsteen* (117)
163 I Still Haven't Found What I'm Looking For *U2* (120)
164 Somebody to Shove *Soul Asylum* (210)
165 No Matter What *Badfinger* (204)
166 #9 Dream *John Lennon* (240)
167 Rock and Roll Music *Chuck Berry* (147)
168 Eight Miles High *Byrds* (144)
169 Drive In Saturday *David Bowie* (176)
170 Back Street Luv *Curved Air* (224)
171 The Letter *Boxtops* (210)
172 Atlantis *Donovan* (165)
173 At the Hop *Danny & The Juniors* (281)
174 Heartbreak Hotel *Elvis Presley* (293)
175 Supernaut *Black Sabbath* (274)
176 Napoleon Bonapart One and Two *Budgie* (137)
177 American Girl *Tom Petty & The Heartbreakers* (227)
178 Echoes *Pink Floyd* (169)
179 The Knife *Genesis* (66)
180 Shape of Things *Yardbirds* (289)
181 Rebel Rebel *David Bowie* (29)
182 Gimme Some Truth *John Lennon* (266)
183 Desperado *Eagles* (137)
184 Soldier Blue *Buffy Sainte Marie* (137)
185 Watching the Detectives *Elvis Costello & The Attractions* (184)
186 Go Your Own Way *Fleetwood Mac* (47)
187 Josephine *John Otway and Wild Willy Barrett* (231)
188 Paris 1919 *John Cale* (92)
189 Someone to Lay Down Beside Me *Karla Bonoff* (112)
190 Get Back *Beatles* (117)
191 Rising Sun *Medicine Head* (249)
192 Sad Eyed Lady of the Lowlands *Bob Dylan* (297)
193 Breathing *Kate Bush* (171)
194 Bela Lugosi's Dead *Bauhaus* (109)
195 Psychotic Reaction *Count Five* (278)
196 Autobahn *Kraftwerk* (83)
197 Lust for Life *Iggy Pop* (120)
198 Longview *Green Day* (269)
199 Almost Cut My Hair *Crosby Stills Nash & Young* (153)
200 Truckin' *Grateful Dead* (245)
201 Everlong *Foo Fighters* (63)
202 Little Wing *Jimi Hendrix Experience* (103)
203 Ride Captain Ride *Blues Image* (123)
204 They Don't Know *Kirsty MacColl* (86)
205 Takin' Care of Business *Bachman Turner Overdrive* (253)
206 Jailbreak *Thin Lizzy* (253)
207 Sex and Drugs and Rock and Roll *Ian Dury & The Blockheads* (141)
208 Lay Down *Melanie* (120)
209 Riot in Cell Block #9 *Johnny Winter* (253)
210 Wild Thing *Troggs* (198)
211 Free Bird *Lynyrd Skynyrd* (103)
212 How Soon Is Now *Smiths* (77)
213 Edie *Cult* (109)
214 I Fought the Law *Bobby Fuller Four* (60)
215 Somebody to Love *Jefferson Airplane* (112)
216 Tarkus *Emerson, Lake and Palmer* (134)
217 And You And I *Yes* (31)
218 Badlands *Bruce Springsteen* (294)
219 Welcome to the Jungle *Guns 'n' Roses* (199)
220 In the Ghetto *Elvis Presley* (294)
221 Cryin' *Aerosmith* (237)
222 Pablo Picasso *Modern Lovers* (178)
223 Ramblin' Man *Allman Brothers* (245)
224 Bittersweet Symphony *Verve* (273)
225 Great Balls of Fire *Jerry Lee Lewis* (96)
226 Next (Aux Suivantes) *Sensational Alex Harvey Band* (195)
227 Fire and Rain *James Taylor* (139)
228 It's So Easy *Buddy Holly* (191)
229 Shoot Out at the Fantasy Factory *Traffic* (184)
230 Then He Kissed Me *Crystals* (75)
231 Karma Police *Radiohead* (60)

232 Back in the USA *Chuck Berry* (227)
233 Rock Around the Clock *Bill Haley & the Comets* (189)
234 Answering Machine *Replacements* (210)
235 Black Metallic *Catherine Wheel* (57)
236 After the Goldrush *Neil Young* (138)
237 The Pretender *Jackson Browne* (23)
238 Tangled Up in Blue *Bob Dylan* (217)
239 Submission *Sex Pistols* (124)
240 Johnny Hit and Run Pauline *X* (98)
241 Touch Me I'm Sick *Mudhoney* (285)
242 Fly Like an Eagle *Steve Miller Band* (103)
243 Ooh La La *Faces* (63)
244 You Look Good on the Dancefloor *Arctic Monkeys* (281)
245 Sebastian *Cockney Rebel* (99)
246 Black Sabbath *Black Sabbath* (274)
247 What is Life *George Harrison* (77)
248 In Shreds *Chameleons* (285)
249 Epitaph *King Crimson* (52)
250 Jackson *Nancy Sinatra and Lee Hazlewood* (227)
251 Everything's Alright *Mojos* (289)
252 Tom Traubert's Blues *Tom Waits* (149)
253 It's Alright Ma, I'm Only Bleeding *Bob Dylan* (121)
254 Alternate Title *Monkees* (118)
255 Marie and Joe *Doctors of Madness* (262)
256 Baby Jump *Mungo Jerry* (58)
257 Heart of Gold *Neil Young* (129)
258 Protection *Graham Parker* (113)
259 That's Entertainment *Jam* (224)
260 Rocking in the Free World *Neil Young* (266)
261 It Might as Well Rain Until September *Carole King* (139)
262 Come Together *Beatles* (278)
263 Love Reign O'er Me *Who* (139)
264 Losing My Religion *REM* (31)
265 Pink Moon *Nick Drake* (126)
266 Cortez the Killer *Neil Young* (138)
267 Everything I Own *Bread* (204)
268 Waiting for the Sun *Doors* (249)
269 Creep *Radiohead* (285)
270 Wonderful Tonight *Eric Clapton* (205)
271 Time *Pink Floyd* (189)
272 Night Moves *Bob Seger* (176)
273 You Can Make Me Dance, Sing or Anything *Faces* (205)
274 You're So Vain *Carly Simon* (121)
275 Starting Over *John Lennon* (246)
276 Let's Hang On *Four Seasons* (157)
277 Good Riddance (Time of Your Life) *Green Day* (48)
278 My Sweet Lord *George Harrison* (31)
279 Isis *Bob Dylan* (134)
280 A Hard Day's Night *Beatles* (234)
281 Big Eyes *Cheap Trick* (95)
282 I Get Around *Beach Boys* (246)
283 Little Queenie *Chuck Berry* (116)
284 Powderfinger *Neil Young* (150)
285 Hello It's Me *Todd Rundgren* (218)
286 Not Fade Away *Buddy Holly* (191)
287 Possession *Sara McLachlan* (113)
288 Everybody Hurts *REM* (269)
289 Barbara Ann *Beach Boys* (262)
290 Debris *Faces* (294)
291 Hallelujah *Leonard Cohen* (32)
292 Life During Wartime *Talking Heads* (150)
293 Why Do Fools Fall in Love *Frankie Lymon & The Teenagers* (77)
294 Jessica *Allman Brothers* (169)
295 Lady Rachel *Kevin Ayers* (240)
296 The Only Living Boy in New York *Simon & Garfunkel* (78)
297 Three Stars *Eddie Cochran* (194)
298 Devoted to You *Everly Brothers* (297)
299 Oh Boy *Buddy Holly* (191)
300 So Long Marianne *Leonard Cohen* (48)
301 Suspicious Minds *Elvis Presley* (48)
302 Space Truckin' *Deep Purple* (36)
303 Paranoid *Black Sabbath* (269)
304 The Carny *Nick Cave & The Bad Seeds* (213)
305 Roadrunner *Bo Diddley* (83)
306 Jeremy *Pearl Jam* (99)
307 Out Demons Out *Edgar Broughton Band* (266)
308 Killer Queen *Queen* (258)
309 Hey Mr Draftboard *David Peel* (154)
310 Bedsitter Images *Al Stewart* (294)
311 Shaking All Over *Johnny Kidd & The Pirates* (87)
312 The Perfect Drug *Nine Inch Nails* (149)
313 My Death *David Bowie* (195)
314 Heroin *Velvet Underground* (194)
315 Doll Parts *Hole* (114)
316 Pleasant Valley Sunday *Monkees* (294)
317 Born to be Wild *Steppenwolf* (104)
318 Venus in Furs *Velvet Underground* (142)
319 24 *Jem* (52)
320 Lady Eleanor *Lindisfarne* (262)
321 Who Knows Where the Time Goes *Fairport Convention* (77)
322 Honky Tonk Woman *Rolling Stones* (29)
323 Court of the Crimson King *King Crimson* (41)
324 Tutti Frutti *Little Richard* (88)
325 The Show Must Go On *Queen* (237)
326 Soho Square *Kirsty MacColl* (196)
327 Total Eclipse of the Heart *Bonnie Tyler* (58)
328 Don't Bring Me Down *Pretty Things* (289)
329 Nite Klub *Specials* (188)
330 96 Tears *Question Mark & The Mysterians* (237)
331 Basket Case *Green Day* (278)
332 Lady Jane *Rolling Stones* (224)
333 Song for Europe *Roxy Music* (92)
334 Clocks *Coldplay* (190)
335 A Salty Dog *Procol Harum* (124)
336 Baker Street *Gerry Rafferty* (197)
337 Badge *Cream* (210)
338 Coney Island Baby *Lou Reed* (79)
339 For No One *Beatles* (49)
340 Blitzkrieg Bop *Ramones* (281)
341 Revolution Blues *Neil Young* (67)
342 Ghost of Tom Joad *Bruce Springsteen* (291)
343 There Goes a Tenner *Kate Bush* (60)
344 Barracuda *Heart* (199)
345 Fairytale of New York *Pogues* (26)
346 Johnny Mekon *Radio Stars* (299)
347 Maggie May *Rod Stewart* (180)

348 Proud Mary *Creedence Clearwater Revival* (124)
349 Soft Wolf *Grant Lee Buffalo* (199)
350 Get Off of My Cloud *Rolling Stones* (139)
351 Till the End of the Day *Kinks* (155)
352 Up the Junction *Squeeze* (172)
353 Hold Your Head Up *Argent* (121)
354 Winona *Matthew Sweet* (109)
355 Stuck Inside of Mobile with the Memphis Blues Again *Bob Dylan* (227)
356 Days of Pearly Spencer *David McWilliams* (225)
357 Positively 4th Street *Bob Dylan* (118)
358 Funeral Party *Cure* (53)
359 Running Up That Hill *Kate Bush* (242)
360 Happy Xmas War Is Over *John Lennon* (27)
361 Tales of Brave Ulysses *Cream* (134)
362 Purple Haze *Jimi Hendrix Experience* (32)
363 Locomotive Breath *Jethro Tull* (172)
364 Firth of Fifth *Genesis* (159)
365 Nights in White Satin *Moody Blues* (126)
366 Those Were the Days *Mary Hopkin* (49)
367 Wake Up Little Susie *Everly Brothers* (110)
368 Something Else *Eddie Cochran* (83)
369 Chestnut Mare *Byrds* (199)
370 Make Me Smile (Come Up and See Me) *Steve Harley and Cockney Rebel* (297)
371 Amoruese *Kiki Dee* (112)
372 Knockin' on Heaven's Door *Bob Dylan* (53)
373 John I'm Only Dancing *David Bowie* (281)
374 Alice's Restaurant *Arlo Guthrie* (154)
375 Jumping Jack Flash *Rolling Stones* (73)
376 Paradise by the Dashboard Light *Meatloaf* (222)
377 Me and Bobby McGee *Janis Joplin* (246)
378 Somewhere in Hollywood *10CC* (110)
379 Dreaming *Blondie* (188)
380 Here There and Everywhere *Beatles* (247)
381 Madame George *Van Morrison* (262)
382 Life in Dark Water *Al Stewart* (124)
383 Carol *Chuck Berry* (263)
384 Jailhouse Rock *Elvis Presley* (254)
385 Peggy Sue *Buddy Holly* (191)
386 Midnight Rider *Greg Allman* (43)
387 Wedding Bell Blues *Laura Nyro* (277)
388 Memphis, Tennessee *Chuck Berry* (211)
389 Tomorrow Never Knows *Beatles* (86)
390 Paint It Black *Rolling Stones* (129)
391 Crazy On You *Heart* (278)
392 Big Bad Moon *Joe Satriani* (274)
393 Come Dancing *Kinks* (177)
394 White Winter Hymn *Fleet Foxes* (231)
395 Mona *Quicksilver Messenger Service* (263)
396 Invisible Sun *Police* (150)
397 Marquee Moon *Television* (126)
398 Angie *Rolling Stones* (263)
399 I'm in Love with a German Filmstar *Passions* (110)
400 Rain on the Scarecrow *John Mellencamp* (103)
401 Ruby *Kaiser Chiefs* (263)
402 Hello I Love You *Doors* (297)
403 Born Too Late *Poni Tails* (190)
404 War Pigs *Black Sabbath* (151)
405 This Wheel's on Fire *Julie Driscoll, Brian Auger & The Trinity* (96)
406 Boxers *Morrissey* (222)
407 You Ain't Seen Nothing Yet *Bachman Turner Overdrive* (205)
408 Go Now *Moody Blues* (100)
409 10:15 Saturday Night *Cure* (190)
410 Down in the Boondocks *Gregory Philips* (273)
411 Universal Soldier *Donovan* (151)
412 Bad Things *Jace Everett* (58)
413 Psycho Killer *Talking Heads* (184)
414 C'est La Vie *Emerson Lake & Palmer* (202)
415 You Can't Put Your Arms Around a Memory *Johnny Thunders* (177)
416 Light My Fire *Doors* (104)
417 California Girls *Beach Boys* (162)
418 Fireball *Deep Purple* (216)
419 Road to Cairo *Julie Driscoll, Brian Auger & The Trinity* (93)
420 Hey Hey My My *Neil Young* (147)
421 Anyone Who Had a Heart *Cilla Black* (101)
422 My Life *Dido* (121)
423 Black Water *Doobie Brothers* (228)
424 Massachussetts (The Lights Went Out In) *Bee Gees* (228)
425 Ashes to Ashes *David Bowie* (145)
426 Nobody's Fault But Mine *Led Zeppelin* (216)
427 Showroom Dummies *Kraftwerk* (45)
428 News From Spain *Al Stewart* (93)
429 Lullaby *Cure* (274)
430 Come As You Are *Nirvana* (45)
431 Black Juju *Alice Cooper* (41)
432 We Are the Dead *David Bowie* (291)
433 In the Air Tonight *Phil Collins* (131)
434 Plaistow Patricia *Ian Dury & The Blockheads* (258)
435 Astronomy Domine *Pink Floyd* (36)
436 Rock Lobster *B-52's* (199)
437 This Flight Tonight *Joni Mitchell* (167)
438 Kool Thing *Sonic Youth* (45)
439 I Don't Want to Talk About It *Rod Stewart* (218)
440 Chapel of Love *Dixie Cups* (277)
441 Self Esteem *Offspring* (285)
442 Sweet Little Rock'n' Roller *Chuck Berry* (147)
443 Black Magic Woman *Fleetwood Mac* (42)
444 Girl Don't Come *Sandy Shaw* (49)
445 Meet on the Ledge *Fairport Convention* (53)
446 Who Does Lisa Like *Rachel Sweet* (77)
447 Rock'n'Roll High School *Ramones* (174)
448 Space Oddity *David Bowie* (37)
449 Summer Breeze *Seals and Croft* (249)
450 It's the End of the World As We Know It *REM* (165)
451 How Long *Ace* (77)
452 Where Do You Go to My Lovely *Peter Sarstedt* (23)
453 Too Much to Dream Last Night *Electric Prunes* (145)
454 Jeepster *T Rex* (63)
455 We're an American Band *Grand Funk* (228)
456 It's My Life *Animals* (121)
457 Under Pressure *Queen & David Bowie* (89)
458 A Whiter Shade of Pale *Procol Harum* (130)
459 Faith Healer *Sensational Alex Harvey Band* (275)
460 White Punks on Dope *Tubes* (271)

461 Tusk *Fleetwood Mac* (143)
462 Sunny Afternoon *Kinks* (249)
463 It's All Over Now Baby Blue *Bob Dylan* (118)
464 Hey Lord Don't Ask Me Questions *Graham Parker & The Rumour* (33)
465 Fifteen Minutes *Kirsty MacColl* (114)
466 Bachelor Boy *Cliff Richard* (277)
467 It's My Party *Lesley Gore* (49)
468 Alive *Pearl Jam* (185)
469 Subterranean Homesick Blues *Bob Dylan* (276)
470 Hasten Down the Wind *Linda Ronstadt* (74)
471 Another Girl Another Planet *Only Ones* (37)
472 Sara Smile *Hall & Oates* (264)
473 When We Were Fab *George Harrison* (177)
474 Dead Man's Curve *Jan and Dean* (84)
475 Jack the Ripper *Morrissey* (185)
476 Have You Ever Seen the Rain *Creedence Clearwater Revival* (71)
477 Gold *John Stewart* (114)
478 Dead End Street *Kinks* (295)
479 Passion *Rod Stewart* (143)
480 It Doesn't Matter Anymore *Buddy Holly* (191)
481 Suzanne *Leonard Cohen* (264)
482 Eve of Destruction *Barry McGuire* (154)
483 Down in the Tube Station *Jam* (197)
484 Berlin *Udo Lindenberg* (93)
485 The Night They Drove Old Dixie Down *Band* (138)
486 Death Disco *Public Image Ltd* (281)
487 (I Don't Want to Go to) Chelsea *Elvis Costello & The Attractions* (197)
488 I Don't Like Mondays *Boomtown Rats* (175)
489 Ghost Town *Specials* (267)
490 Anarchy in the UK *Sex Pistols* (67)
491 No Rain *Blind Melon* (140)
492 Promised Land *Johnny Allen* (162)
493 Change *Sparks* (140)
494 Johnny Remember Me *John Leyton* (53)
495 Blind Willie McTell *Bob Dylan* (276)
496 White Light White Heat *Velvet Underground* (130)
497 Song for Guy *Elton John* (169)
498 Gimme Some Loving *Spencer Davis Group* (143)
499 Little Deuce Coupe *Beach Boys* (84)
500 Rosalyn *Pretty Things* (289)
501 Spirit of Christmas *Steve Ashley* (27)
502 Blockbuster *Sweet* (61)
503 Can't Get Enough *Bad Company* (205)
504 Standing Outside a Broken Phone Booth with Money in My Hand *Primitive Radio Gods* (211)
505 Journey from Eden *Steve Miller Band* (240)
506 California Dreamin' *Mamas & The Papas* (162)
507 Three Steps to Heaven *Eddie Cochran* (297)
508 Emma *Hot Chocolate* (53)
509 Criminal World *Metro* (58)
510 It's Only Love *Beatles* (156)
511 Wishing Well *Free* (214)
512 Whole Lotta Shakin' Goin' On *Jerry Lee Lewis* (87)
513 Wild World *Cat Stevens* (114)
514 Burning of the Midnight Lamp *Jimi Hendrix Experience* (97)
515 Love Me Tender *Elvis Presley* (166)
516 City of New Orleans *Arlo Guthrie* (173)
517 Zombie *Cranberries* (151)
518 Zoom Club *Budgie* (281)
519 Parisienne Walkways *Gary Moore* (93)
520 Rita Mae *Bob Dylan* (264)
521 Ace of Spades *Motorhead* (286)
522 One of These Nights *Eagles* (275)
523 Tomahawk Cruise *TV Smith* (171)
524 Willin' *Little Feat* (247)
525 Brothers in Arms *Dire Straits* (151)
526 Jennifer Juniper *Donovan* (203)
527 Berlin *Lou Reed* (93)
528 This Is Hardcore *Pulp* (110)
529 Pretty in Pink *Psychedelic Furs* (130)
530 All I Have to Do Is Dream *Everly Brothers* (205)
531 Rikki Don't Lose That Number *Steely Dan* (157)
532 Werewolves of London *Warren Zevon* (197)
533 Porpoise Song *Monkees* (199)
534 Metal Guru *T Rex* (211)
535 Since I've Been Loving You *Led Zeppelin* (297)
536 Hey Joe *Jimi Hendrix Experience* (105)
537 Friday on My Mind *Easybeats* (289)
538 Fox on the Run *Sweet* (200)
539 Lucille *Little Richard* (166)
540 Virginia Plain *Roxy Music* (178)
541 The Weight *Band* (234)
542 Jack and Diane *John Mellencamp* (99)
543 Leader of the Gang *Gary Glitter* (43)
544 Ever Fallen in Love *Buzzcocks* (206)
545 Leader of the Pack *Shangri-Las* (43)
546 Radio Activity *Kraftwerk* (160)
547 First of May *Bee Gees* (177)
548 Halloween Parade *Lou Reed* (34)
549 Rock On *David Essex* (148)
550 I've Seen All Good People *Yes* (154)
551 The Witch *Cult* (42)
552 Never Turn Your Back on Mother Earth *Sparks* (163)
553 Bat Out of Hell *Meatloaf* (200)
554 I Don't Want to Know *Nils Lofgren* (118)
555 Pride (in the Name of Love) *U2* (53)
556 I Want to Kill You *David Peel* (163)
557 The Air That I Breathe *Hollies* (132)
558 Young Americans *David Bowie* (228)
559 Muswell Hillbillies *Kinks* (225)
560 Dance Me to the End of Love *Leonard Cohen* (282)
561 Andmoreagain *Love* (105)
562 Woodstock *Joni Mitchell* (242)
563 Folk Song *Jack Bruce* (95)
564 Maybe Baby *Buddy Holly* (181)
565 Glory Box *Portishead* (237)
566 16 Again *Buzzcocks* (188)
567 Money *Pink Floyd* (24)
568 Immigrant Song *Led Zeppelin* (138)
569 The Wind Cries Mary *Jimi Hendrix Experience* (74)
570 Iron Man *Black Sabbath* (251)
571 Blackberry Way *Move* (130)
572 Oliver's Army *Elvis Costello & The Attractions* (267)
573 Californication *Red Hot Chili Peppers* (162)

574 Walk Away Renee *Left Banke* (29)
575 For Your Love *Yardbirds* (101)
576 We Gotta Get Out of This Place *Animals* (254)
577 Apache *Shadows* (170)
578 Village Green *Kinks* (177)
579 Roundabout *Yes* (214)
580 Brass in Pocket *Pretenders* (24)
581 All Shook Up *Elvis Presley* (87)
582 The Sounds of Silence *Simon & Garfunkel* (122)
583 Hippy Hippy Shake *Swinging Blue Jeans* (87)
584 Matchstalk Men and Matchstick Cats and Dogs *Brian & Michael* (178)
585 I Want You, I Need You, I Love You *Elvis Presley* (181)
586 Hello Spaceboy *David Bowie* (251)
587 Sharp Dressed Man *ZZ Top* (46)
588 I Hate Banks *Mojo Nixon and Skid Roper* (25)
589 Cathy's Clown *Everly Brothers* (214)
590 Rubber Bullets *10CC* (254)
591 Expecting to Fly *Buffalo Springfield* (167)
592 God Save the Queen *Sex Pistols* (116)
593 To Know Him Is to Love Him *Teddy Bears* (206)
594 Big Yellow Taxi *Joni Mitchell* (242)
595 Blue Jean Bop *Gene Vincent & His Blue Caps* (282)
596 Girls and Boys *Blur* (34)
597 Elenore *Turtles* (264)
598 Red Right Hand *Nick Cave & The Bad Seeds* (89)
599 Johnny B Goode *Chuck Berry* (166)
600 High and Dry *Radiohead* (44)
601 Sunday Bloody Sunday *U2* (67)
602 My White Bicycle *Nazareth* (145)
603 Excerpt from a Teenaged Opera *Keith West* (54)
604 Bo Diddley *Bo Diddley* (156)
605 Ebony Eyes *Everly Brothers* (167)
606 Glad All Over *Dave Clark 5* (101)
607 Speedway *Morrissey* (44)
608 Harvest Moon *Neil Young* (126)
609 Dancing Barefoot *Patti Smith Group* (282)
610 Police Car *Larry Wallis* (61)
611 America *Nice* (229)
612 Mr Soul *Buffalo Springfield* (114)
613 Hurt *Nine Inch Nails* (237)
614 Stay with Me *Faces* (143)
615 Pipeline *Chantays* (170)
616 For You *Judy Tzuke* (298)
617 Young Turks *Rod Stewart* (271)
618 Sheep *Pink Floyd* (200)
619 I Walked with a Zombie *Roky Erickson* (275)
620 Nineteenth Nervous Breakdown *Rolling Stones* (278)
621 Silhouettes *Herman's Hermits* (102)
622 Starman *David Bowie* (251)
623 A Touch of Grey *Grateful Dead* (180)
624 Happy Together *Turtles* (277)
625 Search and Destroy *Stooges* (271)
626 New Ways Are Best *TV Smith* (177)
627 The Jack *AC/DC* (286)
628 Trouble Coming Every Day *Mothers of Invention* (67)
629 Sweet Child of Mine *Guns 'n' Roses* (298)
630 Moonage Daydream *David Bowie* (37)
631 Kiss Me on a Bus *Replacements* (247)
632 Achilles Last Stand *Led Zeppelin* (134)
633 Peaches *Stranglers* (187)
634 Here Comes the Night *Them* (289)
635 Love Will Tear Us Apart *Joy Division* (89)
636 I Can't Explain *Who* (290)
637 Je T'aime *Serge Gainsbourg & Jane Birken* (203)
638 Starless *King Crimson* (292)
639 Veronika *Tricky* (264)
640 Reward *Teardrop Explodes* (114)
641 AC/DC *Sweet* (72)
642 Sonic Reducer *Dead Boys* (272)
643 Hypnotized *Fleetwood Mac* (214)
644 Dead Leaves & The Dirty Ground *White Stripes* (232)
645 In a Gadda Da Vida *Iron Butterfly* (105)
646 Roxette *Dr Feelgood* (259)
647 Eight Days a Week *Beatles* (155)
648 Memory Motel *Rolling Stones* (295)
649 Cincinatti Fatback *Roogalator* (229)
650 Volunteers *Jefferson Airplane* (151)
651 Blinded by the Light *Bruce Springsteen* (214)
652 I Wanna Be Sedated *Ramones* (278)
653 The State That I Am In *Belle and Sebastian* (269)
654 Tupelo *Nick Cave & The Bad Seeds* (165)
655 Vincent *Don McLean* (178)
656 California Uber Alles *Dead Kennedys* (162)
657 Eastbourne Ladies *Kevin Coyne* (225)
658 1984 *Spirit* (292)
659 The End *Doors* (134)
660 Saturday Gigs *Mott the Hoople* (46)
661 Haitian Divorce *Steely Dan* (218)
662 Centerfield *John Fogerty* (223)
663 Sweet Home Alabama *Lynyrd Skynyrd* (229)
664 Daydream *Lovin' Spoonful* (250)
665 First We Take Manhattan *Leonard Cohen* (79)
666 Song to Comus *Comus* (135)
667 Rooster *Alice in Chains* (103)
668 Perfect Day *Lou Reed* (250)
669 It Don't Come Easy *Ringo Starr* (276)
670 Flash *Queen* (252)
671 SWLABR *Cream* (63)
672 2000 Light Years From Home *Rolling Stones* (37)
673 Capital Radio *Clash* (160)
674 Ballroom Blitz *Sweet* (282)
675 Run Run Run *Jo Jo Gunne* (247)
676 Melissa *Allman Brothers* (265)
677 I Am a Rock *Simon & Garfunkel* (90)
678 Let's Make the Water Turn Black *Mothers of Invention* (163)
679 China Girl *Iggy Pop* (247)
680 Death Is Not the End *Nick Cave & The Bad Seeds* (54)
681 Shots *Neil Young* (152)
682 Overnight Sensation *Raspberries* (115)
683 Cygnet Committee *David Bowie* (68)
684 New Age *Velvet Underground* (110)
685 No Fun *Stooges* (272)
686 The Last Resort *Eagles* (163)
687 Itchycoo Park *Small Faces* (145)
688 Rat Trap *Boomtown Rats* (68)
689 Moondance *Van Morrision* (127)

690 White Riot *Clash* (68)
691 Band on the Run *Paul McCartney & Wings* (255)
692 Ballad of John and Yoko *Beatles* (277)
693 24 Hours from Tulsa *Gene Pitney* (229)
694 Andy Warhol *David Bowie* (179)
695 I Feel Like I'm Fixing to Die Rag *Country Joe & The Fish* (152)
696 Are Friends Electric *Tubeway Army* (252)
697 Say Hello Wave Goodbye *Soft Cell* (118)
698 Saturday Night *Bay City Rollers* (155)
699 Rebellion *Arcade Fire* (122)
700 Needles and Pins *Searchers* (102)
701 August Day *Hall and Oates* (95)
702 Hold the Line *Toto* (190)
703 Abacab *Genesis* (64)
704 Where Have All the Good Times Gone *Kinks* (290)
705 Da Doo Ron Ron *Crystals* (64)
706 Telstar *Tornadoes* (40)
707 Fell in Love with a Girl *White Stripes* (218)
708 A Lover's Concerto *Toys* (298)
709 The Only Living Boy in New Cross *Carter USM* (267)
710 Sheena Is a Punk Rocker *Ramones* (265)
711 Mad Eyed Screamer *Creatures* (188)
712 Devil Woman *Cliff Richard* (42)
713 Strange Brew *Cream* (149)
714 Play with Fire *Rolling Stones* (273)
715 When Will I Be Loved *Everly Brothers* (77)
716 Broken English *Marianne Faithfull* (203)
717 Move It *Cliff Richard* (148)
718 Alone Again Or *Love* (283)
719 Alley Oop *Hollywood Argyles* (138)
720 Deuce *Kiss* (286)
721 To Bring You My Love *PJ Harvey* (248)
722 Cherry Bomb *Runaways* (272)
723 Two Princes *Spin Doctors* (116)
724 Maybe *Chantels* (218)
725 Living Next Door to Alice *Smokey* (295)
726 Brown Sugar *Rolling Stones* (166)
727 Jane Says *Jane's Addiction* (265)
728 Surf's Up *Beach Boys* (187)
729 I'm Going Home *Ten Years After* (216)
730 The Joker *Steve Miller Band* (287)
731 Atomic *Blondie* (206)
732 Plush *Stone Temple Pilots* (59)
733 Arizona *Alejandro Escoveda* (230)
734 Master of the Universe *Hawkwind* (252)
735 I Wanna Be Your Dog *Stooges* (72)
736 Going Up the Country *Canned Heat* (248)
737 All Apologies *Nirvana* (115)
738 C Moon *Wings* (127)
739 Hole in My Shoe *Traffic* (248)
740 Deal *Grateful Dead* (287)
741 The River *Bruce Springsteen* (122)
742 Carry on Wayward Son *Kansas* (272)
743 Love Will Come Through *Travis* (157)
744 Presence of the Lord *Blind Faith* (33)
745 Piece of My Heart *Big Brother & The Holding Company* (50)
746 Hell Is Round the Corner *Tricky* (295)
747 Aqualung *Jethro Tull* (125)
748 Indian Reservation *Paul Revere & The Raiders* (138)
749 Spinning Wheel *Blood Sweat and Tears* (215)
750 Radio Free Europe *REM* (160)
751 Lovecats *Cure* (200)
752 Queen Bitch *David Bowie* (34)
753 This Corrosion *Sisters of Mercy* (119)
754 Ciao *Lush* (50)
755 Terry *Twinkle* (54)
756 Lake of Fire *Meat Puppets* (295)
757 Jump *Van Halen* (223)
758 Pictures of Lily *Who* (112)
759 Route 66 *Depeche Mode* (84)
760 Metal Postcard *Siouxsie & The Banshees* (267)
761 Coz I Luv You *Slade* (206)
762 I Got You Babe *Sonny and Cher* (207)
763 Sweeter Memories *Todd Rundgren* (95)
764 20 Flight Rock *Eddie Cochran* (181)
765 I'm Ready *Fats Domino* (181)
766 Ruby Tuesday *Rolling Stones* (155)
767 Lola *Kinks* (35)
768 Lithium *Nirvana* (145)
769 When the Sun Goes Down *Arctic Monkeys* (259)
770 Everyday *Buddy Holly* (191)
771 What'd I Say? *Ray Charles* (88)
772 Killing Moon *Echo & The Bunnymen* (279)
773 Something in the Air *Thunderclap Newman* (132)
774 For What It's Worth *Buffalo Springfield* (69)
775 Mrs Robinson *Simon & Garfunkel* (180)
776 San Francisco Nights *Eric Burdon & The Animals* (162)
777 She Sells Sanctuary *Cult* (259)
778 Shattered *Rolling Stones* (79)
779 Gloria *Patti Smith Group* (33)
780 Radio Radio *Elvis Costello & The Attractions* (160)
781 Mississippi Queen *Mountain* (230)
782 Boys and Girls *Bryan Ferry* (269)
783 Green Manalishi *Fleetwood Mac* (275)
784 Monkberry Moon Delight *Paul McCartney* (95)
785 Stoned Soul Picnic *Laura Nyro* (145)
786 A Hard Rain's A-Gonna Fall *Bob Dylan* (171)
787 Jesus of Suburbia *Green Day* (33)
788 Love is Like Oxygen *Sweet* (132)
789 Homeward Bound *Simon & Garfunkel* (173)
790 Pinball Wizard *Who* (215)
791 Close Watch *John Cale* (298)
792 Reconnez Cherie *Wreckless Eric* (203)
793 Jet *Paul McCartney & Wings* (168)
794 The Rocker *AC/DC* (216)
795 Trans-Europe Express *Kraftwerk* (173)
796 It's Different for Girls *Joe Jackson* (86)
797 Song to the Siren *Tim Buckley* (136)
798 Crystallized *XX* (269)
799 Nature's Way *Spirit* (215)
800 A Certain Girl *Yardbirds* (207)
801 Lost Cause *Beck* (238)
802 Termination *Iron Butterfly* (54)
803 Wear Your Love Like Heaven *Donovan* (130)
804 Kiss on the Lips *Joan Jett* (59)
805 Walk Don't Run *Ventures* (170)

806 Soul Sacrifice *Santana* (170)
807 Whole Lotta Love *Led Zeppelin* (75)
808 Dark End of the Street *Linda Ronstadt* (295)
809 Under the Bridge *Red Hot Chili Peppers* (146)
810 Because the Night *Patti Smith Group* (127)
811 Delilah *Tom Jones* (185)
812 Don't Forget to Dance *Kinks* (180)
813 Morning Glory *Tim Buckley* (225)
814 I'm a Man *Bo Diddley* (86)
815 Madman Across the Water *Elton John* (279)
816 Breakdown *Tom Petty & The Heartbreakers* (157)
817 Seether *Veruca Salt* (119)
818 Louie Louie *Kingsmen* (72)
819 Caring Is Creepy *Shins* (59)
820 Holiday on the Moon *Love and Rockets* (40)
821 Angeline *Faithless* (259)
822 Alcohol *Kinks* (149)
823 Tobacco Road *Nashville Teens* (230)
824 Monkey Gone to Heaven *Pixies* (200)
825 Back Street Girl *Rolling Stones* (273)
826 Do the Strand *Roxy Music* (283)
827 The Girl Can't Help It *Little Richard* (279)
828 Pack Up Your Sorrows *Richard and Mimi Farina* (238)
829 I Just Wanna Make Love to You *Rolling Stones* (166)
830 Sunburn *Muse* (250)
831 Star *Stealers Wheel* (115)
832 Everyone Says Hi *David Bowie* (211)
833 Pandora's Box *Procol Harum* (136)
834 The Carnival Is Over *Seekers* (215)
835 No Regrets *Walker Brothers* (219)
836 Stand by Me *John Lennon* (207)
837 Without You *Nilsson* (219)
838 Time of the Season *Zombies* (232)
839 Willie & The Hand Jive *Eric Clapton* (283)
840 Eminence Front *Who* (190)
841 Remember Walking in the Sand *Shangri-Las* (187)
842 Love Is the Drug *Roxy Music* (112)
843 Amos Moses *Sensational Alex Harvey Band* (186)
844 Suffocate *Green Day* (149)
845 Nantucket Sleighride *Mountain* (125)
846 Life's a Gas *T Rex* (132)
847 Surf City *Jan and Dean* (187)
848 Black Heart *Marc & The Mambas* (90)
849 Strange Kind of Woman *Deep Purple* (259)
850 La Grange *ZZ Top* (260)
851 Reno, Nevada *Richard and Mimi Farina* (230)
852 Bullet with Butterfly Wings *Smashing Pumpkins* (115)
853 Big Black Smoke *Kinks* (197)
854 Do Wah Diddy Diddy *Manfred Mann* (64)
855 Hurricane *Bob Dylan* (223)
856 St Petersburg *Robyn Hitchcock* (94)
857 Wrecking Ball *Emmylou Harris* (283)
858 Sister Morphine *Rolling Stones* (146)
859 London Boys *David Bowie* (290)
860 You Can't Judge a Book by Its Cover *Bo Diddley* (156)
861 Walking on Thin Ice *Yoko Ono* (279)
862 When We Meet Again *Nicole Reynolds* (157)
863 The High Road *Broken Bells* (146)
864 A Night In *Tindersticks* (127)
865 SOS *ABBA* (211)
866 Lalena *Donovan* (260)
867 Second Skin *Gits* (238)
868 No Milk Today *Herman's Hermits* (238)
869 Opal *Syd Barrett* (156)
870 Ohio *Crosby Stills Nash & Young* (69)
871 House of Fun *Madness* (112)
872 Do You Realize *Flaming Lips* (77)
873 Straight to Hell *Clash* (152)
874 All the Things She Said *Tatu* (212)
875 Rave On *Buddy Holly* (191)
876 Come Back *Mighty Wah!* (122)
877 Ballad of Easy Rider *Byrds* (44)
878 Tired of Waiting For You *Kinks* (50)
879 Crazy *Gnarls Barkley* (279)
880 Brand new Cadillac *Vince Taylor* (84)
881 Radar Love *Golden Earring* (85)
882 Refugee *Tom Petty & The Heartbreakers* (206)
883 Freshmen *Verve Pipe* (175)
884 Whole Wide World *Wreckless Eric* (94)
885 50 Ways to Leave *Paul Simon* (219)
886 Old Wild Men *10CC* (299)
887 Child in Time *Deep Purple* (152)
888 Back On the Chaingang *Pretenders* (255)
889 Desire *U2* (143)
890 Panic *Smiths* (161)
891 Kick Out the Jams *MC5* (272)
892 Far Far Away *Slade* (248)
893 Southern Pacific *Neil Young* (173)
894 Silver Machine *Hawkwind* (40)
895 Drag *Low* (90)
896 Communication Breakdown *Led Zeppelin* (212)
897 Helen Wheels *Paul McCartney & Wings* (85)
898 No-One Knows *Queens of the Stone Age* (125)
899 Golden Age of Rock'n' Roll *Mott the Hoople* (148)
900 Jenny Was a Friend of Mine *Killers* (186)
901 Maybe I'm Amazed *Paul McCartney* (298)
902 Rol& The Headless Thompson Gunner *Warren Zevon* (275)
903 Tush *ZZ Top* (72)
904 I Can Never Go Home Anymore *Shangri-Las* (90)
905 Whipping Post *Allman Brothers* (255)
906 The Jean Genie *David Bowie* (292)
907 I Want to See the Bright Lights *Richard Thompson* (149)
908 Blank Generation *Richard Hell* (272)
909 Ferry Cross the Mersey *Gerry & the Pacemakers* (102)
910 Runaway Train *Soul Asylum* (173)
911 King of the Rumbling Spires *Tyrannosaurus Rex* (116)
912 Bye Bye Johnny *Chuck Berry* (99)
913 One Headlight *Wallflowers* (85)
914 Stoney End *Laura Nyro* (295)
915 Buddy Holly *Weezer* (194)
916 Nowadays Clancy Can't Even Sing *Buffalo Springfield* (86)
917 Story of the Blues *Wah!* (276)
918 Adam Raised a Cain *Bruce Springsteen* (138)
919 God Gave Rock'n' Roll to You *Argent* (148)
920 Magic Man *Heart* (275)
921 Oxford Comma *Vampire Weekend* (292)
922 Dirty Deeds Done Dirt Cheap *AC/DC* (234)

923 On the Radio *Cheap Trick* (161)
924 Alone Again Naturally *Gilbert O'Sullivan* (55)
925 Another Brick in the Wall *Pink Floyd* (175)
926 Fire *Crazy World of Arthur Brown* (97)
927 Tell Laura I Love Her *Ricky Valance* (55)
928 Here's Where the Story Ends *Sundays* (292)
929 Brand New Key *Melanie* (146)
930 Duncan *Paul Simon* (99)
931 I'm a Boy *Who* (35)
932 Take the Money and Run *Steve Miller Band* (25)
933 Ballrooms of Mars *T Rex* (283)
934 When Do I Get To Sing 'My Way'? *Sparks* (119)
935 Tunnel of Love *Fun Boy Three* (119)
936 Your Woman *White Town* (219)
937 Merry Xmas Everybody *Slade* (28)
938 July Flame *Laura Veirs* (250)
939 New Year's Day *U2* (28)
940 If You Go Away *Marc & The Mambas* (195)
941 Political World *Bob Dylan* (267)
942 As Tears Go By *Marianne Faithfull* (273)
943 TV Eye *Stooges* (110)
944 Seven Nation Army *White Stripes* (115)
945 Hound Dog *Elvis Presley* (75)
946 You Wear It Well *Rod Stewart* (46)
947 Hey Nineteen *Steely Dan* (180)
948 Talking Airplane Disaster Blues *Phil Ochs* (168)
949 This Town Ain't Big Enough For Both of Us *Sparks* (186)
950 My Hero *Foo Fighters* (122)
951 Race with the Devil *Gene Vincent & His Blue Caps* (275)
952 Prince Charming *Adam & The Ants* (116)
953 Sex and Candy *Marci Playground* (143)
954 Love U More *Sunscreem* (143)
955 Sylvia *Focus* (170)
956 Conquistador *Procol Harum* (138)
957 Fun Fun Fun *Beach Boys* (85)
958 Loaded *Primal Scream* (146)
959 On the Beach *Neil Young* (187)
960 Blowing in the Wind *Bob Dylan* (74)
961 Kodachrome *Paul Simon* (130)
962 Vienna *Ultravox* (94)
963 Love and a Molotov Cocktail *Flys* (69)
964 Garden Party *Ricky Nelson* (299)
965 Crying in the Rain *Everly Brothers* (140)
966 Boy in the Bubble *Paul Simon* (40)
967 Everyday is Halloween *Ministry* (232)
968 The French Song *Joan Jett* (203)
969 Worcester City *Eliza Carthy* (186)
970 Dance to the Bop *Gene Vincent & His Blue Caps* (283)
971 Get It On *T Rex* (29)
972 Radio Radio Radio *Rancid* (161)
973 Samba Pa Ti *Santana* (170)
974 End of the World *Skeeter Davis* (285)
975 Fade Into You *Mazzy Star* (35)
976 July Morning *Uriah Heep* (250)
977 In Bloom *Nirvana* (119)
978 Rowche Rumble *Fall* (188)
979 I Wish You Would *Yardbirds* (290)
980 Good Morning Little Schoolgirl *Yardbirds* (175)
981 ME-262 *Blue Oyster Cult* (168)
982 Paraffin *Ruby* (59)
983 I Guess That's Why They Call It the Blues *Elton John* (276)
984 Ex-Girlfriend *No Doubt* (219)
985 March of the Black Queen *Queen* (42)
986 Rock'n' Roll Suicide *David Bowie* (299)
987 In the Summertime *Mungo Jerry* (250)
988 Rock the Casbah *Clash* (94)
989 Megalomania *Black Sabbath* (279)
990 Carrie *Cliff Richard* (265)
991 Dope Show *Marilyn Manson* (146)
992 Shipbuilding *Robert Wyatt* (267)
993 Semaphore Signals *Wreckless Eric* (212)
994 Mandolin Wind *Rod Stewart* (74)
995 Jackie *Scott Walker* (195)
996 Shake Your Money Maker *Fleetwood Mac* (87)
997 Granny Takes a Trip *Purple Gang* (146)
998 Indian Summer *Doors* (232)
999 Jive Talking *Bee Gees* (64)
1,000 Telephone Line *Electric Light Orchestra* (212)

THE FIRST FIVE

The top five songs ever written and recorded, and not one of them is "Bridge Over Troubled Water," "Hey Jude" or "Like A Rolling Stone," or any of those others that so habitually top lists like this that you could almost believe five minutes of "na-na-na' really were the peak of John Lennon and PaulMcCartney's musical endeavors.

The five songs here were selected because they speak not to the rock critic in all of us, but to the music lover... and there is a difference. Hear them and weep.

♫ #1 Bus Stop BY THE HOLLIES (1966)

Composed by Graham Gouldman, the one UK songwriter who seriously rivaled Lennon/McCartney's grasp of melody in the sixties, "Bus Stop" was just one in a stream of hits for Graham Nash and co. But it arrived bedecked with such glorious harmonies and magnificent melody that nothing else they ever did came close. In common with many of Gouldman's compositions—and, by 1965, he was already writing hits for the Yardbirds (575) and Herman's Hermits (868)—the song was at least partially written with his father, Hyme Gouldman.

"The idea for [Bus Stop] came to me one day when I was sitting on the bus, going home from work, looking at a bus stop from the window. I told my father about the idea and another day when I came home, he'd written the words… He'd written *'Bus stop, wet day, she's there, I say please share my umbrella,'* and it's like when you get a really great part of a lyric or, I also had this nice riff as well, and when you have such a great start to a song it's kind of like the rest is easy. It's like finding your way onto a road and when you get onto the right route, you just follow it. So I took that up to my bedroom and then wrote the song, except for the middle eight, which I finished off on the bus going to work."

The Hollies were inducted into the Rock and Roll Hall of Fame in 2010. "Bus Stop" tells you why.

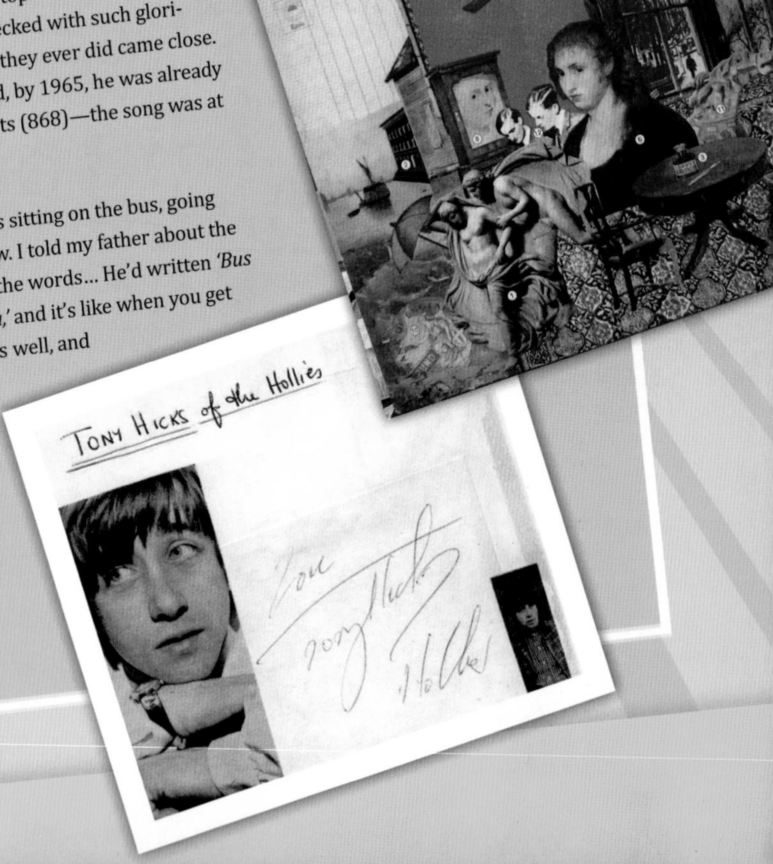

THE HOLLIES' GREATEST HITS
1 BUS STOP
2 CARRIE-ANNE
3 DEAR ELOISE
4 LOOK THROUGH ANY WINDOW
5 STOP, STOP, STOP
6 LONG COOL WOMAN IN A BLACK DRESS
7 LONG DARK ROAD
8 JUST ONE LOOK
9 KING MIDAS IN REVERSE
10 PAY YOU BACK WITH INTEREST
11 ON A CAROUSEL
12 HE AIN'T HEAVY, HE'S MY BROTHER
TONY HICKS of the Hollies

♫ #2 Season of the Witch BY DONOVAN (1966)

"The tune was seminal," Donovan wrote of "Season of the Witch." "The riff is pure feel. My early practice on drums found its way into the groove. The lyric of 'Season of the Witch' proved to be prophetic in the months to come. There is a line in it that goes 'some other cat looking over his shoulder at me,' and there were certainly cats looking over their shoulder at me. Soon these bad cats would come calling at my door."

He told his *The Hurdy Gurdy Man* autobiography, "Led Zeppelin often played 'Season of the Witch' (actually, it was Robert Plant) [and it] would be recorded by Al Kooper and Steven Stills. Julie Driscoll and Brian Auger would also make it a must in their music." He is being modest. Since "Season of the Witch" first fetched up on his *Sunshine Superman* album, majestic covers by, indeed, Driscoll/Auger and Kooper/Stills have been followed by fresh takes by Vanilla Fudge, Terry Reid, Pesky Gee!, Dr John, Hole, Luna, Joan Jett, and Richard Thompson.

Of these, Pesky Gee!'s version is simply shimmering, with Kay Garrett staking her claim amongst the most astonishing, and astonishingly unsung, British vocalists of the late 1960s. Jett's version is strangely spectral; Thompson's is tired and world-weary. But Driscoll/Auger's is perhaps the finest, despite Auger admitting, "I never imagined I would ever be doing a Donovan cover. A lot of those tunes that Julie chose, they were kind of enigmas to me, how to turn them around so they sounded like Julie Driscoll, Brian Auger and the Trinity! If you listen to the Donovan version, it's much, much faster tempo, and so these things were kind of conundrums, how to arrange them so that they fit into our repertoire, and we give them our own stamp?"

♫ #3 Jungleland BY BRUCE SPRINGSTEEN (1975)

The greatest of all Springsteen's street fighting epics (or anybody else's, for that matter), the ultimate American dream-turned-nightmare resets *West Side Story* on the New Jersey Turnpike, where pianos tinkle to the clash of switchblades and every lyric chases the hungry and the hunted round the parking lot battlefield.

#4 Won't Get Fooled Again BY THE WHO (1971)

IN HIS OWN WORDS—JOHN ENTWISTLE (bassist): Of all the songs that Pete wrote during that period of the Who, 'Won't Get Fooled Again' really stands out, because he was saying things that really mattered to him, and saying them for the first time. So those lyrics just came out of him in one long flood of anger and frustration, and then he built everything up around it. By the time he was finished with the demo there really wasn't anything left for the rest of us to do, and that was always when the Who were at their best, because it was like 'you think you're finished? We'll show you, you bastard...."

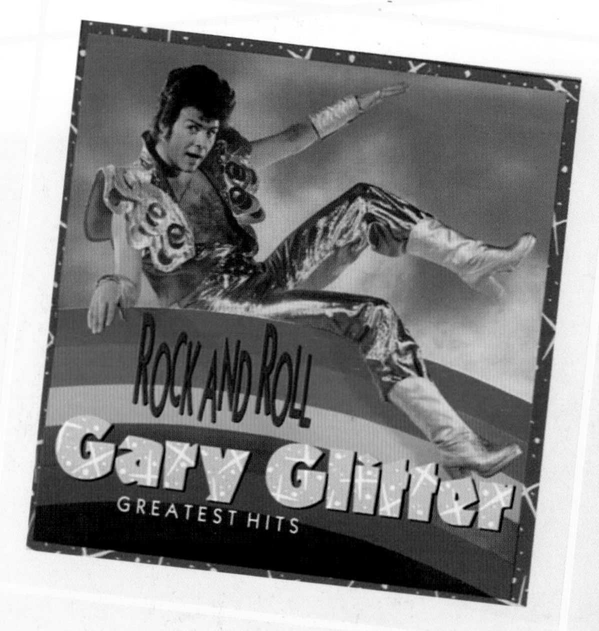

#5 Rock and Roll BY GARY GLITTER (1972)

IN HIS OWN WORDS—MIKE LEANDER (producer/co-writer): "[Gary] was very much into rock'n'roll, so I said to him, 'Let's go into the studio with a couple of friends, and you and I will write something as we go along, and see what we come up with." A tape of one of Glitter's earlier releases, a stomping piece of nonsense called "Shag Rag, That's My Bag," was duly put on the deck, and they began playing along with it. "Friends dropped in during the evening, people came into the studio, played for a while and then drifted away, it was all very loose, and eventually this developed into an impromptu jam session as we started to get into a rock'n'roll rhythm, and then we built it up from there.

"And suddenly it all came together. We had produced something that was like all the records we had ever heard before, and yet was different to them all. We were writing and making the sort of record that we had both loved to listen to when we were 14 and 15 years old, yet it wasn't preconceived. We had not planned it that way. But when we played the tapes back the sound we heard was a revelation." What they came up with was a primeval stomp; 15 minutes long, they called it "Rock and Roll." Edited down to a more manageable length, they renamed it "Rock and Roll (parts One and Two)."

"Rock and Roll" is the tribal war cry of the 20th Century. Forget its absorption into American sporting iconography; forget, too, the fact that Gary built a five-year career at the top of the British charts, from recycling that same primeval formula. You can even forget that, thanks to sundry personal indiscretions, Glitter is widely considered a leper in his homeland. "Rock and Roll" is important because of its lyrics; and those lyrics, the most joyful, meaningful, and utterly, defiantly, triumphant lyrics in the entire history of modern music, go "rock'n'roll, rock'n'roll, rock'n'roll, rock'n'roll." That's part one, anyway. Part two is even better. That one goes "hey, hey, hey, hey, hey."

$MONEY...

THAT'S WHAT I WANT

It is, we are told, the root of all evil. It is also, as the song says, what I want. It makes the world go round and it delineates a rich man's world. And, of course, it rhymes with honey. But while songs about cold hard cash are plentiful, it is not the mere accumulation of so much lovely lolly that exercises the greatest songwriters. Its acquisition, too, is worthy of some consideration—and so is the greed that ensures some people gain a lot more than others. So, forget the old nursery rhyme about singing a song of sixpence... it's time to go for broke.

♫ The Pretender

BY JACKSON BROWNE (1976)

West Coast icon Browne was actually born in Germany and made his first mark in New York, where he wrote songs from former Velvet Underground chanteuse Nico. Then he relocated to California to become the conscience of a generation, from whence this number adopted even greater resonance. A song for every would-be businessman who dismisses every other reason he has to live, in favor of a lifelong pursuit of cash.

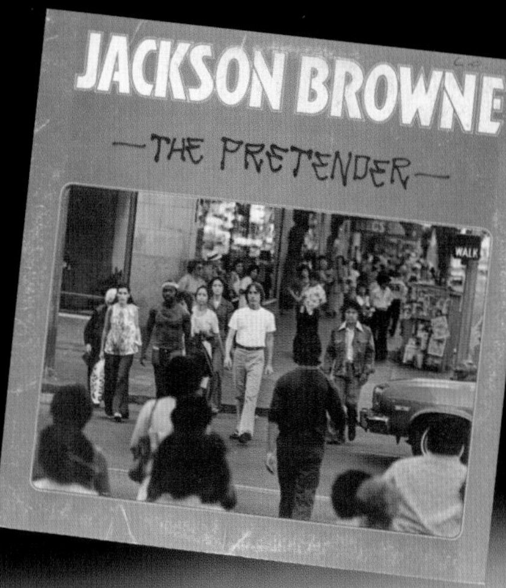

♫ Where Do You Go To, My Lovely

BY PETER SARSTEDT (1969)

Part of the same smash hitting dynasty that gave us Eden Kane, Peter Sarstedt topped charts around the world with the ultimate rags to riches tale, told with a knowing sorry and just a hint of blackmail.

♫ Brass in Pocket

BY THE PRETENDERS (1979)

The song is actually about the Pretenders' first ever live show, and Chrissie Hynde's exposure to a neat piece of British slang—"brass" means money, and the accompanying video sees her working as a waitress, collecting tips.

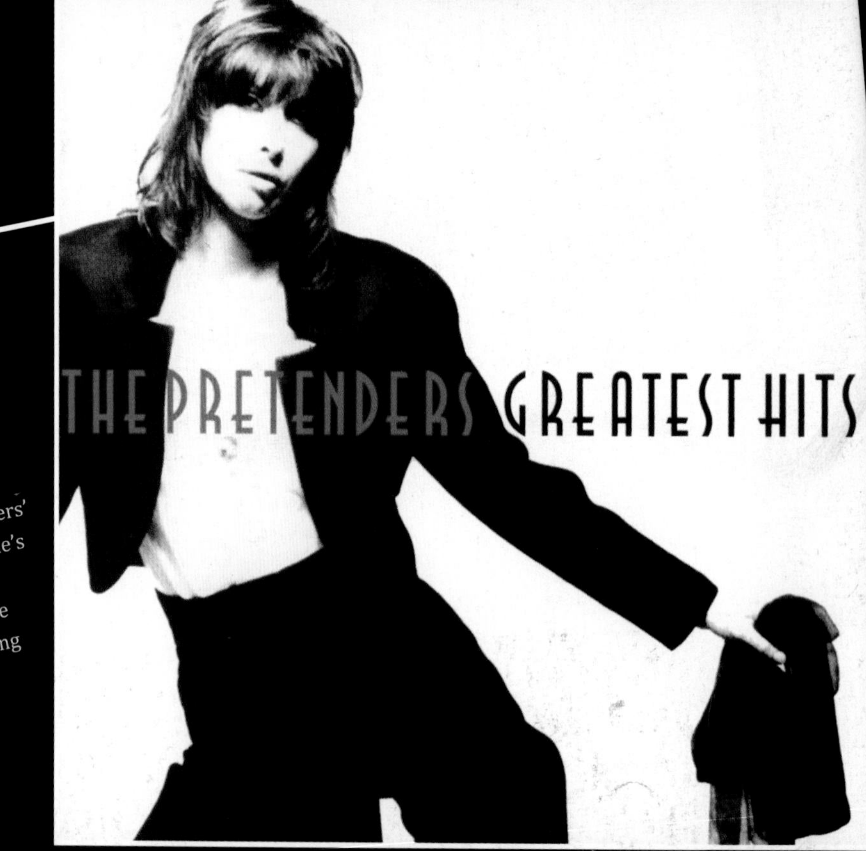

♫ I Hate Banks

BY MOJO NIXON AND SKID ROPER (1986)

Most of the Mojo's songs are hysterically funny, but this mid-80s rant against the banking system took on even greater redolence following the credit crisis in the late 2000s.

♫ Take the Money and Run

BY THE STEVE MILLER BAND (1976)

Spinning off Miller's multi-million selling Fly Like An Eagle, the story of a modern day Bonnie and Clyde. Bank robbing has never sounded so catchy. Or so sexy, come to that.

ALL I WANT FOR CHRISTMAS IS AN ELECTRIC GUITAR (BUT I GOT A BOX OF HANKIES INSTEAD)

The Pogues

There was a time when Christmas music was the province of the old and gray, the annual resurrection of "White Christmas" et al, and maybe a few festive Elvis mumbles to keep the kids quiet. All that changed in the early 1970s, when a host of British rockers... Slade, John Lennon, Showaddywaddy, Roy Wood... started firing their festive offerings chartwards. Today, Christmas songs are as seasonally ubiquitous as credit card bills, stomachache and "thank you auntie Mabel for the socks, they are fabulous." And a few of them can be listened to at any time of year, but especially once the clocks have gone back.

♫ Fairytale of New York

BY THE POGUES (1987)

Possibly the least festive lyric ever applied to a Christmas song, but one of the most singable as well. A duet between two defiant, and deeply-in-love New York City bums, it is already a staple of the modern holiday celebration.

♫ Happy Xmas, War Is Over

BY JOHN LENNON/PLASTIC ONO BAND (1972)

The Lennons' sweetest melody and most hopeful sentiment, dropped with scathing irony into the last years of Vietnam, and still powerful whenever a new war looms.

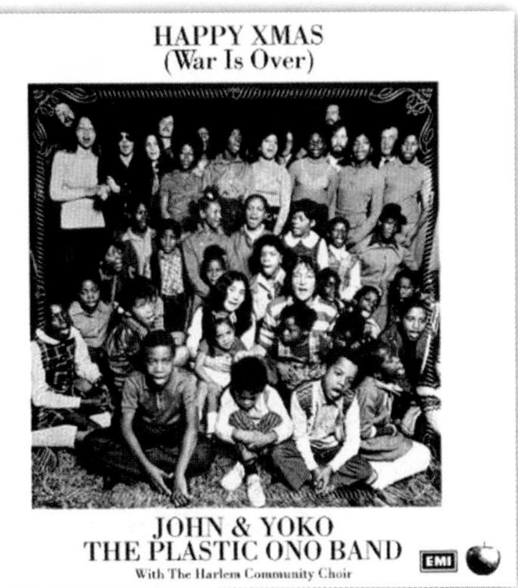

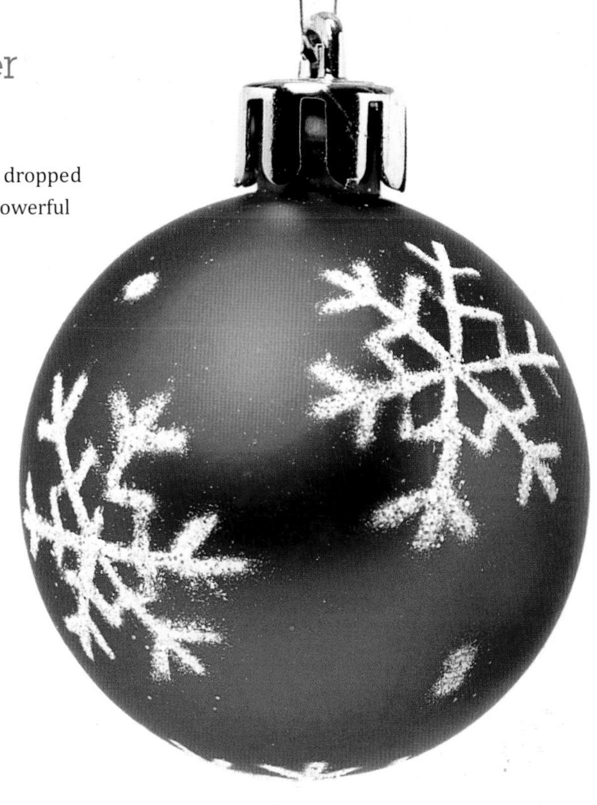

♫ The Spirit of Christmas BY STEVE ASHLEY (1974)

IN HIS OWN WORDS—STEVE ASHLEY (composer): "This came about during a long wander around the streets of Rochester [in southeast England] during the run up to Christmas. It must have been 1968. I was in the duo Tinderbox at that time with Dave Menday. As I remember, the tune came into my head and I had no instrument to help me keep it there. So just kept singing it to myself and it became very mesmeric. It took all day to write the words and my obsession with the these left me no time for food, so I was high as kite on hunger by the end of the day.

"For some reason, I got caught up in the pagan energy that lies at the heart of it all. And it still carries that spirit for me on the rare occasions that I perform it today. Dave worked out a great guitar part and I played the whistle. We've recorded it three times, the first for John Peel's *Nightride* in 1969, the second time was for the *Stroll On* LP sessions 1971 and the third, a live version 35 years later on 60th birthday album. Apart from that, I usually sing it on Christmas Eve."

♫ Merry Xmas Everybody BY SLADE (1973)

The biggest British band of the early1970s, although it took them another decade to have any real success in America, this was Slade's most enduring UK chart topper. Every festive ingredient you could ask for is incorporated into this semi-raucous celebration of the ultimate family celebration.

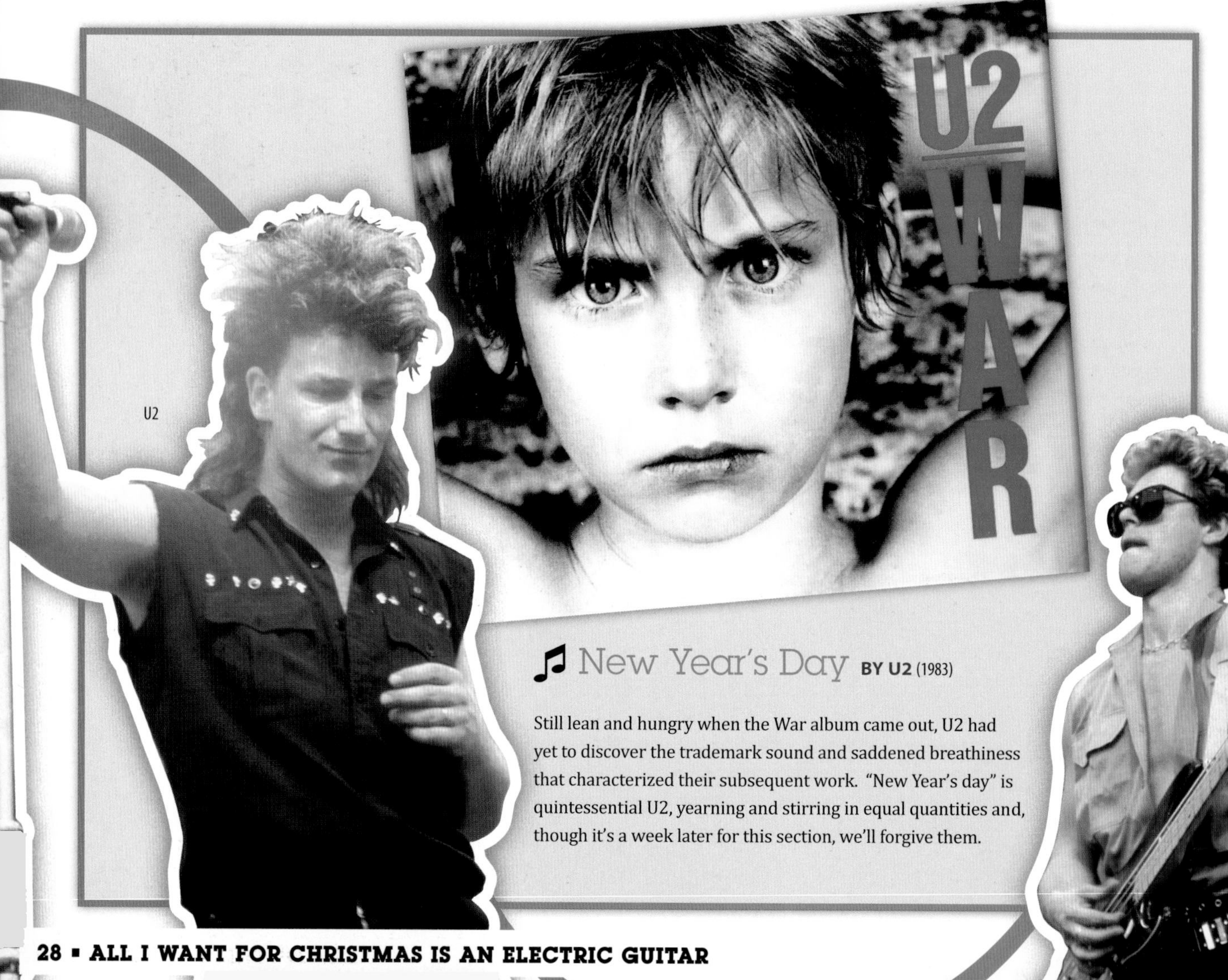

U2

♫ New Year's Day BY U2 (1983)

Still lean and hungry when the War album came out, U2 had yet to discover the trademark sound and saddened breathiness that characterized their subsequent work. "New Year's day" is quintessential U2, yearning and stirring in equal quantities and, though it's a week later for this section, we'll forgive them.

ALAN MERRILL'S TOP FIVE

Born in New York, a superstar in Tokyo, a teenybop idol in London, the man who wrote the National Anthem of Teenaged Rock'n'Roll (or one of them, anyway), "I Love Rock'n'Roll" (139) selects his top five rockers...

Alright Now

BY FREE (1970)

"I heard this song and was immediately impressed by the power and simplicity of it. Andy Fraser is a genius at crafting unforgettable melodies and hooks. Paul Rodgers is one of the best singers I've ever heard. The combination of the two talents was beyond world class. It was supernatural. Factor in soul king Paul Kossoff on guitar, and master of backbeat simplicity Simon Kirke on drums and you have one of the greatest bands ever."

Rebel Rebel

BY DAVID BOWIE (1974)

"One of the best rock records ever made. I played this song live with Derringer, and I loved it every time. Riff, melody, and lyric all perfect."

Honky Tonk Women

BY THE ROLLING STONES (1969)

"My dear old mate Jimmy Miller on the cowbell, with one of Keith's best riffs starting this one off. Killer chorus. The perfectly constructed rock song, in my opinion."

Walk Away Renee

BY THE LEFT BANKE (1967)

"Brilliant tune. A song that will always remind me of New York City in the mid 1960s. First girlfriends, High School. Growing long hair when it was daring to do so!"

Bang a Gong (Get it On)

BY T REX (1971)

"The best of glam rock, and Marc Bolan's biggest international hit. Wonderful lyrical imagery, great production. A perfectly crafted song, right down to the brilliant asides."

GOD IS A CONCEPT

The devil may, as the old saying goes, have all the best songs. But the opposition has some doozies as well.

♫ God Only Knows BY THE BEACH BOYS (1966)

Utterly dismissing the Beach Boys' reputation as a sun, surf and girls-only band, the ultimate rock opera, and it consumes less than three minutes. Even more remarkably, it was supposedly written in just twenty minutes. It will endure forever.

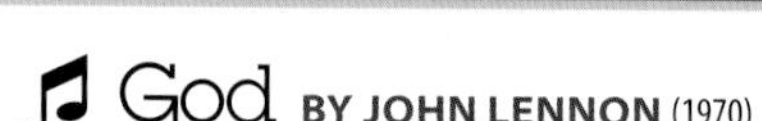

♫ God BY JOHN LENNON (1970)

The penultimate cut on Lennon's first post-Fabs album, John mourns the death of the Beatles by denying everything that his fans ever believed in.

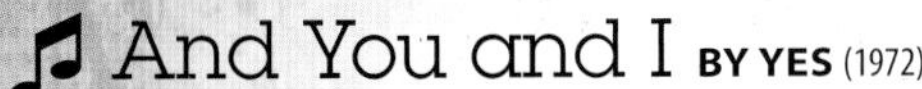

And You and I BY YES (1972)

Typically, Yes songs are so open to interpretation that they could be about anything. This blending of sundry Christian and eastern creation myths, however, remains one of the band's most powerfully focused.

Losing My Religion BY R.E.M. (1991)

REM were college rock favorites long before they hit the mainstream, although few people ever doubted that the transition was inevitable. A lot of the songs mean a lot to many people, but there is something about this one that just hits the spot every time. And they knew it. "I wanted to write a classic obsession song," said Michael Stipe. "So I did."

George Harrison

My Sweet Lord

BY GEORGE HARRISON (1971)

Most people thought George had written a #1 hit, professing his faith in the most melodic terms. But his former manager decided he'd just ripped off the Chiffons, and sued him for the royalties. Nice.

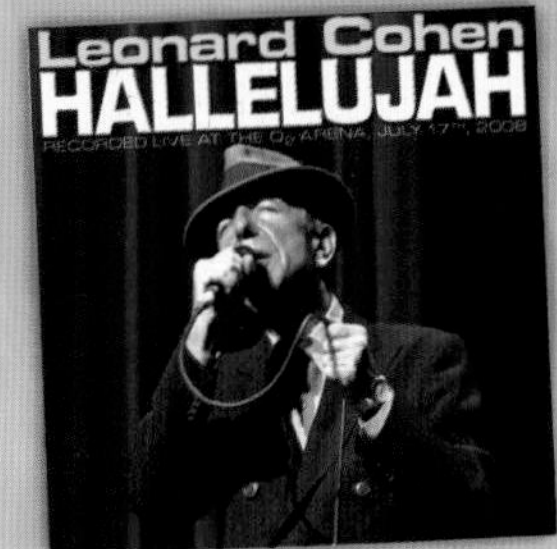

♫ Hallelujah

BY LEONARD COHEN (1985)

From his mid-1980s comeback album *Different Positions*, "Hallelujah" is – incredibly – Canadian Cohen's most oft-covered song. Which means it even beats out "Suzanne"!

♫ Purple Haze

BY THE JIMI HENDRIX EXPERIENCE (1967)

While most ears insist the song is about drugs, and some still smirk over the popularly misheard line "scuse me while I kiss this guy," Hendrix himself once claimed the song was inspired by a dream in which he was walking on the seabed, when he became engulfed by and lost within a purple haze. It was his faith in Jesus, he said, that saved him.

UNCLE RUSS PRESENTS IN DETROIT
JIMI HENDRIX
EXPERIENCE
SOFT MACHINE MC5
RATIONALS
FRI FEB 23
MASONIC
TEMPLE
CASS & TEMPLE

Jimi Hendrix

♫ Hey Lord, Don't Ask Me Questions

BY GRAHAM PARKER AND THE RUMOUR (1978)

Hard to believe, when you hear this song, that writer Graham Parker was "lying around watching the ceiling changing shapes to a backdrop of *Dark Side of the Moon* only a couple of years earlier." Even he wasn't sure where the rage came from!

♫ Presence of the Lord

BY BLIND FAITH (1969)

The Blind Faith supergroup was Clapton's attempt to marry the majesty of Cream with the relaxation of the Band. It failed, but their solitary album was a jewel regardless and this remains one of Clapton's finest ever moments. Even more spectacularly, this was the first full lyric he ever completed.

♫ Gloria

BY THE PATTI SMITH GROUP (1975)

Rewiring and re-envisioning a decade old Van Morrison composition, Patti's opening stanza says it all—"Jesus died for somebody's sins, but not mine." Or does it?

Green Day

♫ Jesus of Suburbia

BY GREEN DAY (2004)

The epic center of the *American Idiot* phenomenon, as Green Day complete their evolution from raw punk mavericks to a centerpiece of the anti-establishment establishment.

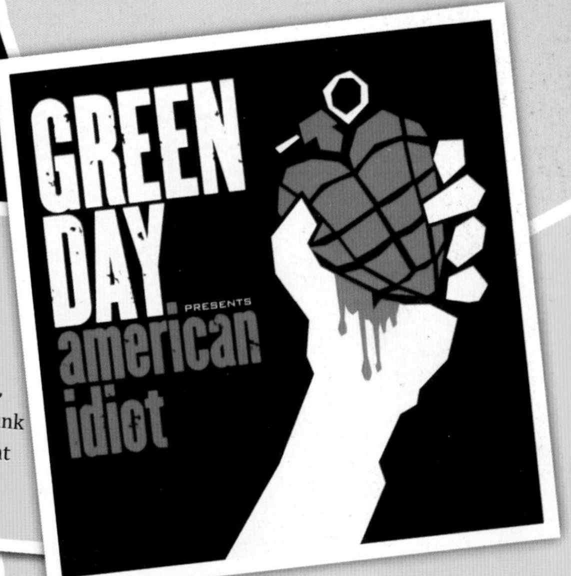

MIXED UP CONFUSION—
GIRLS WILL BE BOYS, BOYS WILL BE GIRLS

Ever since Little Richard first burst out of Georgia in a flurry of rhinestones, satin, and flash, and all the more so after the British Invaders grew hair down past their collars, the older generation have enjoyed nothing so much as a game of "you can't tell the girls from the boys." The Rolling Stones upped the ante even further when they shot a promotional video for "Have you Seen Your Mother, Baby," their satanic selves togged up in streetwalker finest. And then the Kinks released "Lola" and laid the whole thing out on the table. High street fashion would never be the same again.

Halloween Parade

BY LOU REED (1989)

Lou Reed memorializes New York's annual gay parade, name checking a few favorite transvestites but mourning more who are no longer there. One of the saddest songs that the AIDS epidemic ever inspired.

Girls and Boys

BY BLUR (1994)

Scions of the mid-1990s Britpop explosion, although better remembered today for an unseemly squabble with arch-rivals Oasis, Blur broke through to the big time with this insanely compulsive club hopper. It's theme could be the blurring of sexual identity – or, what I wish I did on my summer vacation!

Queen Bitch

BY DAVID BOWIE (1971)

Written in conscious tribute to Lou Reed and the Velvet Underground for Bowie's *Hunky Dory* LP, the still-unknown Bowie gives bisexuality a musical test drive.

Lou Reed

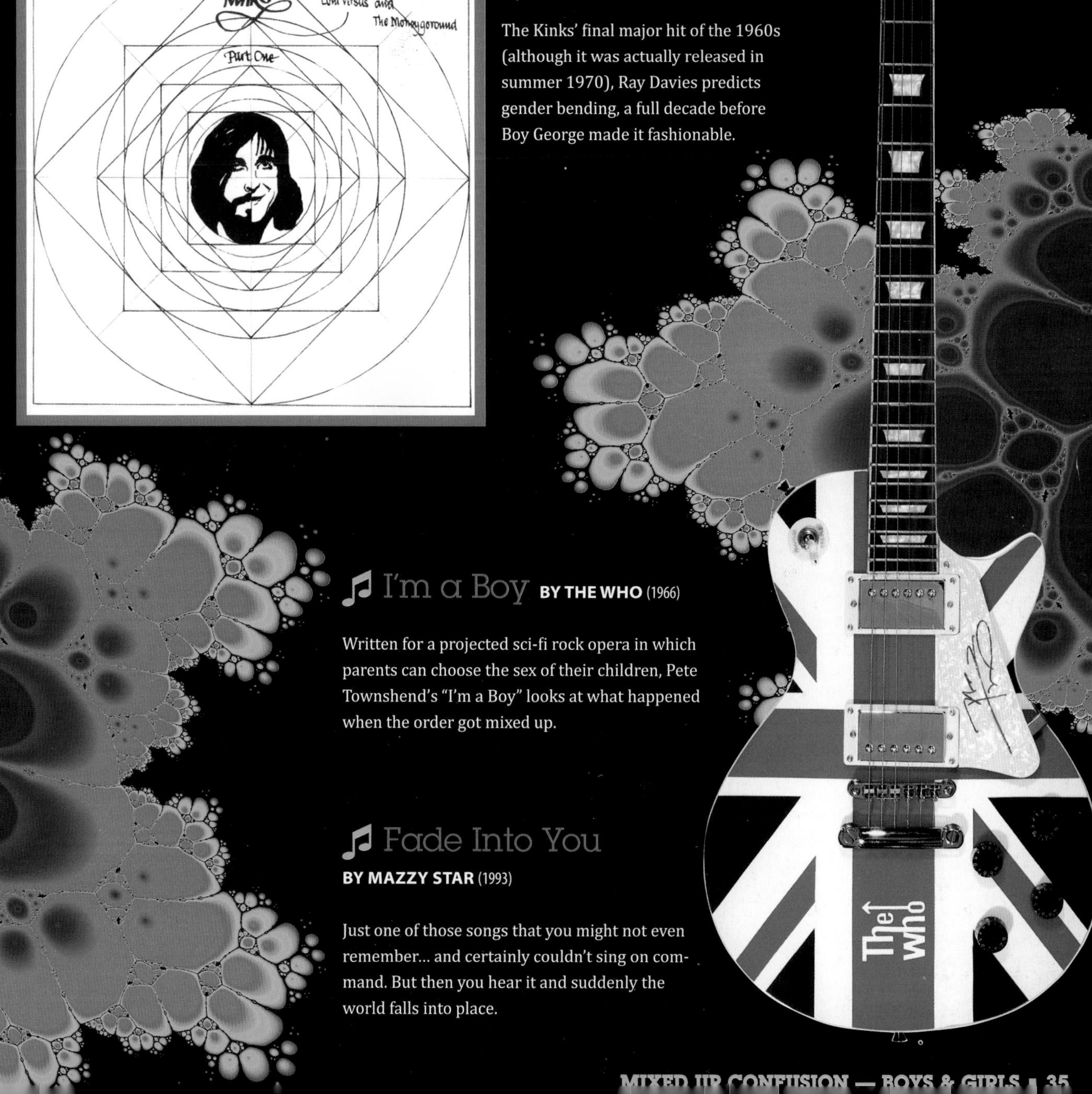

The Kinks' final major hit of the 1960s (although it was actually released in summer 1970), Ray Davies predicts gender bending, a full decade before Boy George made it fashionable.

♫ I'm a Boy **BY THE WHO** (1966)

Written for a projected sci-fi rock opera in which parents can choose the sex of their children, Pete Townshend's "I'm a Boy" looks at what happened when the order got mixed up.

♫ Fade Into You

BY MAZZY STAR (1993)

Just one of those songs that you might not even remember… and certainly couldn't sing on command. But then you hear it and suddenly the world falls into place.

Although man has dreamed, and written, about space travel for centuries, Science Fiction as a
literary genre has only been around since the end of the 19th century, and the likes of Jules Ver
Wells. It didn't take rock'n'roll long to join it there, though—the first burst of music coincided wi
flying saucer mania that entertained America through the mid-1950s, and who can ever forget th
they heard the Randells' "Martian Hop"? Or Billy Lee Riley's "Flying Saucer R

There's no room for either of them here, but unlike the hero of David Bowie's "Space Oddity,"
likely to get lonely out there. Today, sci-fi themes account for so much music that you could prob
spaceship of your own simply from all the vinyl they consumed. It probably wouldn't get very fa

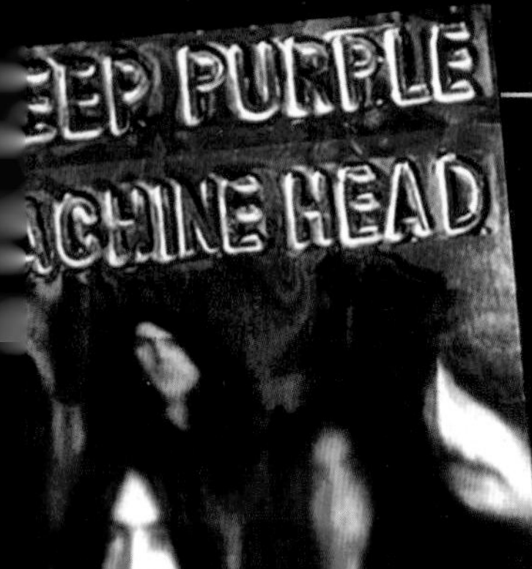

 Space Truckin' **BY DEEP PURPLE** (1972)

From Purple's most punishing period, the early 1970speak when they really could do no wrong. Hyper-anthemic, the lyric remains a seamless porcupine of interstellar punning.

 Astronomy Domine

BY PINK FLOYD (1967)

From their 1967 debut album, with the band still under the aegis of psychdelic warlord Syd Barrett, looking back at earth from the sanctuary of space.

♫ Space Oddity **BY DAVID BOWIE** (1969)

Bowie's first hit, and his last for another three years, the tale of the disillusioned astronaut cutting off all contact with the planet Earth made peculiar accompaniment for British Television's broadcast of the Moon Landing in 1969. Space – the ultimate away-from-it-all vacation place!

♫ Another Girl Another Planet

BY THE ONLY ONES (1978)

British punk rock shot through with a dose of classic pop art, and stating its case in the opening line. "Space travel's in my blood" – what a lyric.

♫ Moonage Daydream **BY DAVID BOWIE** (1972)

A song, Bowie used to say, that was "written by Ziggy"—Mr Stardust's statement of sex and drugs and rock'n'rolling intent.

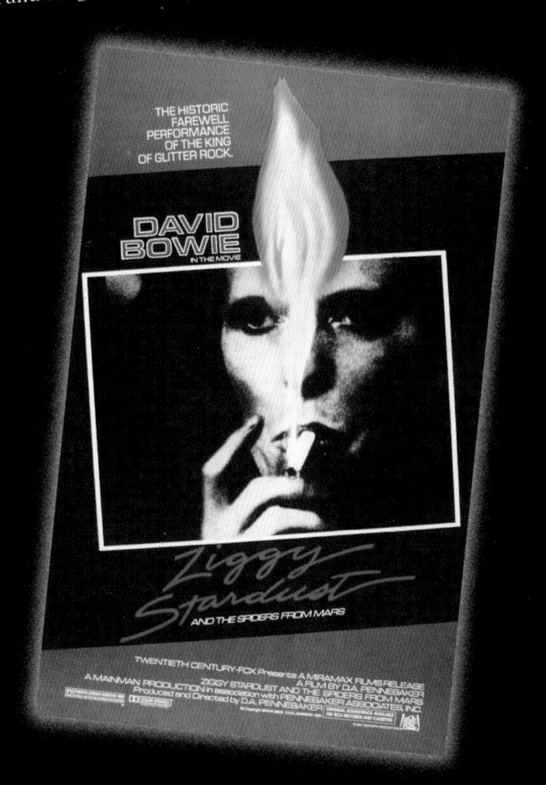

♫ 2000 Light Years From Home

BY THE ROLLING STONES (1967)

The bulk of the Stones' *Their Satanic Majesties Request* LP was locked into inner space. Not this one, though.

The Martian Hop and Other Space Rides

It's true, you know. There never was any important news from space, the Martians never did intend throwing a dance for the entire human race and, if they had, it certainly wouldn't have opened with the words "papa oom mow mow." Or sounds to that effect.

But, for an equally unfeasible three months through the late summer of 1963, three New Jersey-born cousins, local disc jockey Steve Randell, Robert Rappaport (also Randell's real surname) and John Sprit—collectively the Ran-Dells—not only convinced America that there was, they did and it would, they did so with such gusto that their "Martian Hop" climbed all the way into the Top 20. And all over the country, the helium falsetto of several hundred thousand hopping Martians was inescapable.

The Ran-Dells occupy one of those extraordinarily precious places in the annals of American pop—one hit wonders who never came even close to making it two (except maybe in Florida. We need to double-check that). They did release a couple of other singles, but nobody noticed, nobody cared. The dance was over.

Funny thing about science fiction. Set it to music and you're either going to blast off on a career-long journey through the cosmos, with record sales as high as the stars and the sun shining out of the body part you moon with; or you're going to fall to earth with such a crash that they'll still be scraping you off the tarmac when you hit retirement age.

So, on the one hand there's Hawkwind, Pink Floyd, Parliament and David Bowie, intrepid cosmopopsters one and all. And on the other, there's the Five Blobs, Lothar & The Hand

People, Billy Riley & His Little Green Men and Milton Delugg—names so long on the dusty shelves of oblivion that even they've probably forgotten the identities they conceal.

But maybe they're not forgotten, really. After all, you're reading about them now, aren't you?

Steven Randell appears to have been the guiltiest of the three members, a student of electronic music at a time when it was still the preserve of rocket scientists, nuclear physicists and English producer Joe Meek—whose effects-ridden chart-topping ode to the satellite "Telstar" (706) masterpiece had just fallen off the Top 100. Laboring over his sine wave oscillators and electronic thingummyjiggies, Randell would be responsible for the ear-catching effects which made "Martian Hop" so instantly memorable, ultimately emerging with what history now recalls as the first pop record ever to use "additive synthesis." So now you know.

But that wasn't the only reason it proved such a hit. It was also very topical indeed.

By 1963, the space race was in full swing. A year earlier, John Glenn became the first human to orbit the planet earth; a year later, an unmanned satellite would transmit back the first ever photographs of the lunar surface and, even as "Martian Hop" hit the stores, the world watched as Soviet cosmonaut Valentina Tereshkova became the first woman into space, completing a dizzying 48 orbits before heading for home. Glenn, by comparison, managed three.

President Kennedy was vowing to land men on the moon by the end of the decade (he succeeded); scientists were confidently predicting the wholesale human colonization of at least a handful of nearby moons and planets by the end of the century (no comment); and television was launching into a brave new world of its own, with a network debut for The Outer Limits and plans already afoot for Lost in Space. (In Britain, Dr Who was also born that year). Space was out there, it was everywhere, and the only nagging doubt in anybody's mind was, what would we find when we got there?

The answer to that question, of course, was one of the very staples of science fiction in all its guises—print, radio, TV, cinema. Today, of course, nobody denies that intelligent life exists elsewhere in the universe—where do you think we get electricity from? Back then, however, it was a dilemma that exercised some of the finest minds in society, most of whom seemed convinced that the scariest ones were undoubtedly the denizens of Mars, the Red Planet.

Literary precedent agreed with them. H.G. Wells had conjured up living, breathing Martians at the end of the 19th century; Orson Welles reanimated the same fiendish intelligence just before the outbreak of World War Two; and Penguin Books had only recently published Nigel Kneale's chilling Quatermass & The Pit, in which the insect-like protagonists were, of course, Martians.

The difference was, they weren't dancing—and dancing was teenaged America's other big preoccupation during the early 1960s. The Twist, the Hully-Gully, the Mashed Potato, the Swim, the Locomotion, the Popcorn, the One Which Made You Look Like An Otter... if a vaguely synchronized body movement could be named, it could be danced as well.

The "Martian Hop" itself was apparently composed within a matter of minutes—which perhaps isn't too surprising, when one considers that the key lyric was a repeated "eeee-eeee-eeee, eeee-eeee the Martian Hop." Making the actual record, however, took somewhat longer, as Steve Randell took over Bell Sound Studios, New York, to piece together the complex array of sounds and effects which were the heart of the piece. Again, "Telstar" would appear to have served as a role model, a tour de force of technical wizardry and space age imagination, around which Randell constructed a boisterous universe of cosmic whooshes, bleeps and burps, distorting and disturbing the very fabric of Robert Rappaport's falsetto vocals.

It was an expensive procedure. Despite the finished performance clocking in at just two minutes and 17 seconds, the master tape cost over $300—which actually places it in much the same economic ballpark as "Strawberry Fields Forever" and "Good Vibrations." But even before the recording was complete, the Ran-Dells had a record deal. Gerry Goffin was visiting the studio while Randell worked; hearing the performance, he recommended Don Kirschner pick it up for release on his newly formed Chairman label. "Martian Hop" was released in June, 1963, the third ever single on the imprint.

The song's progress was mercurial. Within a couple of weeks, WABC DJ Cousin Brucie was spinning it regularly; by mid-July, it had gone nationwide and, on August 3, "Martian Hop" entered the chart. Three weeks later, on August 22, the Ran-Dells appeared on American Bandstand, and if their somewhat humanoid appearance disappointed any potential purchasers, it didn't hurt the record's sales any. "Martian Hop" peaked at #16; more remarkably, it topped the listings in West Germany, Israel, and France, scored elsewhere around Europe and at least picked up a few complimentary reviews in the UK, where it was released by London Records.

Was there a dance to accompany the record? Common sense insists there had to be, although nobody seems to remember it. One hopes, however, that it required copious quantities of green paint, a pair of those fake antenna that were so popular during the late 1970s, and a death-dealing stun gun to be wielded at the appropriate moment in the dance. It must have taken hours to prepare.

"Martian Hop" finally hopped out of the chart in November, although it was early 1964 before Chairman got round to following it up. "The Sound of the Sun," appeared in the new year, toting more groovy sci-fi effects, but it went nowhere. A shift to the RSVP label brought a second 45, "Beyond the Stars," later in the year—it, too, splashed down long before blast off, and the Ran-Dells faded off the inter-planetary radar soon after. Rappaport went on to become a hotelier, Sprit an artist, Randell an attorney, and "Martian Hop" itself was last heard of on Rhino's Brain in A Box sci fi box set, where it rubs shoulders with a host of other too-good-to-be-forgotten weirdoes... Spirit's "Space Child" and the Rubinoos' "Surf Trek," Leonard Nimoy's "Music to Watch Space Girls By," a super-spooky theremin solo, a slice of the Rocky Horror Show... almost all extra-terrestrial life is there.

And the rest is hovering over your house, making a funny whirring sound while preparing to probe your private parts. I'd sit down now, if I were you.

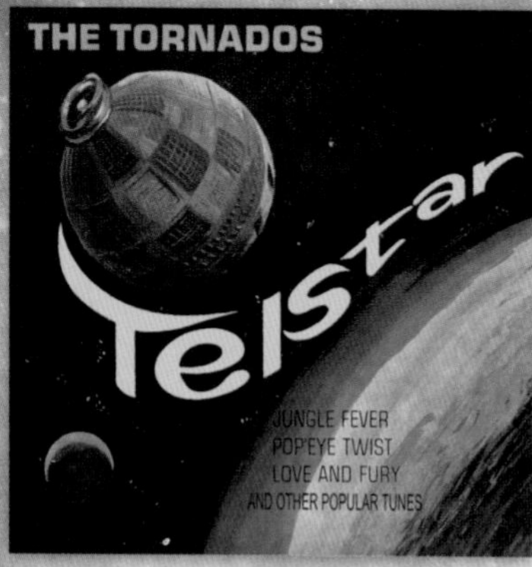

THE TORNADOS
Telstar
JUNGLE FEVER
POP'EYE TWIST
LOVE AND FURY
AND OTHER POPULAR TUNES

Telstar **BY THE TORNADOES** (1962)

Titled for the communications satellite of the same name, but in truth, a self-made tribute to producer Joe Meek's own genius. As producer Roy Thomas Baker put it, "Joe was attempting to do the Wall of Sound thing, but instead of using echo and things like that, he was using compressors. And it worked..."

"People say he was the father of low-fi, because the equipment he was using is considered primitive by today's standards," added Wreckless Eric. "When, actually, he was incredibly far ahead of his time. They needed to bring computers and samplers into the studio to even begin recreating what he was doing, and they still couldn't capture the feel of it."

Holiday On The Moon **BY LOVE AND ROCKETS** (1986)

Originally, incredibly, released only as a b-side, but hastily bundled onto the CD of the band's second album *Express*, "Holiday on the Moon" is laconic, lazy and lovely, a song of supreme solitude.

Silver Machine **BY HAWKWIND** (1972)

British free festival favorites Hawkwind all but single-handedly invented Space Rock—and here's how they did it.

The Boy In The Bubble

BY PAUL SIMON (1986)

The song discusses the mixed blessings of modern technology—the better we get at staving off death, the more ingenious we become at finding new ways of killing people. Science without the fiction.

THE WITCHING HOUR

It's all got so confusing. Time was, witches were either haggard old crones with warts and pointy hats, or they were stunningly beautiful nymphettes, who could turn into cats at a moment's notice. They lived in gingerbread cottages and ate children for fun, they turned princes into frogs and made princesses fall asleep. Yeah, you knew where you were with a witch back then. And then Samantha Stevens came along, twitched her perfect little nose, and now the things are everywhere. Bookstores groan beneath the weight of How To Be A Witch *type textbooks, the Internet is littered with pagan-dot-commery, and as for television...* Bewitched *might itself have bewitched the networks. By the time rock'n'roll joined the circle, then, how much could it possibly teach us? Quite a lot, actually.*

♫ Rhiannon BY FLEETWOOD MAC (1975)

Stevie Nicks' saga of a Welsh witch remains one of the era's most evocative soft rockers, and the only regret is that Mac never got round to releasing the eight-plus minute version that highlighted period live shows.

♫ The Court Of The Crimson King BY KING CRIMSON (1969)

Puppets dance, the fire witch smiles... the title track for prog rock mavens King Crimson's debut album. The entire album is majestic... shards of light falling through the windows of a Gothic cathedral is how one critic described it at the time of release. But this cut sets a stage that is the stuff of true nightmares.

♫ Black Juju BY ALICE COOPER (1971)

IN HIS OWN WORDS—MICHAEL SMITH (drummer): "'Black Juju' was written by [bassist] Dennis Dunaway—he didn't get the nickname Dr Dreary for nothing. He was one of the main creators of 'Dead Babies' (116) too. It was worked on in hotel rooms. We really didn't have a rehearsal studio, our rehearsal studio was the stage, so we sketched it out in hotel rooms on telephone books, and we all agreed it needed a heavy dark African percussion. I wanted to work on the percussion way beyond anything I'd done before. I wanted it to be a big feature drum song, and it was the perfect vehicle. There's a lot of music that uses that tribal primitive vibe, but for me it was like taking Gene Krupa and putting him on floor Toms. Gene Krupa in Haiti. It was the end of the show, the finale, when we strapped Alice into the electric chair and fried him. And then Alice comes back to life...We'd have the smoke bombs and Alice was ripping up the feather pillows, and Mike Bruce had some CO2 canisters and would blast the feathers into the audience, and that was the finale of the show. It was very explosive."

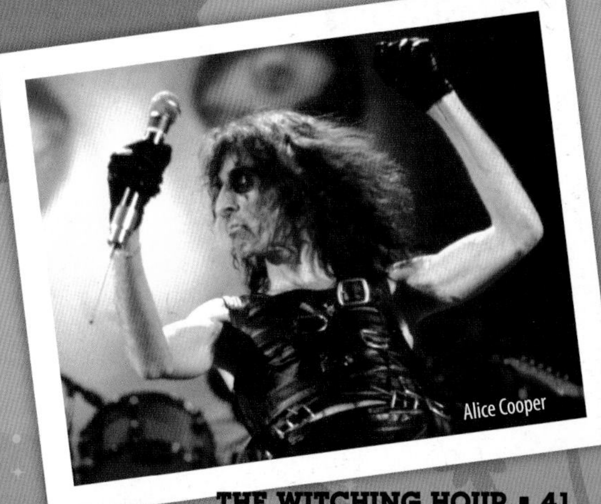
Alice Cooper

♫ Black Magic Woman BY FLEETWOOD MAC (1968)

Composed by British bluesman Peter Green, Santana may have had the hit, but Green and Fleetwood Mac's original had the juju.

♫ The Witch BY THE CULT (1992)

IN HIS OWN WORDS—IAN ASTBURY (vocalist): "The thing about 'The Witch' was, it was a song I'd written, back in December 1989, way ahead of the pack, and I don't think it ever received the attention it deserved. It was an impressive song, an influential song, and it was completely overlooked. We recorded it with Rick Rubin in 93, 94, but it only ever came out on a soundtrack [*Cool World*] and it was buried because that was a cool soundtrack, there was so much great stuff on there. It wasn't overshadowed, but it did have competition."

♫ Devil Woman BY CLIFF RICHARD (1976)

The ultimate bad girl, lame30nted by the ultimate good boy – packing with all the standard paraphernalia of her trade, from crystal balls to black cats, the devil woman is gonna getcha… from behind!

Cliff Richard

♫ March Of The Black Queen BY QUEEN (1974)

Taken from Queen's so-stellar second album, where a side of out and out rockers is backed by a side of maniacal conceptual sound, "March of the Black Queen" is *Alice in Wonderland* meets a Shakespearean epic, somewhere in the forests of Narnia. Guess which side of the LP it was on?

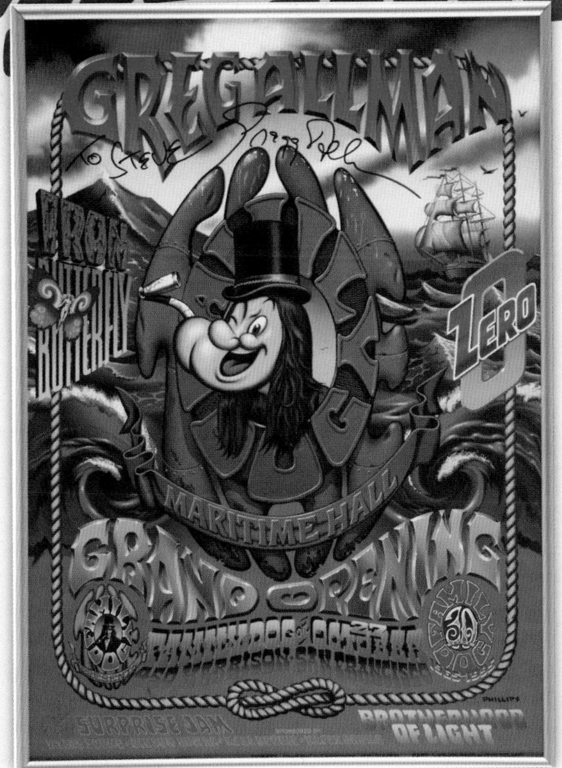

GET ON YOUR BIKES AND RIDE!

Your motor's running, you're out on the highway, you're heading for adventure… and you suddenly realize, you can't hear your 8-Track player over the roar of the engine. It's no wonder that Easy Rider was such an ultimately depressing movie.

♫ Midnight Rider BY GREG ALLMAN (1973)

On the road with his very last silver dollar, Gregg sounds desperate enough to do anything. Or maybe he's already done it. A lot of folk have flaunted outlaw chic as a way of life, but Allman was one of the first to make it sound a little less than fun.

♫ Leader of the Gang BY GARY GLITTER (1973)

While motorcycles roar and his Glitter Band crash, a stamping, stomping and supercharged chant remains one of *the* all-time rabble rousers. And the King of Glam invites us all round to play.

♫ Leader of the Pack BY THE SHANGRI-LAS (1964)

The myrmidons of melancholy, the Shangri-Las created some of the most memorable teen anthems of all time – and most of them ended up badly. The tale of young love on the back of a motorcycle and one of the all-time great death songs, "Leader of the Pack" tells the story of Betty, Jimmy and the consequences of parental disapproval.

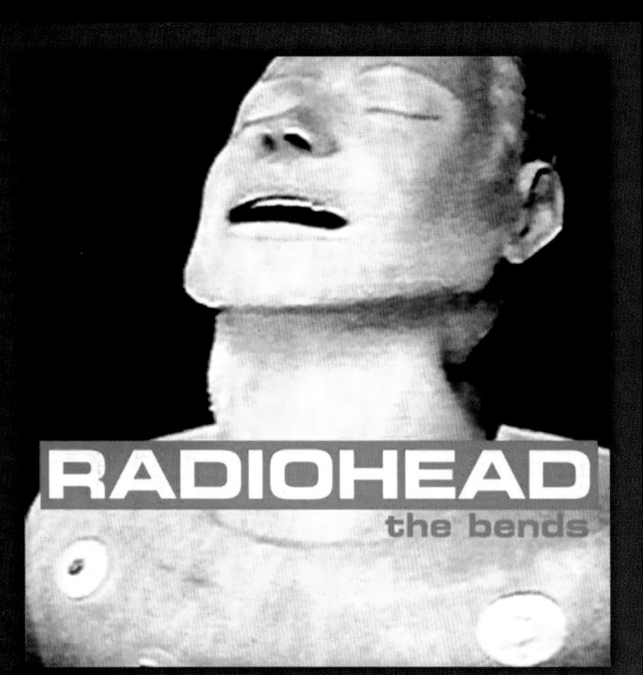

♫ High and Dry BY RADIOHEAD (1995)

Arguably the most important (and certainly the most influential) band of the late 1990s and beyond, Radiohead rarely indulged in what we might call traditional songwriting structures. But these perils of the high riding stunt cyclist were enacted to a heart-breaking melody regardless.

♫ Speedway BY MORRISSEY (1994)

IN HIS OWN WORDS—BOZ BOORER (co-writer): "'Speedway' had my working title rock of ages. The two e-bows in harmony were on it from the start, but the chainsaw sound at the beginning was Morrissey's idea. We started with a drill, but it sounded like a hairdryer, then a big lawn mower also sounded weak, so eventually we brandished the chainsaw in living stereo! For effect, the drums were recorded in the wooden dining room at Hook End Manor, with no dampening, and gradually the compressed room mics at the end were turned up, so I think at the end, you can hear the snare rattle on the last hit."

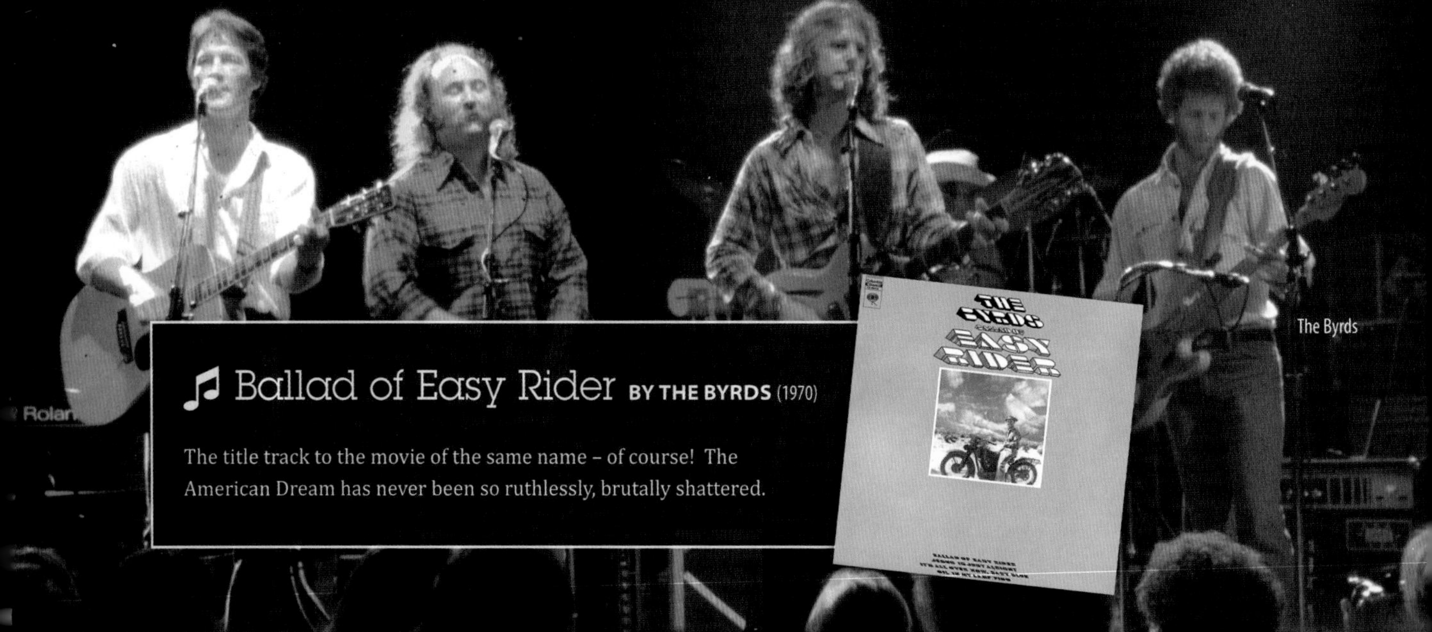

The Byrds

♫ Ballad of Easy Rider BY THE BYRDS (1970)

The title track to the movie of the same name – of course! The American Dream has never been so ruthlessly, brutally shattered.

DRESSED FOR SUCCESS

Clothes, they say, maketh man. Tell that to RuPaul's tailor.

♫ Showroom Dummies **BY KRAFTWERK** (1977)

Television's *Doctor Who* had already been down this particular route, but still Kraftwerk's vision of shop window mannequins coming to life was strangely powerful.

♫ Come As You Are **BY NIRVANA** (1991)

Which, at the heyday of the flannel shirt and work boot Grunge movement, most people did... Taken from the epochal *Nevermind* album, the landmark that sent a whole generation sliding into fuzz and introspection, "Come As You Are" is one of the songs that reminds us why Cobain is still so sadly missed.

♫ Kool Thing **BY SONIC YOUTH** (1990)

Sonic Youth are usually regarded as simply a prototype for what became Grunge. But newly signed to a major label after years spent in unremitting indy-dom, "Kool Thing" is also New York sassiness at its vitriolic finest.

♫ Sharp Dressed Man BY ZZ TOP (1983)

"Sharp-dressed depends on who you are," explained Top's Dusty Hill. "If you're on a motorcycle, really sharp leather is great. If you're a punk rocker, you can get sharp that way. You can be sharp or not sharp in any mode. It's all in your head. If you feel sharp, you be sharp."

♫ Saturday Gigs BY MOTT THE HOOPLE (1974)

A requiem for Glam Rock. "Did you see the suits and the platform boots?" asks Mott frontman Ian Hunter. "Oh dear, oh gawd, oh my oh my," reply his bandmates.

♫ You Wear It Well BY ROD STEWART (1972)

A love letter in song, "You Wear It Well" was allegedly written for Stewart's ex-girlfriend Jojo, a litany of private in jokes and observations that so effortlessly translated into every day life that it became his second monster smash.

ZZ Top

GLAD TO SEE YOU GO

GREAT BREAK-UP SONGS

The best part of breaking up, the song says, is when you're making up. Wrong. The best part of breaking up is when you lock yourself away in your room, turn out the lights and heap a pile of really sad songs on the stereo, and then wallow in self-pity until daybreak. And then you play them all again.

♫ The Next Time BY CLIFF RICHARD (1962)

A love song so perfect, it would be worth being heartbroken, just so you could play it again and again.

♫ She's Gone BY HALL & OATES (1974)

Philadelphia soul sirens Daryl and John at their most archetypically blue-eyed. Their first hit, and their first classic, too.

Fleetwood Mac

♫ Go Your Own Way BY FLEETWOOD MAC (1977)

With the band riven by shattered relationships, the entire *Rumours* album was a Dear John letter from one musician or another. But this is one of the harshest.

Hall & Oates

♫ Good Riddance (Time of Your Life) BY GREEN DAY (1997)

Written when singer Billie Joe Armstrong's girlfriend moved to Ecuador, "Good Riddance" was, he admitted, "the first time we attempted a ballad. The first time we ever played that song was during an encore in New Jersey—I had to pound a beer backstage to get up the courage. I knew we were gonna take a tomato to the face."

♫ So Long Marianne BY LEONARD COHEN (1968)

Marianne (Jensen) is the woman whose picture hangs on the back of Cohen's *Songs From A Room* album, but her song appears on the preceding *Songs Of...* a duet for lament and clattering percussion.

♫ Suspicious Minds BY ELVIS PRESLEY (1969)

Elvis' final number one, at least during his own lifetime, reminds us that it wasn't *all* downhill once the rock stopped rolling.

For No-One BY THE BEATLES (1966)

Paul McCartney ponders his then on-going relationship with actress Jane Asher. "I guess there had been an argument," he explained later. "I never have easy relationships with women."

Those Were the Days BY MARY HOPKIN (1968)

A 19th century Russian melody that did not receive an English lyric until 1963, and topped the chart six years later.

Girl Don't Come BY SANDY SHAW (1964)

According to legend… the shoeless Ms. Shaw's debut single was banned by a number of American radio stations, after the lyric was misheard as "Girls Don't Come."

IT'S MY PARTY
Lesley Gore
Hi – Thanks to you and my many wonderful friends for making my first record a hit! Love Lesley Gore
Mercury RECORDS
72119

It's My Party BY LESLEY GORE (1963)

Another of those impeccable teen dramas with which early 1960s pop was so populated, the tale of the ultimate Bad Hair Birthday packs one of the most heartbreaking pay-offs in lyrical history. It's her party, and she'll cry if she wants to.

Piece of My Heart BY BIG BROTHER AND THE HOLDING COMPANY (1967)

Erma (sister of Aretha) Franklin had the first hit with this Bert Berns' number, but Joplin and Big Brother made it their own, regardless.

Ciao BY LUSH (1966)

IN HER OWN WORDS—MIKI BERENYI (composer): "Nancy and Lee's version of 'Jackson' (250) is one of my all-time favorite singles (I have a very crackly 7" copy still). Most duets I grew up with were unbearably wet and involved two people gazing dreamily into each other's eyes, wittering on about Endless Love. I thought it was so much more passionate and real to have a couple bitching and bantering with each other, yet they still have this spark. Also, the woman gets just as many great lines as the bloke! So I wanted to write a duet that was just as smart-mouthed, with a fuck-you edge.

"Most of my songs for Lush took a bloody age to write. This is because we didn't write as a band, so any song I wrote I had to compose rhythm and lead guitar, drums, bass line, vocal, backing vocal and lyrics, not to mention any extra instrumentation. 'Ciao' was written in an afternoon. I have never written a song so fast, before or since.

"I remember asking Jarvis [Cocker] to sing on the track… I made him a demo tape with both vocal parts on it for him to learn. It probably sounded like a sick frog duetting with a squeaky toy because I had to sing the parts an octave apart to make it clear which bits were his. I heard back from someone that it took him a day to stop laughing.

"When *Lovelife* was released, some reviews said the song was rather nasty and pretty unrealistic. Maybe I have very twisted relationships, but I really felt it was a true representation of the things people say and think when they split up! It's childish and it's petulant and you have two people trying to outdo each other with insults, but they protest too much about how brilliant their life is without the other, no? I think it's rather obvious that they are still in love."

Tired of Waiting for You BY THE KINKS (1965)

I say potato, you say tomato. In the ultimate lament for a contrary lover, Ray Davies stands on the sidelines, waiting… waiting… waiting. And finally despairing. She is never going to be finished in the bathroom.

DEATH IS NOT THE END

Maybe it is, maybe it isn't. The problem is, you won't know for sure until it happens to you, which may be why songs about what Wreckless Eric calls "the final taxi" have always been so popular. It gives you something to think about on those long and lonely nights, when everything that could go wrong already has, and the only people who smile at you are the Goth kids down the block. And teleevangelists, of course.

♫ A Day in the Life BY THE BEATLES (1967)

Famously composed from two separate numbers, both unfinished till they were married together, the last song on *Sgt Pepper* ranks among the most over-analyzed compositions in history. Famously, it was "A Day IN The Life" that crystallized the entire "Paul McCartney is Dead" hoax in 1969. But, somewhere in the world, that final chord is reverberating right now.

♫ Caroline Says II BY LOU REED (1973)

Following up the monster hit Transformer in 1973, Lou Reed did what every newborn pop star would. He created a concept album about divorce and death. "Caroline Says II" is remorseless and relentless, but it reaches parts that other laments simply cannot touch.

♫ Don't Fear The Reaper BY THE BLUE ÖYSTER CULT (1976)

"It's basically a love song where the love transcends the actual physical existence of the partners," vocalist/author Buck Dharma explained. But it sounds like a lot more than that.

Funeral for a Friend/Love Lies Bleeding

BY ELTON JOHN (1973)

Whooshing synths, stately piano, somber guitar, you can see the mists swirl round the gravestones, the mourners' heads all bent in silence... if music was in color, "Funeral for a Friend" would be grays and blacks. Even when the rest of the band steps in, the mood doesn't lift. Most people think of "Funeral for a Friend" as simply a lengthy preamble to the rocking "Love Lies Bleeding." But it exists in such perfect isolation that Elton didn't need to say a word.

Dead Babies **BY ALICE COOPER** (1971)

Although period critics accused the Alice Cooper band of advocating the wholesale slaughter of the nation's youth, "Dead Babies" actually mourned the foolishness with which some parents brought up baby... the pills that were left on the shelf, the plastic bag on the floor, the box of snakes in the bedroom closet.... Do you know what your children are listening to tonight?

Epitaph **BY KING CRIMSON** (1969)

The boiling percussion and psilocybic Mellotrons of "Epitaph" coupled with Greg Lake's most guileless vocal to deliver foreboding dread into even the brightest heart.

24 **BY JEM** (2003)

Racked by guitars and a beat that burns, "24" was inspired, apparently, by Jem's love of the TV show of the same name. The lyric, meanwhile, counts down the last hours before its own protagonist's death.

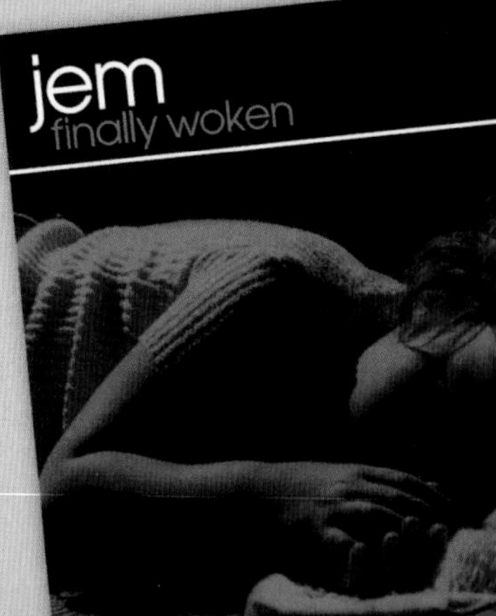

IN HIS OWN WORDS—ROBERT SMITH (composer): "I've always tried to make records that are of one piece, that explain a certain kind of atmosphere to the fullest. That's why I've always liked Nick Drake's albums, or Pink Floyd's *Ummagumma*. I like a lot of music which is built around repetition. Benedictine chants and Indian mantras. These musics are built around slow changes, they allow you to draw things out."

♫ Meet on the Ledge

BY FAIRPORT CONVENTION (1968)

"Meet on the Ledge" was never intended to be a requiem, but the tragedies that weave through the Fairport story decreed that it would become one regardless.

♫ Knockin' on Heaven's Door

BY BOB DYLAN (1973)

Written for the soundtrack to the western *Pat Garrett & Billy the Kid*, but taking on a whole new life thereafter.

♫ Johnny Remember Me

BY JOHN LEYTON (1961)

The eerie Gothic ghost drama that gave British producer Joe Meek his first ever #1, "Johnny Remember Me," tapped both the contemporary mood for death songs, and the spiritualist beliefs that Meek supported. Recorded with every last ounce of enthusiasm and ingenuity Meek could muster, "Johnny, Remember Me" emerged, and remains, a sonic milestone drenched in echo and stormy FX.

♫ Emma BY HOT CHOCOLATE (1974)

Named by John Lennon and originally signed to the Beatles' Apple label, Hot Chocolate went on to become one of the 1970s' most reliable hitmakers – so powerful, in fact, that they could even set the suicide of a struggling actress to music.

♫ Pride (In the Name of Love) BY U2 (1984)

U2's tribute to Martin Luther King, as powerful today as it was in 1984.

♫ Excerpt from a Teenaged Opera **BY KEITH WEST** (1967)

Titled because it was, indeed, a mere excerpt. But the teenaged opera would not be released for another thirty years, and a lot of people still think this slice is called "Grocer Jack." Because that's who dies.

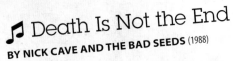

♫ Death Is Not the End

BY NICK CAVE AND THE BAD SEEDS (1988)

All but ignored when composer Bob Dylan recorded it in the 1980s, this song of hope and redemption was reborn when Cave used it to wrap up his *Murder Ballads* opus.

♫ Terry **BY TWINKLE** (1964)

The British "Leader of the Pack," banned in that country because it was considered even more morbid!

♫ Termination **BY IRON BUTTERFLY** (1968)

Most people recall the Butterfly purely for the leviathan "In A Gadda da Vida." But "Termination" is arguably just as magnificent a creation; it just doesn't go on for so long. The title says it all, by the way.

♫ Alone Again (Naturally)

BY GILBERT O' SULLIVAN (1972)

The first ever British chart-topper to open with the promise of suicide (before outlining all of the protagonist's reasons for doing so), "Alone Again (Naturally)" hit the headlines again in 1991 when rapper Biz Markie was sued for his use of an unauthorized sample from the song. Prior to that, many people didn't even realize they needed permission to cut up their favorite oldies.

Gilbert O'Sullivan

♫ Tell Laura I Love Her

BY RICKY VALANCE (1960)

Tommy wants to buy Laura a ring, so he enters a stock car race, hoping to win the cash prize. Instead he winds up dying in the twisted wreckage of his vehicle, but with his dying breath, he looks up at his rescuers and says… "boom boom boom boom." Rarely have the backing vocalists been so badly positioned.

KINDA SEXY, KINDA SCARY....

You know exactly what this means... those love songs that feel just a teensy bit too lovey. The smile that's just a little too sincere. The coworker who stands a few inches too close... and the little girl with the croquet stick, who has mistaken your head for the ball. Yeah, that's really scary.

♫ The Musical Box BY GENESIS (1971)

In which little Cynthia beheads playmate Henry with a croquet mallet, only to meet his disembodied spirit when she opens up his musical box. Standing before her, Henry then ages through all the stages and lusts of life, until he vanishes while still demanding "why don't you touch me?" Proof that not all great prog is about unicorns and computers.

♫ Number One Crush BY GARBAGE (1995)

True love or sheer stalkerville? You choose, but when "Number One Crush" was adapted as the theme to BBC TV's supernatural thriller *Hex*, it took on even darker connotations. "All real love is a form of obsession," explained singer Shirley Manson. "If you love someone more than anything else, that degree of exclusivity requires an abnormal amount of passion and care. And that can be positive. It's just that keeping it short of unhealthy, short of violence, really requires a bit of moderation. You can't let something like that take over all of your thought processes."

♫ Past, Present, Future BY THE SHANGRI-LAS (1966)

Incredibly, the Shangri-Las' final single for the Red Bird label faltered at #59 on the chart. Or maybe it's not so incredible, after all. Is any record more disturbing than this?

Bad to the Bone

BY GEORGE THOROGOOD AND THE DESTROYERS (1982)

I get dem ol' seething, sinister, wicked old blues again, momma.

Don't Think Twice, It's Alright

BY BOB DYLAN (1963)

One of those break-up songs that we've all wished we could have recited when the time was right.

Black Metallic

BY CATHERINE WHEEL (1991)

Grinding over close to eight minutes, "Black Metallic" was the early 1990s band's breakthrough hit, and its lyric remains as mystifying today as it ever was. What does it mean? *And do we really want to know?*

♫ Baby Jump

BY MUNGO JERRY (1971)

Following up the international chart-topper "In The Summertime," the similarly successful "Baby Jump" started life as a cover of Vince Taylor's "Brand New Cadillac," but quickly took on a whole new perspective. Quite possibly one of the most brutally sexual songs ever to have gone to number one in any country.

♫ Total Eclipse of the Heart **BY BONNIE TYLER** (1983)

Originally written for Meatloaf, but scrapped after 'Loaf's label refused to pay for composer Jim Steinman's involvement, the song was then handed over to Tyler, a Welsh songstress best remembered for sounding a bit like Rod Stewart. The ensuing combination sold over six million copies and topped the charts worldwide.

♫ Bad Things **BY JACE EVERETT** (2005)

Based by Everett on Steve Earle's "Poor Boy," Indiana-born country singer Jace Everett cut "Bad Things" for his self-titled debut album, and there it might have remained were it not for "a really cool story of synchronicity." He explained, "my friends at iTunes gave me the opportunity to be the iTunes Single of the Week in 2006. So 'Bad Things' was downloaded by about 210,000 people, and one of those people happened to be Alan Ball, the creator of the HBO TV series *True Blood*." He dropped the song over the credits during the production phase, intending to find something more suitable later on. Except he never did.

♫ Criminal World **BY METRO** (1976)

David Bowie popularized the song with his *Let's Dance* album, and a flaccid little thing it was. Metro's original, on the other hand, is proud as Priapus.

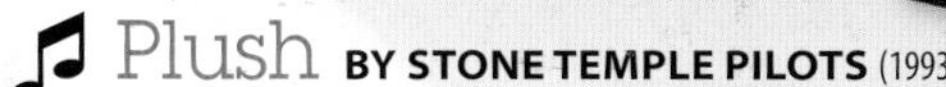

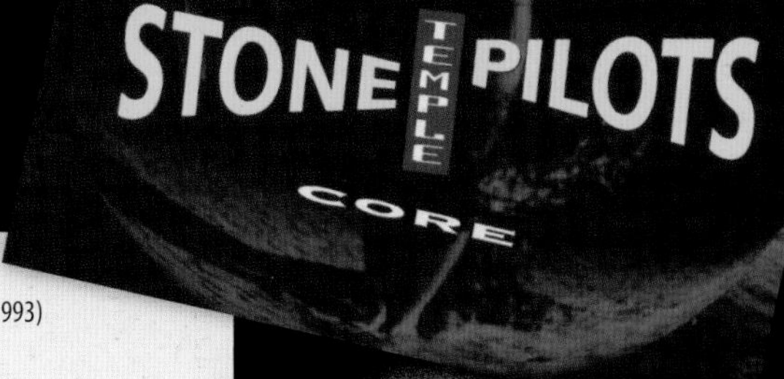

Plush **BY STONE TEMPLE PILOTS** (1993)

Imagine Pearl Jam playing Lynyrd Skynyrd's "Free Bird," and you really can't go wrong.

Kiss on the Lips

BY JOAN JETT AND THE BLACKHEARTS (2004)

A polite second cousin for Jett's "Fetish," "Kiss On The Lips" is a song for those moments when straight sex just seems a little too tame.

Caring Is Creepy **BY THE SHINS** (2001)

Hmmm, you have a point....

Portland's Shins are one of the most intriguing bands of the 2000s, with frontman James Mercer's Broken Bells side project swiftly emerging as another.

Paraffin **BY RUBY** (1995)

How many girls have ever sung about an old man's ass? Seriously, how many? Scots lass Ruby may never have truly followed up the sheer magnificence of "Paraffin" but, in fairness, not many people could have.

Stone Temple Pilots

I FOUGHT THE LAW, AND OTHER ODES OF LAW AND ORDER

The writers and publishers of this book do not condone illegal activities of any kind. But golly gosh, we love listening to songs about them.

♫ I Fought the Law

BY THE BOBBY FULLER FOUR (1966)

And the law won. But they never found out who murdered Bobby....

♫ Karma Police

BY RADIOHEAD (1997)

The Karma Police, Radiohead insisted, were an in-joke they shared among themselves, whenever one of them did something wrong. Look out, the Karma Police are gonna get you....

♫ There Goes A Tenner

BY KATE BUSH (1982)

From Bush's career-best *The Dreaming* album, an idiot's guide to how to plan a bank heist... take movie stars as your role models.

Blockbuster BY THE SWEET (1972)

In late 1972, record buyers were faced with a very unusual dilemma. Two new singles, recorded by two of the biggest acts in the world, linked together by one common factor. David Bowie's "The Jean Genie" (906) and the Sweet's "Blockbuster" were released in the same month, by the same record label… nothing unusual there. And they both had the same old Yardbirds riff driving them to perfection.

Andy Scott (Sweet guitarist): "It's one of those anomalies! I can't believe David Bowie would think 'that's a good old riff' [or song title, for that matter—the Sweet's "Jeanie," after all, was just a few weeks old at the time] and immediately go off and write something, and I can't get my head around the thought that Mike Chapman would be skulking around RCA, he'd hear 'Jean Genie' and think 'what a wag, what a great thing it would be to have two singles out there at the same time, with the same guitar riff.' That would be a nightmare from his point of view."

Steve Priest (Sweet bassist): "I never knew what that was all about. I have a feeling… I can remember when 'Wig-Wam Bam' was out, [songwriter] Mike Chapman went 'I've got a great idea for a new song,' and he had an acoustic guitar and I went 'hey, that's "I'm a Man",' and he went 'yeah, I know. Shut up.' And he went 'you better take care, you better beware,' and that was it. So it was quite a while before 'Blockbuster' was made that he played it to us. But at RCA, people would walk around with the doors open, people playing songs and ideas, so who knows who heard what?"

Who knows, indeed? Bowie and his band departed for their American tour the following week, and "The Jean Genie" was written in New York a few days later. And, while his version rose to #2 in the UK, the Sweet went all the way to the top.

Mick Ronson (David Bowie guitarist): "I kinda liked some of the Sweet's singles around that time. The Sweet were alright."

Police Car BY LARRY WALLIS (1977)

Released in 1978 on the much-beloved Stiff Records label, Former Pink Fairy Larry Wallis wrote "Police Car" while watching Angie Dickinson in *Police Woman.*

WORDS YOU WON'T FIND IN THE DICTIONARY

A wop bop a loo bop, a lop bam BOOM!

Supernaut BY BLACK SABBATH (1972)

IN HIS OWN WORDS—OZZY OSBOURNE (Vocalist and Co-Writer): "Frank Zappa—who was a very techno guy—invited us to a restaurant once where he was having a party. He said 'The song "Supernaut" is my favorite track of all time'. I couldn't believe it—I thought 'this guy's taking the piss: there's got to be a camera here somewhere...' We never consciously knew what we were doing: we were just four innocent guys—very awkward and very unorthodox—who played what we were feeling, trying to make ourselves feel good."

Black Sabbath

♫ Everlong BY THE FOO FIGHTERS (1997)

A song of undying love, apparently written in the darkest hour of all—composer Dave Grohl had lost his girlfriend, his band was breaking up, he was homeless and he'd been frozen out of his bank account. And in the midst of all that, he wrote "Everlong' in forty-five minutes.

♫ Ooh La La BY THE FACES (1973)

Actually, you probably would find it in a French dictionary. It means… well, *ooh la la!* The late Ronnie Lane wrote this gorgeous lament for a life-gone-by, and sang it too on his final LP with Rod Stewart, Ronnie Wood and co.

♫ Jeepster BY T REX (1971)

Most composers, stuck for a rhyme, either reach for the thesaurus or abandon the lyric altogether. Marc Bolan simply made one up, and in the process created a whole new language—half nonsense, half mystery, but wholly intoxicating.

♫ SWLABR BY CREAM (1967)

"SWLABR," claimed co-writer Jack Bruce, "was definitely influenced by the Monkees." There was something about the song's bridge, he said, that was inescapably conjured out of the Prefabricated Foursome's music; and there was something about the way Bruce smiled as he said it that suggested he knew precisely how far up people's noses it would go, to hear him utter a sacrilege like that.

♫ Abacab BY GENESIS (1981)

The title is taken from the chords that the song was constructed from – which could have been one clever notion too far. Fortunately, Genesis selected some good-sounding chords.

♫ Da Doo Ron Ron BY THE CRYSTALS (1963)

"Da Doo Ron Ron," co-writer Ellie Greenwich merrily confessed, meant absolutely whatever you wanted it to. Although countless interpretations of the title have been delivered up over the years, Greenwich and Jeff Barry's own recollection is that they'd simply run out of words to fit the tune, so they ad-libbed in the hope that something better would present itself. When it didn't, they relied on the listener's imagination to fill in the blanks. Which, of course, it did.

♫ Do Wah Diddy Diddy BY MANFRED MANN (1964)

"There she was, just a-walking down the street"—so many Invasion hits kicked off with a first line that you'll never forget, but the Manfreds did it best of them all.

♫ Jive Talking (999) BY THE BEE GEES (1975)

The Brothers Gibb's return from almost five years in the commercial wilderness... the song that kickstarted the white disco boom... Yeah, that's what we're sayin'!

STREET FIGHTING MAN

You probably wouldn't believe it today, but there was a time when rock'n'roll was considered dangerous, rebellious, anti-social and crude; a time when record companies didn't first run a performer's new image through committee, to see what the focus groups thought about it; a time when rhetoric was something that the authorities feared and the revolution was waiting for. Marlon Brando started it, Punk Rock more or less ended it—the music industry was never going to be caught off-guard like that again. But in between times, Babylon blazed like the Fourth of July. Or it would have, if people had just put down their guitars for a moment.

♫ All Along the Watchtower

BY THE JIMI HENDRIX EXPERIENCE (1968)

IN HER OWN WORDS—KATHY ETCHINGHAM (Hendrix's girlfriend and muse): "Jimi had got hold of advance tapes of the new Bob Dylan album, *John Wesley Harding*, and there were two tracks on it which he really, really loved, 'I Dreamed I Saw St. Augustine,' and 'All Along the Watchtower.' Now Jimi wanted to do 'St Augustine,' he really liked that particular track. But for some reason, he felt it was too much Bob Dylan's song, it was too personal. So I said, or maybe he said, 'do "Watchtower" instead'; I can't remember who said what, but I do remember I had to sit there and convince him that this would be a great honor for Dylan, that Dylan wouldn't mind in the slightest that Jimi covered one of his songs.

"So he rehearsed it a bit at home, and on the day we went into the studio, Dave Mason and Brian Jones came round to the flat, and I remember Brian had this great big sitar with him, this huge thing. We all piled into the taxi, Jimi had his guitar, Dave had his, and Brian had this bloody great sitar, so we were all squashed in the back there, and it was quite a long journey down to Olympic Studios. Anyway, we got all the way down there, piled into the studio, Brian was in that little cubicle on the left hand side, Dave was in the main studio, Mitch was there, and I think Noel came along, but left again."

Either way, the result was pure Hendrix magic.

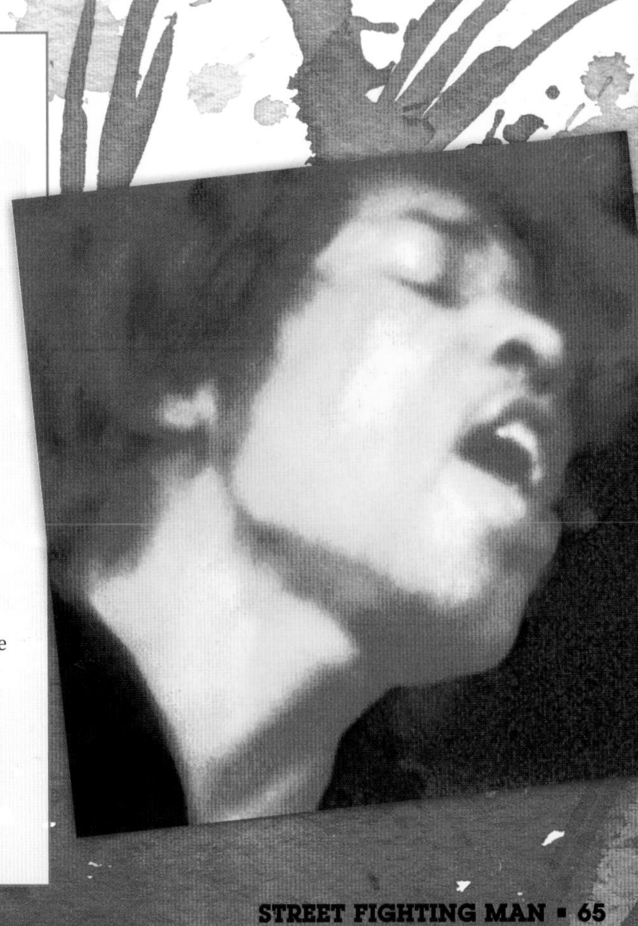

♫ Low Spark Of High Heeled Boys

BY TRAFFIC (1971)

The theme, said composer Jim Capaldi, for an imaginary movie, street toughs in cowboy boots radiating immutable cool. It is, as well.

♫ The Boys Are Back In Town

BY THIN LIZZY (1976)

"The Boys Are Back in Town" is *the* crucial Thin Lizzy song, capturing a moment in time so perfectly that, like "All You Need Is Love" in 1967, or "School's Out" (32) in 1972, it's *impossible* to recall the summer of 1976 without that jukebox in the corner blasting out your favorite songs.

♫ The Knife **BY GENESIS** (1970)

If "The Knife" wasn't written in response to the Kent State Massacre, then it predicted it with frightening accuracy. The heaviest, most brutal, electric and electrifying song Genesis *ever* recorded, this manifesto for civil disorder and rebellion climaxes several minutes before its conclusion, as the army roll in on the protestors and, with six words… "okay men, fire over their heads" …. Well, we know where *that* usually ends up. The rebels do, it seems, ultimately triumph. But at what cost?

Revolution Blues

BY NEIL YOUNG (1974)

The Manson family reborn in mid-1970s LA, creepy-crawling their dune buggies down to Laurel Canyon. One of Young's most merciless lyrics.

Anarchy in the UK

BY THE SEX PISTOLS (1976)

A declaration of intent? Or a word of warning? Either way, "Anarchy" remains a benchmark for all who would be young, loud and very, very dangerous.

Sunday Bloody Sunday

BY U2 (1983)

Not, insisted Bono, a rebel song, although it was difficult not to align it with Northern Ireland's Bloody Sunday—a peaceable protest march broken up in a hail of British army bullets in 1972.

Trouble Coming Everyday

BY THE MOTHERS OF INVENTION (1966)

Mid-sixties inner city America seen through the melting pot of growing social and cultural discontent, set to one mutha of a riff.

♫ Cygnet Committee BY DAVID BOWIE (1969)

Whatever happened to the hippie dream? A longwinded but nevertheless provocative muse on the manner in which even revolutionaries can become fascists in the end.

♫ Rat Trap BY THE BOOMTOWN RATS (1978)

Springsteen's New Jersey restaged in Dublin suburbia. Hopelessness and despair ooze from every pore, but it still topped the British chart.

♫ White Riot BY THE CLASH (1977)

One of the first recorded blasts of British punk, a seething insistence on social change. Back then, it seemed, we *all* wanted to riot.

The Clash

For What It's Worth BY BUFFALO SPRINGFIELD (1967)

It feels like an anti-war song, but "For What It's Worth" was far more domestic than that; a protest against LA's anti-loitering laws, and the closure of the Pandora's Box nightclub in Hollywood.

Ohio BY CROSBY STILLS NASH & YOUNG (1971)

Neil Young's partnership with Crosby Stills and Nash was at its peak when four Kent State students were shot and killed by National Guardsmen policing an anti-war demonstration on the college campus, and there are few more stirring moments in their (or any other contemporary) catalog than this. Recorded and released within days of the slayings, the outrage remains as immediate today as it ever was.

Love and a Molotov Cocktail BY THE FLYS (1978)

Bright pop jangles over a punkoid tale of discontent and devotion.

THE HUMAN JUKEBOX—
THE JOAN JETT HIT LIST

You could (and many of you probably have) compiled a complete LP from the wealth of cover versions that Joan Jett has thrown into her career over the years. But her first album of the 1990s went all out for that particular jugular.

Recorded at the Hit Factory in New York, The Hit List *would pull songs from across the musical spectrum. "Usually they're just songs that I'm a fan of," Jett explained. "To some degree, the message has to be something I can live with, something I believe in. I try to be little bit obscure, and try not to pick songs that are really obvious. I think it's fun. People might bitch about cover songs, but, hey, I write songs, too. A lot of the songs I've recorded are songs I write. But why not? I've got no ego involved here. I don't have to prove myself as a writer to myself or anyone else."*

Besides, she added, "Even though I'm in a band, I'm a fan, too, and it's fun to be able to play some of these songs just for the hell of it. If it's a message that you believe in and a riff that you like, why not?"

The songs included here are not all taken from The Hit List. *But all have been covered by Joan Jett in the years since she launched her solo career, and all join together to remind us of one crucial fact. She really does love rock'n'roll.*

Jukebox Jive

The jukebox is rock'n'roll. No period scenario could be considered complete without a classic style Wurlitzer or Rock-Ola whirring in the corner... the things had style, they had class and they looked sensational. It was a privilege to drop your money into the slot, and then press the buttons that would bring the tunes to life, and in the days when the very notion of a portable personal music selection was an unimaginable dream... even the 8-Track didn't come into being until 1966... the jukebox was the nearest you could get to hearing your music under your terms.

They're a dead issue now, of course, although they ruled for a long time, and their descendents are still around today in places. But they're just computerized boxes which gobble your cash. You don't look at them anymore, you don't lean on then, admire them, fall in love with them. And when the bar owner takes them out, you don't notice.

♫ Roadrunner **BY THE MODERN LOVERS** (1975)

Everything that Route 66 is to the song of that title (759), so "Roadrunner" is to Route 128, circling songwriter Jonathan Richman's hometown of Boston.

♫ Let It Bleed **BY THE ROLLING STONES** (1969)

A handful of late sixties Stones songs epitomize everything that the band represented in the eyes of the establishment, and the title track to their final album of the decade seems to round it all up.

♫ I Love Rock and Roll **BY ARROWS** (1981)

American songwriter Alan Merrill wrote "I Love Rock'n'Roll" as "a knee-jerk reaction to the Rolling Stones' "It's only Rock'n'Roll." Unsuccessful when Merrill's band Arrows released it as a single in 1975, it caught Joan Jett's attention nevertheless—she heard it for the first time during the Runaways' first UK tour in 1976. Three years later she recorded it with Sex Pistols Steve Jones and Paul Cook, and that version too flopped. But a recut in 1981, the title track to her second LP, soared to the top of the chart, while a generation wondered just what might possibly happen if you put another dime in a jukebox. They took quarters at least, by that time.

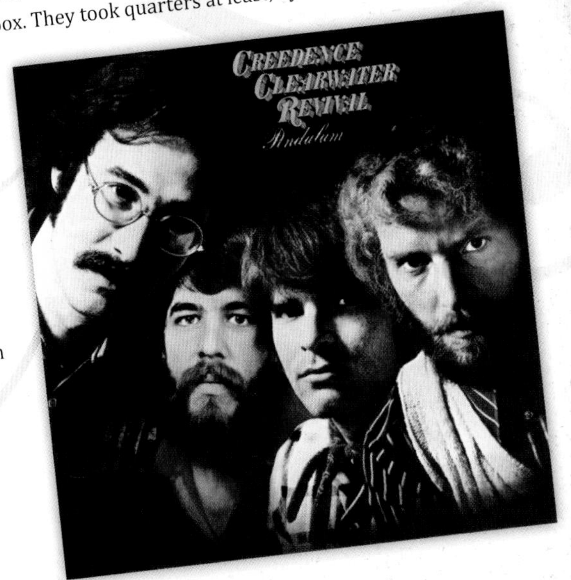

♫ Have You Ever Seen The Rain **BY CREEDENCE CLEARWATER REVIVAL** (1970)

Songwriter John Fogerty laments brother Tom's imminent departure from what was, at that point, one of the most successful bands in the world.

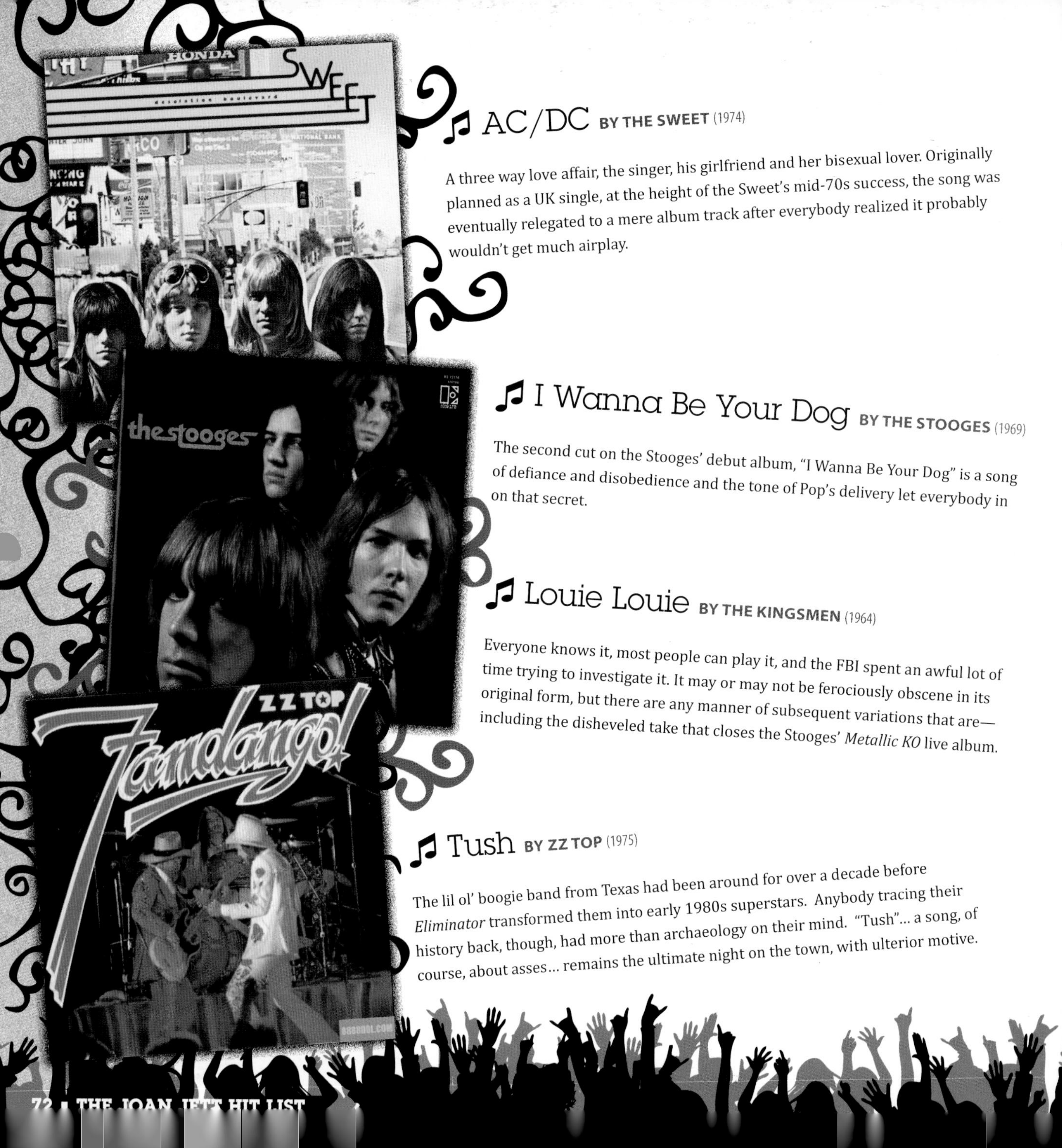

♫ AC/DC BY THE SWEET (1974)

A three way love affair, the singer, his girlfriend and her bisexual lover. Originally planned as a UK single, at the height of the Sweet's mid-70s success, the song was eventually relegated to a mere album track after everybody realized it probably wouldn't get much airplay.

♫ I Wanna Be Your Dog BY THE STOOGES (1969)

The second cut on the Stooges' debut album, "I Wanna Be Your Dog" is a song of defiance and disobedience and the tone of Pop's delivery let everybody in on that secret.

♫ Louie Louie BY THE KINGSMEN (1964)

Everyone knows it, most people can play it, and the FBI spent an awful lot of time trying to investigate it. It may or may not be ferociously obscene in its original form, but there are any manner of subsequent variations that are—including the disheveled take that closes the Stooges' *Metallic KO* live album.

♫ Tush BY ZZ TOP (1975)

The lil ol' boogie band from Texas had been around for over a decade before *Eliminator* transformed them into early 1980s superstars. Anybody tracing their history back, though, had more than archaeology on their mind. "Tush"... a song, of course, about asses... remains the ultimate night on the town, with ulterior motive.

THE ANSWER IS BLOWING IN THE WIND

Let's talk about the weather....

♫ Like a Hurricane **BY NEIL YOUNG** (1977)

Young had just two lines of the song written when he presented it to his band, Crazy Horse, and it took them ten days of struggle to get past that point. Guitarist Poncho Sampedro explained, "We kept playing it two guitars, bass, drums, but it wasn't in the pocket. Neil didn't have enough room to solo. He didn't like the rhythm I was playing on guitar. One day we were done recording and the Stringman was sitting there. I started diddling with it, just playing the chords simply, and Neil said, 'Y'know, maybe that's the way to do it—let's try it.' If you listen to the take on the record, there's no beginning, no count-off, it just goes *woom!* They just turned on the machines when they heard us playing again, 'cause we were done for the day. Neil goes, 'Yeah, I think that's how it goes. Just like that.' And that was the take. That's the only time we ever played it that way."

♫ Dust in the Wind **BY KANSAS** (1977)

It was a line in a collection of Native American poetry that caught guitarist Kerry Livgren's eye—"For All We Are Is Dust in the Wind."

♫ Jumping Jack Flash **BY THE ROLLING STONES** (1968)

Coming down from the psychedelic smorgasbord which was *Their Satanic Majesties' Request*; coming to terms with the departure of creative guru Andrew Oldham; and coming to grips with the harshening aura of late '60s rock, the Stones' first studio dates of 1968 saw them cut what Mick Jagger called "the most basic thing we've done." He could have added, "and the most violent."

The riff belonged to Bill Wyman. He was waiting around the rehearsal room, picking it out on the piano. When Watts and Jones turned up, Wyman says, "we messed around with it for about twenty minutes. When Mick and Keith walked in, they both said 'hey! What's that? Sounds good.' "Depending on which memory Wyman employs, either an instant Jagger lyric followed, and "we recorded it straight off," or it took another couple of weeks for the blistered bluesman autobiography to be married to Richards' scathing guitar, the logical conclusion of the prototype piano. It doesn't matter. Like the song says, it was born in a cross-fire hurricane.

♫ Hasten Down the Wind

BY LINDA RONSTADT (1976)

A Warren Zevon classic, given heartbreaking force by Ronstadt.

♫ The Wind Cries Mary

BY THE JIMI HENDRIX EXPERIENCE (1967)

IN HIS OWN WORDS—NOEL REDDING (bassist): "The song was written about Jimi's girlfriend, Kathy Etchingham. She and Jimi had had an argument. He'd thrown a plate at her or something, and she threw a saucepan, or a frying pan at him, it was one of these domestic things. She walked out, went out with Angie Burdon on the razzle, and when she got back, Hendrix had cleared up the mess, and written 'The Wind Cries Mary' for her. If you listen to the lyrics, it's about a domestic argument."

♫ Blowing in the Wind

BY BOB DYLAN (1963)

With the possible exception of "We Shall Overcome," the most over-sung, over-played and over-wrought protest song of all time. But strip away all that baggage, and it's still a jewel.

♫ Mandolin Wind **BY ROD STEWART** (1971)

The only solo Stewart composition on his *Every Picture Tells a Story* breakthrough album tells the story of a Midwestern farmer, thanking his wife for sticking with him through the worst winter in decades....

JOHN FIDDLER'S TOP FIVE

The composer of "Rising Sun" (191) and a host of other Medicine Head classics, John Fiddler is also renowned for the guiding hand he lent to the post-Mott the Hoople British Lions, and the Yardbirds-inflected supergroup Box of Frogs. Still recording and touring today, Fiddler remains one of the most idiosyncratically brilliant songwriters of our era.

♫ Like a Rolling Stone **BY BOB DYLAN** (1965)

"Rock'n'Roll SHAKESPEARE, truly the Bard of popular music."

♫ Summertime Blues **BY EDDIE COCHRAN** (1958)

"The Riff Maker, so influential to Jimmy Page, Pete Townshend and the next generation."

♫ Then He Kissed Me **BY THE CRYSTALS** (1963)

"Or almost any other Phil Spector or Shadow Morton production, for their "sound sculptures."

♫ Whole Lotta Love **BY LED ZEPPELIN** (1969)

"'You Need Love' by Muddy Waters was the basis for one the greatest ever more 'modern' Rock'n'Roll songs, "Whole Lotta Love."
I put these two together."

♫ Hound Dog **BY ELVIS PRESLEY** (1956)

"Straight out of the birthplace of Rock'n'Roll, THE BLUES! Big Mama Thornton recorded the original, but it's been covered by so many of the Kings of Rock'n'Roll including, of course, The King. Thank you Lieber and Stoller!"

ASK A STUPID QUESTION

Really, you should just make up your own answers to most of these. Or let the music do the talking.

♫ Do Ya Think I'm Sexy?

BY ROD STEWART (1978)

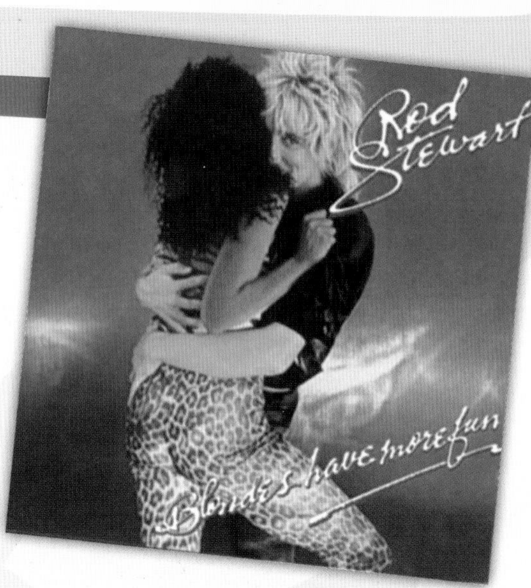

IN HIS OWN WORDS—CARMINE APPICE (co-composer): "Rod would always listen to the chart—'who's number one now, let's see if we can get a song like that.' And, at the time, it was the Stones' 'Miss You,' so we said okay, we want a song like that. So we got the tempo and all of us went home and we put together ideas for Rod. I put together this idea on the keyboard, with a chorus and bridges, then went up to my buddy Wayne Hitchings' house. He had a studio and he played keyboards and drum machines, and we put together a really good version which we presented it to Rod and he loved it.

"Then we went into the studio to record, and we recorded it so many freaking times it was unbelievable. As a matter of fact, we recorded one version which was a really good heavy rock version of it, hard rock, all the guitars and drums and bass, it was rocking. He didn't use that version… we had changed some of the chord structures, so I took that version and I rerecorded it with a Japanese female singer I was producing at the time, we wrote a new song called 'I Just Fell in Love Again,' with a whole different melody, but it had the feel and some of the parts I wrote.

"Finally we did it, and we got a good version that Rod liked, so he wrote the chorus and some other parts, I wrote the verses and the bridge melodies, and then Tom Dowd came in and put strings on it, David Foster's on it, Tom Scott played the sax solo, Linda Lewis came in to do the really high vocals and, little by little, a track that started out as a big track with the band is now shrinking, because of all this other stuff on it and by the time it came out, it was a real disco song instead of a great rock song. And, from then on, Rod hated it!"

♫ How Soon Is Now? **BY THE SMITHS** (1985)

♫ What Is Life? **BY GEORGE HARRISON** (1971)

♫ Why Do Fools Fall in Love? **BY FRANKIE LYMON AND THE TEENAGERS** (1956)

♫ Who Knows Where The Time Goes? **BY FAIRPORT CONVENTION** (1968)

♫ Who Does Lisa Like? **BY RACHEL SWEET** (1978)

♫ How Long? **BY ACE** (1974)

♫ When Will I Be Loved? **BY THE EVERLY BROTHERS** (1960)

♫ Do You Realize? **BY THE FLAMING LIPS** (2002)

BIG APPLE BALLADS

New York is the thing that seduced me
New York is the thing that formed me
New York is the thing that deformed me
New York is the thing that perverted me
New York is the thing that converted me
New York is the thing that I love."

(Patti Smith – BBC TV, 1971)

Simon & Garfunkel

♫ Strawberry Fields Forever

BY THE BEATLES (1967)

The original Strawberry Field was a Salvation Army children's home near John Lennon's childhood home. Since his murder, however, it has become better associated with the 2.5 acre memorial to Lennon that stands in Central Park.

♫ The Only Living Boy in New York **BY SIMON & GARFUNKEL** (1970)

Paul Simon's view of the impending breakup with Art Garfunkel—the "Tom" on the song refers to Garfunkel's pre-fame stage name; he and Simon were a duo called Tom & Jerry.

♫ Coney Island Baby BY LOU REED (1975)

It's hard to imagine Lou wanting to play football for the coach. But, apparently, he did.

♫ First We Take Manhattan BY LEONARD COHEN (1988)

Written by Cohen but first recorded by Jennifer Warnes. A view of the course of his own musical career, Cohen explained, "I had been driven over the edge and I had decided to take matters into my own hand. This is a geopolitical plan. People have asked me what it means. It means exactly what it says."

Leonard Cohen

♫ Shattered BY THE ROLLING STONES (1978)

Closing the Stones' classic *Some Girls* LP with a discordant dance beat and Mick Jagger's sassiest yelp," Shattered" is the tale of life in New York, from the wrong end of the bottle.

BABY, YOU CAN DRIVE MY CAR

Songs about cars are as old as rock'n'roll. From Chuck Berry chewing up the blacktop, to Don McLean taking his Chevy to the levee; from the Beach Boys daring daddy to take away the T-bird, to the Beatles shouting "beep beep YEAH!," rock rides the Interstate with both feet on the gas and even the speed cops are just a blur in the rear view mirror.

And why? Because the people who wrote these songs are exactly the same as the rest of us. They remember the day they passed their driving test, they remember the first car they ever called their own—and they remember everything that happened in that car as well. You could fill a jukebox factory with every song that's ever put the pedal to the metal, but for now, here's a road trip that you'll never forget.

The Legacy of James Dean

One of the most gorgeous hunks of manhood ever to stalk the silver screen, a smoldering mass of burning eyes, silent smiles and grimly thoughtful expression, James Dean had been a star for just three movies when he passed away, wiping out his Porsche 500 on a stretch of US Route 466.

Three movies, but countless dreams and imaginings—at a time when the term "teenager" was still brand new, and an entire generation was struggling to ally its sense of personal entitlement with the Depression-fed humility of its parents, Dean stepped out of that still unformed sense of discontent and frustration and told his audience that life didn't have to be so gray. You could have yourself some fun as well, and if anybody tried to stop you, then head for the horizon. There's a whole world out there and it's yours.

Alongside Elvis's hips and Bill Haley's bluster, the living Dean completed the holy trinity that would rewire teen ambition for the rest of the century—and beyond. The dead Dean was simply the icing on the iconographical cake.

Born in Marion, Indiana, on March 8, 1931, Dean's parents split when he was still a child and, following his mother's death in 1940, he was raised by his sister and her husband. He had spent a few years in Santa Monica, California, before his mother's death and, following graduation, he returned there to study at UCLA. Originally majoring in pre-law, he switched to drama and, having earned a few small roles, dropped out of school altogether, to concentrate on acting.

His first television appearance found him simmering through a Pepsi commercial—setting the stage for a host of other would-be rebels to make their own contributions to the world of fizzy drinks (Cream, the Vanilla Fudge and the Bee Gees all recorded commercials for either Pepsi or its rival Coke; the Rolling Stones and Michael Jackson accepted sponsorship from the soft drink empires). From there, Dean scored small but, according to the standards of the day, memorable parts in the movies, Fixed Bayonets, Sailor Beware, and Has Anybody Seen My Gal?. At the same time, he continued making television appearances, while studying method acting with the famed teacher Lee Strasbourg. And a hitherto competent actor suddenly became a hero for a new age.

Dean's performance in Rebel Without a Cause remains a breathtaking portrayal of youthful surliness crossed with teenaged angst and, even before he died, his trademark glower, quaffed hair and belligerent pout were being imitated by every tough teen in the land. Dean's example taught them what to wear, how to stand, how to walk, how to comb their hair. The actor's love of speed and motor racing only amplified his appeal—he frequently competed in racing in his trademark Porsche 356 Speedster (which replaced a bright red MG TD in his garage) and, had he been so inclined, he might easily have carved himself a reputation as a racing car driver. Two dreams for the price of one, and Thunder Roads the length and breadth of America echoed to the roar of countless would be drag-racing Deans.

Had he lived, he could probably have run for President.

But it was not to be. In late summer 1955, Dean traded in his Speedster for an even faster Porsche 550 Spyder, and was already eyeing a Lotus Mk X when he set out for a race at Salinas, California, on September 30, 1955. He never arrived.

Following his death, Dean ascended to legend, a spirit to be named, invoked or simply just suggested whenever the theme of true teenaged rebellion was raised. Other troubled young men have come and gone since he died, and a few of them have been convincing. But not one of them has added more than a sneer or two to Dean's original role model—because not one of them has needed to. James Dean was perfect.

Interestingly, he was also gay—although only the U.S. Army, who rejected him for that very reason, seemed aware of that at the time.

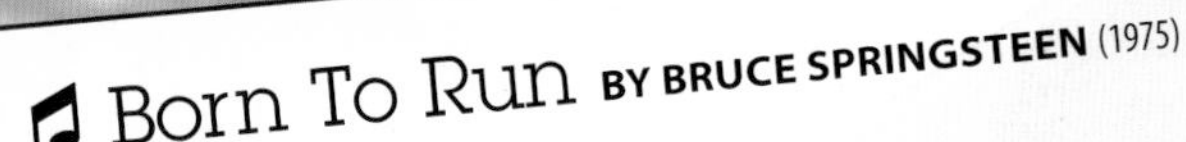

♫ Born To Run BY BRUCE SPRINGSTEEN (1975)

The song that blew Springsteen out of the slow lane and onto superstardom, teenaged lust loops into automotive allegory, and some of the most breathless pauses ever set to music.

♫ Trampled Underfoot BY LED ZEPPELIN (1975)

The song is about an automobile… or, at least, a woman who does not seem to mind being compared to one. But it hit the dance floors like a bulldozer, frantic guitar and drop dead rhythm, and it didn't let up, five and a half minutes of such compulsive, copulating frenzy that, even when you think you're going to get some respite, it's only the song taking a breath. It comes back just as wild straight after.

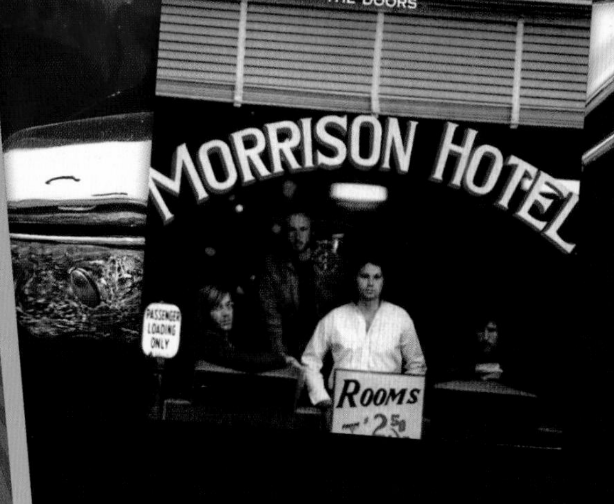

♫ Roadhouse Blues BY THE DOORS (1970)

IN HIS OWN WORDS—RAY MANZAREK (organist): "Roadhouse Blues!" What a tell tale lick, what a signature lick, that's all you have to hear and you know what that song's meant to be. And that great last stanza by Morrison… I got up this morning and got myself a beer. Is that rock'n'roll or what?

Highway to Hell

BY AC/DC (1979)

Australia's AC-DC have ripped out some of modern rock's most remarkable anthems and timeless riffs. "Highway To Hell" is the pinnacle of both, even if it does remind you of a summer's day with roadworks on the Interstate.

Autobahn **BY KRAFTWERK** (1975)

IN HIS OWN WORDS—WOLFGANG FLUR (musician): "Driving is fun. We had no speed limit on the autobahn, we could race through the highways, through the alps, so yes, fahren fahren, fahren, fun fun fun, but it wasn't anything to do with the Beach Boys! We used to drive a lot, we used to listen to the sound of driving, the wind, passing cars and lorries, the rain, every moment the sounds around you are changing, and the idea was to rebuild those sounds on the synth."

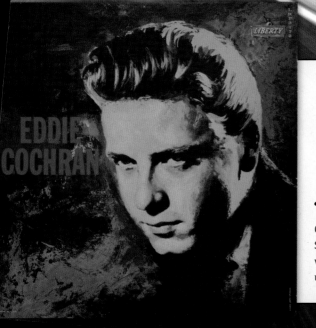

Roadrunner **BY BO DIDDLEY** (1960)

Is it a car? Is it a bird? Bo's "beep beep" leaves you wondering, but there's not many songs that sound better when the sun's out and the road is clear.

Somethin' Else **BY EDDIE COCHRAN** (1959)

Cowritten on the back of a matchbook by Cochran's girlfriend Sharon Sheeley, and finished off by Eddie and his brother Bob, the sad tale of a boy who can't afford the convertible he wants, and the girl who won't date him unless he has the right car.

Dead Man's Curve BY JAN AND DEAN (1964)

Named for a deadly bend on a stretch of Sunset Boulevard, "Dead Man's Curve" came just inches from proving a self-fulfilling prophecy when Jan Berry was almost killed in a car wreck just two miles further down the road.

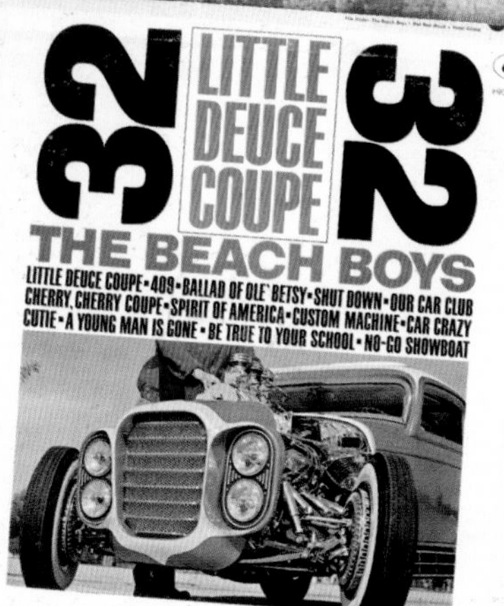

Little Deuce Coupe BY THE BEACH BOYS (1963)

Of all the Beach Boys car songs, this ode to a 1932 Ford Model B was Brian Wilson's favorite. The customized four windowed beauty pictured on the accompanying album cover, by the way, was the property of hot rod aficionado Clarence "Chili" Catallo.

Route 66 BY DEPECHE MODE (1987)

The most famous strip of highway in America has been immortalized by so many bands that it seems unfair to choose just one. In terms of rewiring the old guitar anthem for the eighties, however, Depeche take a lot of beating.

Brand New Cadillac BY VINCE TAYLOR (1958)

There's nothing like that new car smell… unless, of course, it's your girlfriend's, and she won't let you take it for a spin.

♫ Radar Love BY GOLDEN EARRING (1973)

One for all-night road trips, with a beat as hypnotic as the street lights passing, a guitar that sounds like passing horn blasts, and the promise of a real treat once you reach your destination. "We got a thang," sang frontman Barry Kooymans, and it sounds like he did.

♫ Helen Wheels BY PAUL MCCARTNEY AND WINGS (1973)

Paul McCartney's other group was a band on the run when this baby first drove up. The title is a punning reminder for what we all wished our teenaged auto could be... hell on wheels!

♫ One Headlight BY THE WALLFLOWERS (1997)

According to composer Jakob Dylan, the song is about "the death of ideas." But the imagery, of driving through life with only one headlight, is too good to pass up here.

♫ Fun Fun Fun BY THE BEACH BOYS (1964)

"Hey pops, can I borrow the car to go to the library and study?"

"Sure you can, but don't go showing it off to those other teenaged drivers you hang out with."

"Of course I won't...."

STATING THE BLEEDING OBVIOUS *Well, it is.*

They Don't Know BY KIRSTY MACCOLL (1979)

Perfectly styled after an early sixties American girl group classic, by one of 1980s Britain's most remarkable songwriters.

Tomorrow Never Knows

BY THE BEATLES (1966)

Sounds more like a James Bond movie than a psychedelic classic, but no matter.

It's Different for Girls BY JOE JACKSON (1980)

Not, as has occasionally been suggested, a song about visiting the bathroom.... Unfortunately.

I'm a Man BY BO DIDDLEY (1955)

Yes, I expect you are.

One more in that long line of pounding, hypnotic Bo benders, an unequivocal statement of fact.

Nowadays Clancy Can't Even Sing

BY BUFFALO SPRINGFIELD (1966)

Neil Young, Stephen Stills... the Springfield were a supergroup long before Crosby and Nash joined them. And, as for Clancy... well, we just do not know why.

BO DIDDLEY

ALL SHOOK UP— SONGS THAT JUST CAN'T KEEP STILL

Because there aren't many words that rhyme with "agitate."

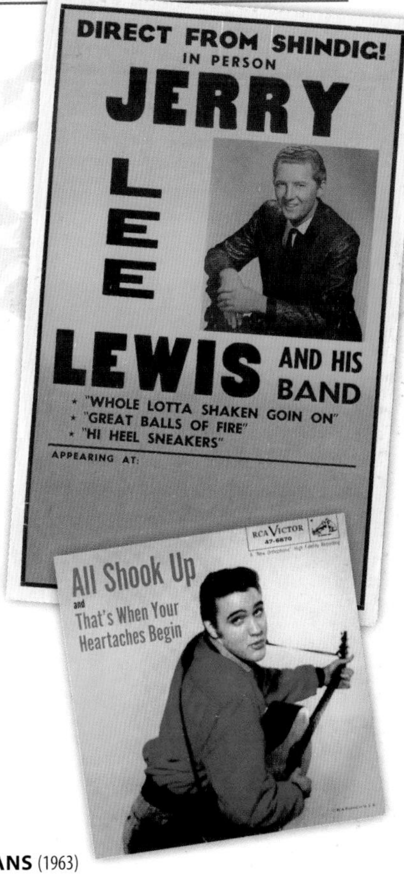

Shake Some Action BY THE FLAMING GROOVIES (1976)

The song that birthed, sired, and single-handedly built the power pop boom of the mid-late 1970s, the quintessential sixties rocker updated for a decade later, and still the essence of pop perfection today.

Shakin' All Over BY JOHNNY KIDD AND THE PIRATES (1961)

Britain's first homegrown rock'n'roll chart-topper, in 1960, the distinctive shaking effects on the guitar were created by running a cigarette lighter across the strings.

Whole Lotta Shaking Goin' On' BY JERRY LEE LEWIS (1957)

The song that proved rock'n'roll wasn't all a bunch of noisy guitars. It could be noisy pianos as well.

All Shook Up BY ELVIS PRESLEY (1957)

Elvis' second number one, and *Billboard*'s Single of the Year for 1957.

Hippy Hippy Shake BY THE SWINGING BLUE JEANS (1963)

Opens with another of those classic opening lines, an impassioned cry of "for goodness sake...." Nothing the Swinging Blue Jeans ever did in the future sounded as glorious as this (although subsequent singles did sound very similar to it), but they'd already snatched immortality.

Shake Your Money Maker BY FLEETWOOD MAC (1968)

Elmore James out of Peter Green, a raw reminder that there was a lot more to Mac than Welsh witches and Sara.

STEVE ASHLEY'S TOP FIVE

English singer-songwriter Steve Ashley might be celebrated here for the festive "Spirit of Christmas" (501) alone, but a forty-plus year career has seen him craft some of the finest songs in the entire history of British folk rock. Still performing and recording today, Ashley's back catalog is essential listening for anybody wishing to trace the recent career of electric folk-with-bite.

♫ Hey Jude **BY THE BEATLES** (1968)

"I like this because, like 'What'd I Say,' it has a great build-up. It may be a little soft for a rock song, but the compassion carries it through and the singalong coda gets my mindless participation every time."

♫ Like A Rolling Stone **BY BOB DYLAN** (1965)

"So many brutal questions. Folk Rock's finest moment?"

♫ Lily, Rosemary and the Jack of Hearts **BY BOB DYLAN** (1974)

A classic Dylan story song, taking the listener through a series of scenarios but never explaining precisely what is happening. There have been at least two attempts to turn this song into a movie, and both have foundered.

♫ Tutti Frutti **BY LITTLE RICHARD** (1957)

"Little Richard was the most amazing of all the early rock'n'roll singers (closely followed by Chuck Berry and Jerry Lee Lewis) and 'Tutti Frutti' is the song for me."

♫ What'd I Say **BY RAY CHARLES** (1959)

"I love this Ray Charles one because it was the first long buildup rock song I ever heard. And he's one of the greatest singers of all time."

GLOOMY SUNDAY
IS THE ONE DAY THAT I LOVE…

More songs about moodiness and blues.

♫ Under Pressure BY QUEEN AND DAVID BOWIE (1981)

IN HIS OWN WORDS—BRIAN MAY (guitarist, Queen): "We hooked up with David via one of those lovely pieces of chance. He was in Montreaux, I think he was living in Switzerland at that time, his very early days there, and we'd just bought the studio because we liked it so much and it was a nice refuge away from the hurly-burly of England. And David just happened to be passing, that's the truth, it wasn't any more planned than that. He came in and we said 'do you fancy kicking a few ideas around?' and he said 'yeah, what have you got?' and we just started playing in the studio and that's what happened."

♫ Red Right Hand BY NICK CAVE AND THE BAD SEEDS (1994)

IN HIS OWN WORDS—NICK CAVE (composer): "Mick [Harvey] and Thomas [Wydler] sat around playing a kind of Latin like thing that I sang a creepy little lyric to. I took it away and wrote 'Red Right Hand.' The lyrics were only half written when I came to cut it at the sessions, and sections of it were improvised on the spot."

♫ Love Will Tear Us Apart BY JOY DIVISION (1980)

"Love Will Tear Us Apart" is frequently described as the quintessential Joy Division song, although listened to dispassionately, and with no reflection on the tangled skeins of doomed frontman Ian Curtis' own private life, it is difficult to understand what all the fuss is about. Frequently overlooked, after all, is the humorous subtext of the lyric, as Curtis purposefully set about writing a scathing rebuttal of the Captain & Tenille's 'Love Will Keep Us Together.'

His own personal dilemmas might indeed have been reflected in the song's examination of a crumbling relationship, as he and wife Deborah parted after five years, and Curtis pledged his heart, instead, to new love Annik Honore. But the jaunty keyboard line that travels behind the melody is as sweet as cheesecake; and, though the title would soon become Curtis' epitaph (the single was released a month after his May 18, 1980 suicide), the song stands as his most lasting legacy.

♫ I Am a Rock **BY SIMON & GARFUNKEL** (1966)

Originally written and recorded for Simon's first solo album in 1965, "I Am a Rock" is indeed a song about going it on your own, because trust and companionship can only lead to suffering.

♫ Black Heart **BY MARC AND THE MAMBAS** (1983)

Bridging Marc Almond's career between Soft Cell and solo stardom, Marc and the Mambas was a darkly beautiful, but utterly uncommercial sideline whose two LPs (this is from the second) stand in absolute opposition to anything he's recorded, before or since.

♫ Drag **BY LOW** (1994)

Low-fidelity was the buzzword for a lot of rock in the mid-1990s, but few bands ever took it to the extremes that Low managed. Like the Velvet Underground if they were buried even deeper underground than usual, and taken from Low's *I Could Live In Hope* debut album, the title and the band name alone say it all.

♫ I Can Never Go Home Anymore **BY THE SHANGRI-LAS** (1965)

Producer Shadow Morton calls it the greatest of all the Shangri-Las' mini epics, and when one considers the company which that raises it above—"Leader of the Pack," "Past Present Future," "(Remember) Walking in the Sand"—that's called not bad. The tale of a girl leaving home following a row about a boy (what else?), only for her mother to die of a broken heart, wrung an equally heartbreaking vocal from Mary Weiss. "I love the performance that I got from Mary on that one," Morton enthuses. "She had to convince people by talking, no sight, which is very difficult. We spent a lot of time on that performance, and I was very tough on her."

The key moment follows the spectral lullaby which haunts the singer midsong; an anguished cry of "momma!" drawn from the very depths of despair. Weiss just conjured it out of nowhere. "It was very believable," Morton continues. "She was 16, had no professional background, no training, no nothing, and I'll be honest, I was making demands on this girl that you would not make of top-notch actresses. She should have got an Oscar for it."

The Shangri-Las

ALL AROUND THE WORLD

The first map of the world, that students readily agree is both a map and the world, was published in Lubeck, Germany, in 1475. But songs about packing your bags and heading off to such places are a lot older than that, as half an ear clasped to the European folk tradition will remind you. The times, and the maps, have changed a great deal since then, but the very human urge to seek out new horizons, or simply grab a change of scenery, has not changed one iota.

♫ Wish You Were Here BY PINK FLOYD (1975)

The title track of an album whose overall theme is absence, "Wish You Were Here" was based on a poem that vocalist Roger Waters wrote for one-time Floyd frontman " and founder Syd Barrett.

Led Zeppelin

♫ D'yer Maker BY LED ZEPPELIN (1973)

The title's a pun, but the melody's in reggae, in case you're still trying to figure it out.

♫ Kashmir BY LED ZEPPELIN (1975)

Robert Plant's choice for the "definitive" Led Zeppelin number, "Kashmir" is s certainly one of their most ambitious. Phased percussion and Page's unlikely tuning (DAGDAD) combine with a mood that Plant slipped into while driving from Goulimine to Tantan, in Morocco. "The whole inspiration came from the fact that the road went on and on and on. It was a single-track road, which neatly cut through the desert. Two miles to the East and West were ridges of sandrock. It basically looked like you were driving down a channel, this dilapidated road, and there was seemingly no end to it."

♫ Solsbury Hill BY PETER GABRIEL (1977)

Named for a landmark close to Gabriel's home in Bath, England, where he would walk to clear his head, "Solsbury Hill" was inspired by his recent departure from Genesis.

♫ "Heroes" BY DAVID BOWIE (1977)

The image of two lovers kissing in the shadow of the Berlin Wall remains one of the most hopeful visions to emerge from the hope*lessness* of the then-divided city.

♫ Paris 1919 BY JOHN CALE (1973)

The title evokes the conference that wound up World War One, but Cale's literary imagery invokes a sense of sadness and doom that history alone would anticipate.

♫ Song for Europe BY ROXY MUSIC (1973)

Alone in a Parisian café, mumbling into his absinthe, Bryan Ferry has rarely sounded quite so supremely alone as here. And no matter how many times you hear the song, the mood and surroundings remain palpable.

♫ The Road to Cairo **BY JULIE DRISCOLL, BRIAN AUGER AND THE TRINITY** (1968)

A David Ackles composition, the follow-up single to "This Wheel's on Fire" (405) remembers the North African pilgrimages that it was once de rigueur for young seekers to undertake.

♫ The News from Spain **BY AL STEWART** (1972)

Written about Stewart's break-up with a girlfriend, and his subsequent flight to Spain to try and win her back—a personal tragedy that saw him stop writing songs for a year.

♫ Berlin **BY UDO LINDENBERG** (1981)

For an entire generation of young Germans, the question of what their parents did during World War Two was one that few truly wanted to have answered. "Berlin," released at a time when the far Right seemed again to be rising in western European politics, brought the subject to the surface.

♫ Parisienne Walkways

BY GARY MOORE (1979)

With Thin Lizzy's Phil Lynott on reflective vocals, and Moore's guitar crying to the sky, the kind of song that reminds you why Paris is considered the city of lovers.

♫ Berlin **BY LOU REED** (1972)

The title track to Lou Reed's death and divorce concept album in 1973, but even before then, a sweet and sweeping portrait of the city's sparkling underbelly.

Al Stewart

♫ St. Petersburg BY ROBYN HITCHCOCK (1982)

A murder? A suicide? A love song? You decide.

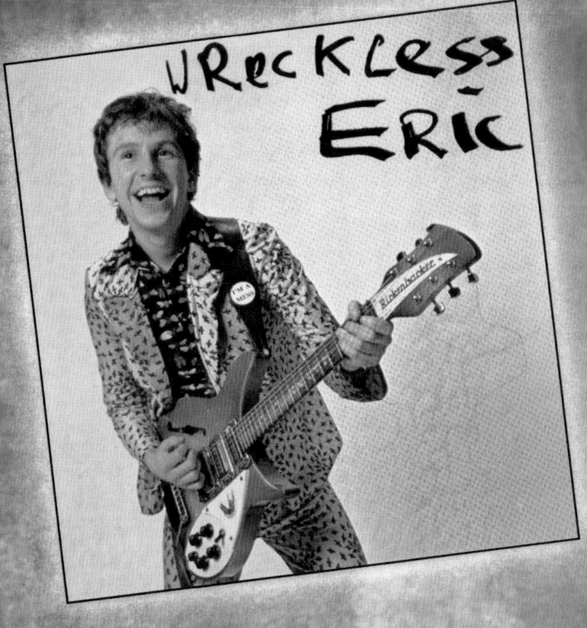

♫ Whole Wide World BY WRECKLESS ERIC (1977)

One of the most astonishingly gifted songwriters to emerge from the punk explosion, Wreckless Eric debuted with a song that proves that the search for true love knows no boundaries.

♫ Vienna BY ULTRAVOX (1981)

Pioneers of what the early 1980s called Synthipop, and fronted by the irrepressible Midge Ure, Ultravox's first hit single took them to the capital city of Austria. Which meant nothing to them. Apparently.

♫ Rock the Casbah BY THE CLASH (1982)

The unofficial anthem of the U.S. forces during the first Gulf war, "Rock the Casbah" was originally written about the then-newly declared Islamic Republic of Iran's outlawing of disco music.

MARTIN GORDON'S TOP FIVE

Bassist with Sparks for their* Kimono My House*/"This Town Ain't Big Enough for Both of Us" (949) breakthrough; a founding member of Jet, Radio Stars, and the Blue Meanies, composer of the immortal "Johnny Mekon" (346), Martin Gordon is today five installments into "the Mammal Trilogy," a series of solo CDs that prove his pen is as sharp today as it ever was.

♫ Big Eyes **BY CHEAP TRICK** (1977)

"In fact any tune from the *In Color* album would qualify. They encapsulate a social ritual from the late seventies in London put on the Cheap Trick album, get fired up and out we go to see what the world has to offer. Raucous but tuneful, perfect pop for grownup people. And it's got guitars, innit.... Paul McCartney clearly loved it (as you can hear on 'Only Mama Knows,' from *Memory Almost Full*)."

♫ Folk Song **BY JACK BRUCE** (1971)

"Celtic melancholy from a master bassist. Magical and mysterious, the meaning is hidden in layers of impenetrable chordage. But who cares, when transported by Bruce's peerless vocal?"

♫ August Day **BY HALL AND OATES** (1978)

Another melancholy, post-summer, Melodica-driven ballad, best heard overlooking the Mediterranean from the top of the Golden Cliffs in Malta. I won't give the exact location; we don't want the world and his wife turning up. Guaranteed jam-proof unless you know the chords, you cannot play along. And what a vocal performance from the master of melisma, before reality TV wannabees decided to adopt it as their favored vocal trick."

♫ Sweeter Memories **BY TODD RUNDGREN** (1972)

"A bittersweet ballad, with a peerless vocal evoking times passed. Real music for real people, and the essence of music literacy and skill."

♫ Monkberry Moon Delight
BY PAUL AND LINDA MCCARTNEY (1971)

"Bonkers rocker with no apparent lyrical meaning ('I sat in the attic with a piano up my nose...') but oozing with *esprit, joie de vivre, je ne sais quoi* and probably also some *savoir faire* if you were to listen closely. Entire careers have been carved out of his little finger. Wait until he gets to the coda, and lets rip with Maccascat. A revelation! Don't go out without it."

GOODNESS GRACIOUS, GREAT BALLS OF FIRE

Resisting the temptation to simply sing the Stones' "Hot Stuff," four aural conflagrations.

♫ Great Balls of Fire

BY JERRY LEE LEWIS (1957)

Nerve shaking, frame rattling, brain charring—rock'n'roll at its most primal.

♫ This Wheel's on Fire

BY JULIE DRISCOLL, BRIAN AUGER AND THE TRINITY (1968)

IN THEIR OWN WORDS – BRIAN AUGER: "[Our manager] called me up one day and said 'I have a tape coming from Bob Dylan,' which was the original *Basement Tapes* recording. I asked him where it was and he said 'bloody Manfred Mann has it.' Well, I thought that was it, by the time they'd finished, there'd have been nothing left, and of course they took 'Mighty Quinn'; and, by the time we finally got the tape, the only things of any quality were 'Tears of Rage' and 'This Wheels on Fire.' We went with 'This Wheels On Fire.'

"Dylan's version was simply him singing and playing guitar, with this walking bass going through it. I tried setting a heavy back-beat to it, but it just sounded so wrong, so corny, so I went about it a different way, losing the beat, keeping the walking bass and adding a string line with this horrible great Mellotron which

Burning of the Midnight Lamp

BY JIMI HENDRIX (1967)

Written on a flight from New York to LA, and notable for its pioneering use of a wah wah guitar effect, "The Burning of the Midnight Lamp," said Hendrix, "is a song I'm proud of. Some people say this is the worst track we have ever done. I think it is the best. Even if the technique is not great, even if the sound is not clear and even if the lyrics can't be properly heard, this is a song that you often listen to and come back to. I don't play neither piano nor harpsichord, but I had managed to put together all these different sounds. It was the starting point."

Fire **BY THE CRAZY WORLD OF ARTHUR BROWN** (1968)

A lot of songs have invoked the Devil, but few are actually introduced by him. "I am the God of Hellfire!" declares Brown as the needle touches vinyl and, by the end of the record, you'll be believing him.

WHAT'S IN A NAME?

THE BOYS

According to the 1978 Guinness Book of Records, *the record for the longest name was claimed by one Adolph Blaine Charles David Earl Frederick Gerald Hubert Irvin John Kenneth Lloyd Martin Nero Oliver Paul Quincy Randolph Sherman Thomas Uncas Victor William Xerxes Yancy Wolfeschlegelsteinhausenbergerdorffwelchevoralternwarengewissenschaftschafe rswessenschafewarenwohlgepflegeundsorgfaltigkeitbeschutzenvonangreifeudurch ihrraubgierigfeindewelchevoralternzwolftausendjahresvorandieerscheinenersch einenvandererersteerdemenschderraumschiffgebrauchlichtalsseinursprungvonkraft gestartseinlangefahrthinzwischensternaitigraumaufdersuchenachdiesternwelche gehabtbewohnbarplanetenkreisedrehensichundwohinderneurassevonverstandigmens chlichkeitkonntefortpflanzenundsicherfeuenanlebenslanglichfreudeundruhemitn icheinfurchtvorangreifenvonandererintelligentgeschopfsvonhinzwischenternart Zeus igraum, Senior. Born in Bergedorf, near Hamburg, Germany, on 29 Feb. 1904, he spent most of his life in Philadelphia, and was best known to his friends as Mr. Wolfe + 585, Senior.*

♫ Sweet Baby James BY JAMES TAYLOR (1970)

Written on a road trip to visit brother Alex, "Sweet Baby James" was Taylor's lullaby for his newly born nephew, also named James.

♫ Daniel BY BAT FOR LASHES (2009)

It's scarcely a name you'd want to rhyme too often (spaniel, manual...) but both Bat and Elton John have drawn considerable mileage from a moniker that, in its original Hebrew form, means "God is my judge."

TWO SUNS
JAMES TAYLOR IS THE DRIVER
WARREN OATES IS GTO
LAURIE BIRD IS THE GIRL
DENNIS WILSON IS THE MECHANIC
TWO-LANE BLACKTOP IS THE PICTURE
TWO-LANE BLACKTOP
JAMES TAYLOR · WARREN OATES · LAURIE BIRD · DE

♫ Johnny Hit and Run Pauline BY X (1980)

Death and drugs in the LA punk underbelly.

Sebastian BY COCKNEY REBEL (1973)

A labyrinthine epic that might well be little more than a wealth of linguistic nonsense. But it conjures worlds and eras far beyond the pop norm, and is the best excuse for combing rock with an orchestra that the seventies ever came up with.

Jeremy BY PEARL JAM (1992)

The Seattle band's first major hit was inspired by the 1991 suicide of Dallas teen Jeremy Wade Delle, who shot himself in front of his classmates and teacher, after being sent to pick up an admittance slip from the school office. His final words were, "Miss, I got what I really went for."

Jack and Diane BY JOHN MELLENCAMP (1982)

The artist formerly known as Cougar, with a tale of young love.

Bye Bye Johnny BY CHUCK BERRY (1960)

Having given the world "Johnny B Goode," Berry now snatches him away again.

Duncan BY PAUL SIMON (1972)

The son of a fisherman and "a fisherman's friend," a wry saga of adolescent discovery, set in the kind of motel room where you can hear everyone's business.

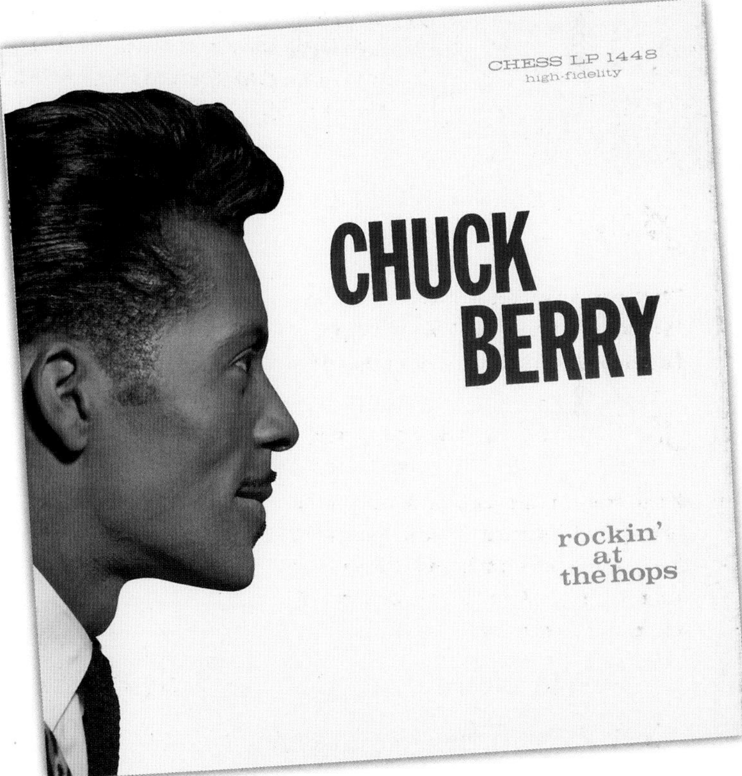

THE BRITISH INVASION

The British Invasion was the moment when music came of age—not in America, where rock'n'roll was already a healthy seven year old; nor in the UK, where the likes of Lonnie Donegan, Cliff Richard, the Shadows and Joe Meek had already made a massive mark. It was on a global scale that the Invasion mattered, translating for a worldwide audience the thoughts and dreams of a truly provincial musical movement... for what else were Manchester, St. Albans, Newcastle and Birmingham (the home cities of our first four listings) if not provincial? And between 1964 and 1966, it was towns and cities like these that ruled the world, dictating hair, clothing, even language and slang, to teens across the planet.

♫ She's Not There **BY THE ZOMBIES** (1964)

Colin Blunstone's beautifully breathy voice leads this half-ballad, half-lament to glory, and it still seems incredible that the Zombies weren't the biggest thing on ten legs. But they scored just one more hit ("Tell Her No"), and that was more or less it until the end of the decade. By which time of the season, they'd already broken up.

♫ A Groovy Kind of Love **BY THE MINDBENDERS** (1966)

A Carole Bayer Sager lyric that reminds us just how deeply involved with the Invasion homegrown talent was... a proper Fifth Column, in fact. Arguably the last true Invasion hit before the tides of fashion turned and psychedelia took over, "A Groovy Kind of Love" would be a hit again two decades later, under the aegis of Phil Collins. But this version remains the greatest.

♫ You Really Got Me **BY THE KINKS** (1964)

London Mods in red riding jackets, the Kinks more or less invented Heavy Metal with their first hit. They moved on from there... arguably, Metal never did.

♫ Go Now **BY THE MOODY BLUES** (1964)

The old bluesy chest beater rendered in immaculate tones by Denny Laine and the decidedly pre-prog rocking Moodies.

♫ Anyone Who Had A Heart

BY CILLA BLACK (1964)

A U.S. hit for Dionne Warwick, edged out by George Martin's masterful production, and the Beatles' love for the girl from the cloakroom at the cavern.

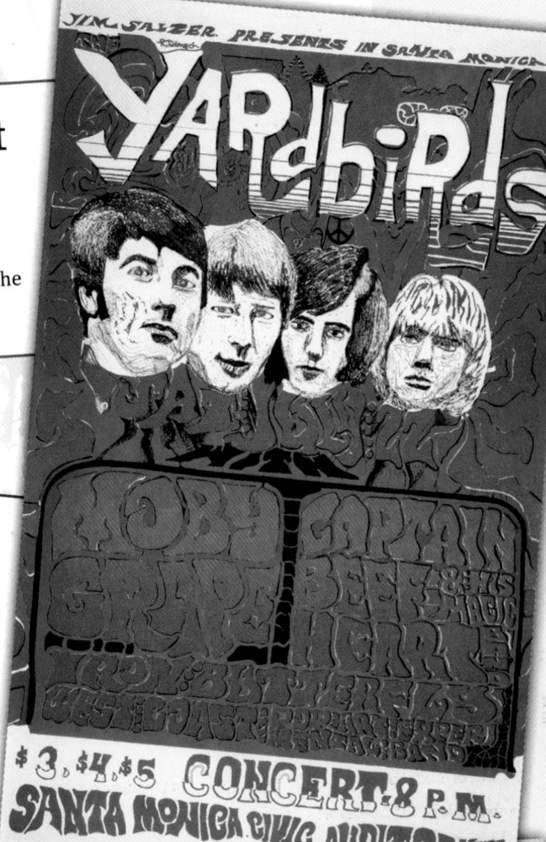

♫ For Your Love BY THE YARDBIRDS (1965)

Second only to Lennon/McCartney, Graham Gouldman was Britain's top songwriting export. Hits for the Hollies, Herman's Hermits and many more followed, but this was his, and the Yardbirds', first. Unfortunately, guitarist Eric Clapton was so outraged by the song's commerciality that he quit the band in protest. The band didn't worry too much—they replaced him with Jeff Beck.

♫ Glad All Over

BY THE DAVE CLARK 5 (1963)

British fans still seem surprised when they discover just how huge the DC5 were in America at one point. But then you play the records (and they had half a dozen in a similar vein to this) and the excitement goes off the Richter scale from the very first thud every time.

THE SEARCHERS / NEEDLES & PINS
B/W
SATURDAY NIGHT OUT
KAPP
K-577
THE GROUP & RECORD THAT KNOCKED "THE BEATLES" OUT OF FIRST PLACE IN ENGLAND!
THE NEW
TUESDAY September 25th 4/6
HJC
Barnston Institute
The BEATLES and GERRY and the Pacemakers

♫ Silhouettes BY HERMAN'S HERMITS (1965)

At one point, the Hermits were as big as the Beatles and the Dave Clark 5 in America, at the same time as their British audience wrote them off as mere teenyboppers. Their earliest hits, however, radiate the cheeky chappiness that American audiences adored.

♫ Needles and Pins

BY THE SEARCHERS (1964)

A Sonny Bono/Jack Nitzsche composition, given the old Merseybeat treatment by a surprisingly resilient (13 hits in five years) beat combo.

♫ Ferry Cross the Mersey

BY GERRY & THE PACEMAKERS (1964)

Not one of their biggest hits, but there was always more to the Pacemakers than Gerry's cracked grin (and the unnatural height at which he held his guitar), and this captures the band as they drifted out of Merseybeat, towards something even more parochial.

FLY LIKE AN EAGLE—
BIRD SONG AND SONGS ABOUT BIRDS

And that's* bird song. *NOT "The Birdie Song." Although there's probably somebody out there who'd include it on this list.

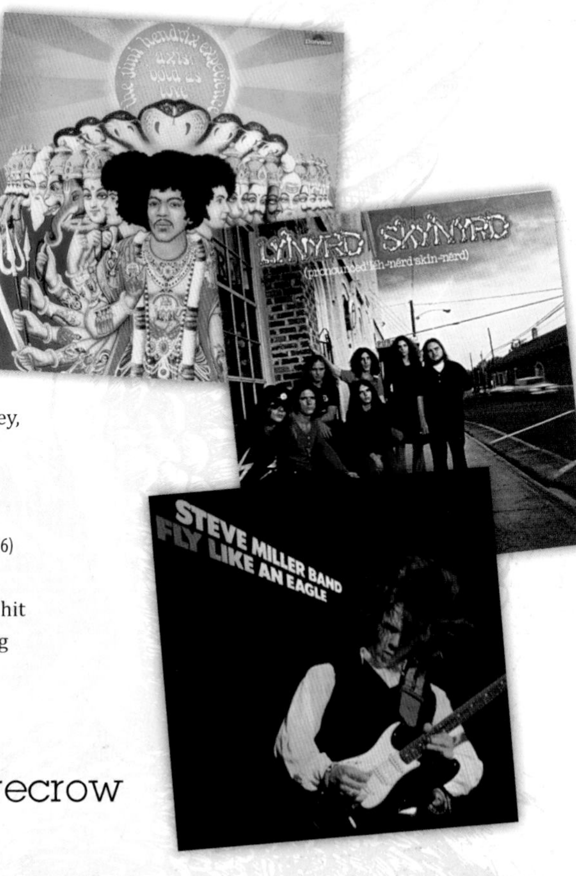

♫ Little Wing **BY THE JIMI HENDRIX EXPERIENCE** (1967)

He made his name on wild guitar, but the tender "Little Wing" is archetypal Hendrix regardless, the lyric oozing love while the solo breaks your heart.

♫ Free Bird **BY LYNYRD SKYNYRD** (1974)

Written as a tribute to departed Allman Brothers Duane Allman and Berry Oakley, but spouting wings of its own the moment it got out there.

♫ Fly Like an Eagle **BY THE STEVE MILLER BAND** (1976)

Still one of the most absurdly likeable albums ever made, and home to a host of hit singles, *Fly Like an Eagle* is nevertheless dominated by its title track, all bubbling synths and breathy boys, while everything percolates furiously beneath.

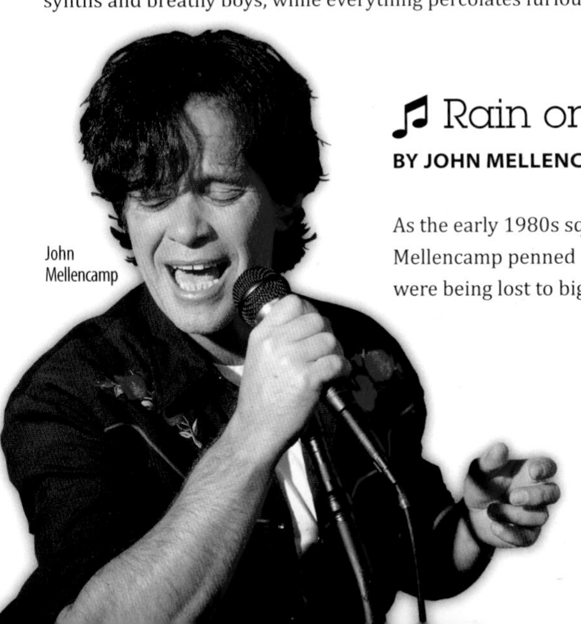
John Mellencamp

♫ Rain on the Scarecrow **BY JOHN MELLENCAMP** (1984)

As the early 1980s squeezed America's farming heartland ever tighter, Mellencamp penned this foreboding number as a reminder of the lives that were being lost to big business.

♫ Rooster **BY ALICE IN CHAINS** (1992)

Seattle grunge stars Alice in Chains, mourning the madness of war. The rooster ain't gonna make it.

NIK TURNER'S TOP FIVE

Founder of psychedelic rock's longest running space soap opera, Hawkwind, as well as such subsequent delights as Sphynx, Inner City Unit, and Space Ritual, saxophonist supreme and vocalist deluxe Nik Turner remains one of rock'n'roll's true supermen.

♫ Born to Be Wild BY STEPPENWOLF (1968)

"I remember raving all night long to this with my friend, the late, great, poet Robert Calvert, in Margate in the late '60's. He was a manic depressive, but in his manic moods, he would keep me awake for days, with his fantastical rantings about all things completely off the wall, phantasmagorical, bizarre, way-out science fictional/fantasical, turning me on to great literature, films, poetry and art. And then later, in the early '70's. I was able to invite him to join Hawkwind as space poet and singer and song-writer. He was then able to write, and devise, with the great Barney Bubble, the Log Book for the Hawkwind album *In Search of Space*, and then to realize, with Barney's design and presentation, his great Space-Rock Opera, *Space Ritual*, also performed by Hawkwind."

♫ Light My Fire BY THE DOORS (1971)

"I danced to it a lot when I lived in Amsterdam, when I was working in the Psychedelic Psyrchus Mobile Freak Out, a big circus tent with bands and a bar which traveled all around Holland in the summer of 1967, where I was working as a roustabout and barman. This was where I met Mick Slattery and Dave Brock, musicians who were playing in their band The Famous Cure in the Psyrchus, and with whom I later formed Hawkwind."

The Doors

Hey Joe BY THE JIMI HENDRIX EXPERIENCE (1966)

"I first heard this in Amsterdam, when I was personal road-manager to Davey Jones, a black New York James Brown actalike soul singer, and Pocomania, his backing band. I used to pick Davey up off the floor every night, after he collapsed with emotion, and thrust me aside to grab the microphone, and resume his song, and spend time afterwards going round the bars of Amsterdam with him and his hip pals. He was writing a dictionary of hip-speak, and turned me on to a lot of good music."

Andmoreagain

BY LOVE (1968)

"I got the album [Forever Changes] from my friend Tony Cooper, a brilliant flute and sax player who was emigrating to U.S.A. when I lived in Margate [in southeast England] where I grew up, and where I then had a couple of stalls selling buckets and spades, kiss-me-quick hats, rude post cards, psychedelia, holding drugs for the mods, and looking after the rockers' bikes. Then the album got stolen, and I heard it again in the car of my girl-friend Stiltz Ska-West, ex-deb society dame, on my way to daddy's flying saucer, and then jammed with the band Love [Arthur couldn't make it at that time] after we supported them at the Roundhouse, at the Speakeasy Club [music biz sleaze joint] in London's Soho. Cool scene."

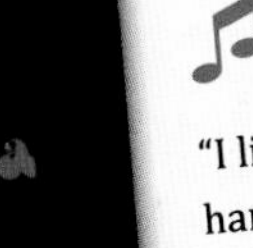

In a Gadda Da Vida BY IRON BUTTERFLY (1968)

"I listened to it a lot in Berlin in 1968 in the Sun Club, a psychedelic club where I used to hang out at night, with Edgar Froese of Tangerine Dream, club owners, dj's, musicians, all the groovy Berlin crowd, as well as the avant-garde jazz crowd that I met, who'd hung out with Eric Dolphy, the modern jazz musician, in the Blue Note Club, and convinced me that you don't need to be technical to express yourself, and inspired me to playing free jazz in a rock band. Which is what Hawkwind was to me."

CELLULOID HEROES

It found its own feet soon enough, but rock'n'roll was more of less birthed by cinema—Bill Haley's "Rock Around the Clock" was the theme to the movie of the same name, and Elvis' immortality would surely have been cheaper if he hadn't made his first few films (politely, we draw a veil over the rest). The Beatles, too, confirmed their command by acting out in a couple of flicks, and that's just the tip of the iceberg.

But Hollywood itself is a song just waiting to be sung, and ever since the Everlys first took Susie to the drive-in, the silver screen has sought out songsmiths to sing its praises.

Bela Lugosi — Fangs for the Memories

Bela Lugosi was born on 20th October 1882, in the Hungarian town of Lugos—Bela Blasko adopted a variation on his hometown's name as his own following his arrival in America in 1921, by which time the youth who had apprenticed as a coal miner, following the early death of his father, had already made a string of movies in both Hungary and Germany.

His impact on his adopted homeland was negligible. Having made his Hollywood debut in 1923's The Silent Command, Lugosi's meager command of the English language saw him confined to mere bit parts, and even there he struggled. Any lines he was given, he learned phonetically, but worse was to come. Having been hired to direct a drama, The Right to Dream, Lugosi was then dismissed when it became apparent that he was incapable of communicating with his cast. He sued for wrongful dismissal, but the court could make no more sense of his complaint than the actors could of his direction. He lost the case and was forced to auction off his own possessions to pay the legal fees.

Undeterred, Lugosi remained on the fringes of the acting world and, in 1927, he was finally offered a role in which his heavily accented, beguilingly faltering English would play to his advantage, the title role in a Broadway adaptation of Dracula. An immediate hit, Lugosi remained in the role for three years, then returned to Hollywood in triumph, to repeat the feat on film.

Universal Studios, the movie's backers, originally had no intention whatsoever of casting Bela Lugosi in the movie role, much preferring Lon Chaney Jr. Chaney, however, was battling cancer at the time and was too ill to work. Other possibilities fell through. Finally, Lugosi was the only name left in the frame, and neither studio nor director Tod Browning were left with any choice. Lugosi became Dracula—in every sense of the phrase.

It is impossible today to recapture the sheer power of Dracula. Vampire movies themselves were new to American eyes and ears—Nosferatu had enjoyed only very limited showings outside of Germany, and other efforts had scarcely caught even a cultish imagination. Dracula, however, rode the renown of the stage-show to the top of the box office, then rode its own moody atmosphere and unparalleled scenes of horror and ugliness even further.

Overnight, Lugosi was reinvented from a litigious mumbler who once had an affair with Clara Bow, to the hottest property in Hollywood, an international star who suddenly found he could take—or turn down—any role he chose.

It was a freedom that he enacted to the full, although not necessarily to his own advantage. Among the offerings he rejected was the title role in director James Whale's forthcoming Frankenstein; Lugosi's eyes were set on another European masterpiece, a remake of The Hunchback of Notre Dame, titled for its main character, Quasimodo.

Unfortunately, while Frankenstein rocketed to peaks approaching Dracula's own, Quasimodo was never made and Lugosi—who had seen that role as essential to proving he was more than a simple stereotype monster—would never really recover. Although he remained constantly in demand, he was indeed stereotyped, if not as Dracula, then at least as a mysteriously sinister eastern European, and few of the movies he made throughout the remainder of his career ever allowed him to break out of that cliché. By 1948, he was reduced to caricaturing his finest moment in the comedy Abbott & Costello Meet Frankenstein, a depth that apparently horrified him so much that he would not return to the screen for another four years.

He resurfaced in 1952, finally resigned to his fate by an appetite for drugs that demanded he take all the employment he was offered. Indeed, he embraced the role with such relish that his every subsequent public appearance found him clad in full costume, while the films he now made were purposefully calculated to play on his reputation: Bela Lugosi Meets a Brooklyn Gorilla, My Son the Vampire, Old Mother Riley Meets the Vampire and a pair of films with the eccentric Ed Wood, Glen or Glenda? And Bride of the Monster.

In 1955, Lugosi voluntarily committed himself in the hope of shaking off his dope habit. He succeeded, but at a dreadful cost. Having shot just a handful of scenes for another Wood spectacular, Plan 9 from Outer Space, Lugosi was felled by a massive heart attack. On August 15, 1956, the world learned that Bela Lugosi was dead. Twenty-three years later, almost to the day, it was reminded that he still was.

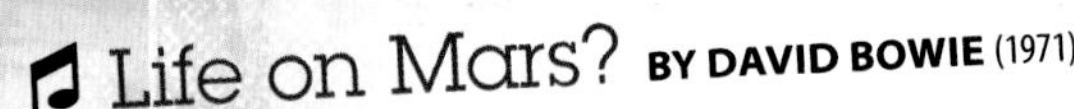

Life on Mars? BY DAVID BOWIE (1971)

Bowie steadfastly refuses to say what the song is about, but its cinematic sweep and the vignettes of action that play across the screen give it a Hollywood glamour regardless.

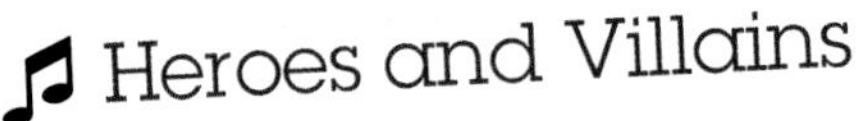

Heroes and Villains

BY THE BEACH BOYS (1967)

An excerpt from the doomed *Smile* project, a cunningly updated and devilishly harmonic tribute to the cops and robbers of days gone by.

Celluloid Heroes BY THE KINKS (1972)

Written after Ray Davies first visited the Hollywood Walk of Fame, a touching reminder of the lives behind the sidewalk legends.

A Man Needs a Maid BY NEIL YOUNG (1972)

Written by Young about his then-lover, actress Carrie Snodgrass—hence the lyric "I was watching a movie with a friend, I fell in love with the actress…"

♫ Ballad of Dwight Frye BY ALICE COOPER (1971)

IN HIS OWN WORDS—NEAL SMITH (drummer): "If 'I'm Eighteen' was the commercial side of the group Alice Cooper, then the 'Ballad of Dwight Frye' was the darker more theatrical side of our group. Most bands are influenced by others bands. But in Alice Cooper's case, we were also influenced by old Hollywood moves, horror movies in particular. The original 1931 Dracula, with Bela Lugosi, one of my favorites, featuring the insect eating character Renfield, a lost soul and disciple of Dracula's. Renfield is played by actor Dwight Frye. Hence the name and direction of our song. This time Michael [Bruce] and Alice craft a song about a misunderstood mental patient who spends a lot of time institutionalized wearing a straight jacket. We brought our version of Dwight Frye to life when Alice appears on stage wearing a straight jacket and makes a Houdiniesqe escapes from its restraints. The recording, on our *Love It to Death* album, was helped along the way with Bob Ezrin's classical musical influence and an atomic bomb explosion!"

♫ Bela Lugosi's Dead BY BAUHAUS (1979)

IN HIS OWN WORDS—PETER MURPHY (co-writer, vocalist): "'Bela Lugosi's Dead' was a very tongue-in-cheek song, which sounds extremely serious, very heavyweight and quite dark. But the essence of the song, if you peel back the first layer, is very tongue-in-cheek, 'Bela Lugosi's dead, undead'—it's hilarious. The mistake we made is that we performed the song with such naive seriousness! That's what pushed the audience into seeing it as a much more serious thing. The intense intention going into the performance actually overshadowed the humor of it."

♫ Edie BY THE CULT (1989)

An impassioned paean to Edie Sedgwick, Warhol's most successful superstar and the inspiration, too, behind the Velvet Underground's "Femme Fatale."

♫ Winona BY MATTHEW SWEET (1991)

Sweet insisted the song was never intended to be about Winona Ryder. But she was "a little movie star," and she was at the height of teenstar fame when the song came out. It was an easy mistake for anyone to make.

♫ Wake Up Little Susie BY THE EVERLY BROTHERS (1957)

Or, the perils of going to see a very long, very dull movie when you should be home in bed. Sparks utilized a similar falling asleep at the movies device in their 1975 track "Gone with the Wind," but the Everlys sounded far more believable.

♫ Somewhere in Hollywood BY 10CC (1974)

IN HIS OWN WORDS—KEVIN GODLEY (co-writer, drummer): "A long and complex song detailing Godley and Creme's abiding love for all things 'movie.' We didn't have the tools or the talent to make a proper film so we made our sonic ode to film instead. The electric piano harp effect that starts the track still gives me goose bumps."

♫ I'm in Love With a German Filmstar BY THE PASSIONS (1981)

Darkly erotic, melancholic *noir*, fandom has never sounded so seductive.

♫ This Is Hardcore BY PULP (1998)

Life is a movie and you don't even get to choose the plot. The mid-90s Britpop scene's most chilling hour recasts us all in a XXX feature.

THE EVERLY BROTHERS
OPENING THE Pit CLUB
LOCATED AT BRONCO BOWL / 2600 FORT WORTH AVE. / DALLAS, TEX.
WITH THE FLOYD DAKIL COMBO / DECEMBER 6, 7, 8

♫ New Age BY THE VELVET UNDERGROUND (1970)

An open letter to an idol, sincerity dashed against a little too much honesty. The Velvets' final album, *Loaded*, was utterly overlooked at the time of its release. Today it is seen as one of the key LPs of its era, and this song is one of the reasons why.

♫ TV Eye BY THE STOOGES (1970)

"TV Eye" was a term used by guitarist Ron and drummer Scott Asheton's younger sister, Kathy. It stood for "twat vibe eye," and was employed if she ever caught anybody staring… "he's got a TV Eye on you." Iggy Pop took the phrase and turned it into something far nastier.

THE LOOK OF LOVE (PART ONE)

Boy meets girl. It's the oldest song in the world, and the most revisited one as well. But the course does not always run as smoothly as it could—and even when it does, there's a few surprises in store.

♫ I'm Not In Love BY 10CC (1975)

"I'm Not in Love," says drummer Kevin Godley, was "the cornerstone of the band's creative and commercial success and a recording experiment that took an initially unloved tune from lightweight bossa nova to seismic choral tsunami. The Gods were with us on those sessions. A text book example of 'studio as musical instrument.' Still gives me goosebumps."

"The title is the first thing that happened," guitarist and co-writer Eric Stewart later revealed. "My wife used to say to me, 'why don't you say I love you more often?' And I talked to Graham [bandmate Gouldman] about this, and came up with the title 'I'm Not in Love,' but here are all the reasons why I am very much in love. And it was also quite quirky and very 10cc to switch something on its head and say 'I'm not in love,' but I am."

Famously, "I'm Not in Love" required in the region of 256 vocal overdubs to complete. Less famously, it also required a guest appearance from Kathy Warren, the receptionist at Strawberry Studios. "They were trying to work out what to put in the middle eight, and a telephone call came through for Eric," Warren recalled. "So I went to the studio door and just opened it quietly and whispered, `Eric, there's a phone call for you.' And they all said, `That's it!' The line they asked me to say was, `[whispered] Be quiet, big boys don't cry'."

The band themselves believed "I'm Not in Love" was a risky release; "we decided to put it out, thinking it would either be a hit, or a resounding flop," Lol Creme admitted, with Gouldman adding, "Phonogram said that as well." 10cc's second British #1, and a #2 smash in America, "I'm Not in Love" was included on the soundtrack to the movie *The Stud* ("I'm dying to see Joan Collins' bum working away to it," Eric Stewart sniggered), and has also spawned a wealth of cover versions, something which Graham Gouldman (one of the song's coauthors) remains uneasy about. "Petula Clarke's 'I'm Not in Love,' disco style, is probably the worst cover I've ever heard of any song. Chrissie Hynde's was a bit plain; her voice is brilliant, so you can't knock her for that, but it sounded a bit like we've got three hours to do this, so let's knock it out."

"There was another version of 'I'm Not in Love,' but it was a completely different feel," Graham Gouldman adds. "It was like a bossa nova, but it didn't work at all. Fortunately, the song stayed with us; we knew the song was good, and then [drummer] Kevin Godley came up with a different beat and [guitarist] Lol Creme came up with the idea of the choirs. And that was it."

Someone to Lay Down Beside Me

BY KARLA BONOFF (1977)

One of the undisputed queens of the mid-1970s West Coast, Bonoff is frequently remembered more as a songwriter than a performer (Linda Ronstadt cut the best known version of this one). Either way, loneliness has never sounded so heartbroken or desperate.

Somebody to Love

BY THE JEFFERSON AIRPLANE (1967)

There might well be an ounce of irony in the lyric, but there's also a degree of tenderness—no matter how bad things seem to be, having someone to love will always make them better. Probably.

Amoruese **BY KIKI DEE** (1973)

It was Foreigner, heaven help us, who said "it feels like the first time." But Gary Osborne's translation (from the original French), and Kiki Dee's performance reminded us what the first time *really* feels like.

Pictures of Lily **BY THE WHO** (1967)

Another straightforward cinema song, right? Lily is Lily Langtree, the silent movie heroine. But it's the pictures that concern us here, as Pete Townshend broaches the sticky subject of masturbation in a way that even AM radio could love.

Love Is the Drug **BY ROXY MUSIC** (1975)

With a lascivious rhythm, a bass that swings your hips and Bryan Ferry's most in your groin vocal, the sexiest one night stand on record.

House of Fun **BY MADNESS** (1982)

The age of sexual consent in England, in case the lyric confuses you, is sixteen. And what better way to celebrate your coming of age by heading down to the House of Fun to purchase some party hats? In other words, a young man remembers buying his first pack of condoms.

FAME AND FORTUNE
(ANDY, WHERE'S MY FIFTEEN MINUTES?)

Some people spend their entire lives trying, and never get off the bottom rung. Others take a few faltering steps, and then plummet back to earth. Rock'n'roll may make heroes of its most honorable failures, but that doesn't change the fact that they were failures to begin with, and a few near-posthumous column inches when they're far too old to care; or a song being snagged for a television commercial once you've been in the ground for forty years … well, they might be nice for the friends and family (the accountants don't mind, either), but for you?

It was Andy Warhol who once decreed that everybody will be a star for fifteen minutes, and multiple social commentators have been reminding us of that ever since—including David Bowie, who's had more fifteen minutes than most people have had hot dinners, but still found time to demand another in the Tin Machine rocker "I Can't Read." But be careful what you wish for, because fame comes with its own sharp teeth.

♫ Superstar BY THE CARPENTERS (1971)

Karen Carpenter was probably nobody's idea of the ultimate rock groupie, but she transforms Leon Russell's lament into a thing of shimmering beauty. See you at the backstage door.

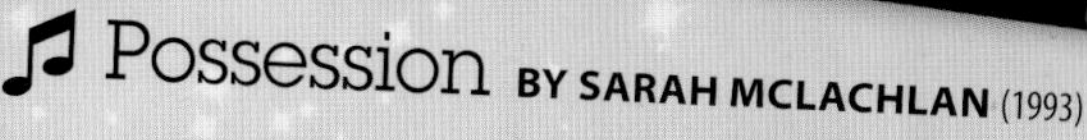

♫ Possession BY SARAH MCLACHLAN (1993)

An open letter to a besotted fan, suggesting he seek out someone more attainable for his desires to fixate upon. Incredibly, a real life stalker, Uwe Vandrei, sued McLachlan in 1994, claiming that it was his letters that inspired the song. The case ended when Vandrei committed suicide.

♫ Protection BY GRAHAM PARKER (1979)

A taut, paranoid rocker with just enough funk to keep the dance floor hopping, Parker looks at life on the other side of the critical pen.

Doll Parts BY HOLE (1995)

Released following the suicide of Hole singer Courtney Love's husband Kurt Cobain, and irrationally reinterpreted in the light of that tragedy, "Doll Parts" is in fact a lament for the manner in which an artist's most basic privacy becomes the public's plaything once the spotlight falls.

Fifteen Minutes BY KIRSTY MACCOLL (1989)

A nightclub jazz feel enfolds one of MacColl's most scathing lyrics, reflecting upon her own moments of superstardom in late-eighties Britain. A BBC tribute documentary produced following Kirsty's death in 2000 handed this song on to Cerys Matthews, whose stark guitar and piano take renders it even more brutal.

Gold BY JOHN STEWART (1979)

The eternal quest for success, transmuting base vinyl into precious million sellers. And if you wonder why it sounds a bit like Fleetwood Mac, Lindsay Buckingham and Stevie Nicks were right up front in the mix.

Wild World BY CAT STEVENS (1971)

"I was trying to relate to my life," Stevens mused. "I was at the point where it was beginning to happen and I was myself going into the world. I'd done my career before, and I was sort of warning myself to be careful this time around, because it was happening. It was not me writing about somebody specific, although other people may have informed the song, but it was more about me. It's talking about losing touch with home and reality— home especially."

Mr Soul BY BUFFALO SPRINGFIELD (1967)

Another early Neil Young jewel, shot through with a tongue in cheek nod to the Stones, "Mr Soul" is a song of defiance and drama. Like... Come on, then, take your best shot...

Reward BY THE TEARDROP EXPLODES (1981)

Liverpool gave us the Beatles, but it also gave us Julian Cope and the Teardrop Explodes, the city's finest export since, indeed, the Fabs. The opening lyric says it all – "bless my cotton socks, I'm in the news."

Cat Stevens

♫ Overnight Sensation BY THE RASPBERRIES (1974)

Eric Carmen would soon be topping the chart as a solo performer. Before that, though, his band came so close to stardom that they could taste it. And this song is their declaration of intent. Fifteen minutes? Gimme gimme!

♫ All Apologies BY NIRVANA (1993)

Oozing ironic intent, "All Apologies" lines up alongside another cut from Nirvana's third album, "Rape Me," as a pointed look at the manner in which the media can so easily forget (or, more appropriately, ignore) the fact that its quarry might have feelings.

♫ Star BY STEALERS WHEEL (1973)

Enjoy it while you can, because you'll be back on the shelf before you know it, and so it proved for Stealers Wheel. Frontman Gerry Rafferty would be back soon enough, though, with the smoky smooch of "Baker Street" (336).

♫ Bullet with Butterfly Wings BY THE SMASHING PUMPKINS (1995)

Frontman Billy Corgan aligns this fragile fury with the band's experiences on the 1994 Lollapalooza tour, tiring of the "alternative" bracket that the Pumpkins had risen so high in, and the demands that the acclaim made on the group.

♫ Seven Nation Army BY WHITE STRIPES (2003)

A simple road lament, tiring of a life spent eternally on tour, and forever being on display. Which is a fair enough complaint for any pop star to make, although you do sometimes want to grab them by the throat and remind them, if you wanted anonymity, you should have found a real job.

NIRVANA
IN UTERO
White Stripes
The Smashing Pumpkins
Mellon Collie and the Infinite Sadness
The Paybacks
Sat Nov 29, 2003
Masonic Temple
Detroit
Art © 2003 Gary Grimshaw • Dedicated to the memory of Jared Ditcher • #JC6

QUEEN FOR A DAY

Do you want a serious discussion on the value of royalty in the modern world? A searing indictment of the hypocrisy of privilege? A mumbled apology for an outdated system, justified by its value to the tourist trade? Or should we just accept, different folks for different strokes, that no system of government is perfect, but at least a royal family keeps the paparazzi occupied?

Unfortunately, that's not always a good thing, either—as anyone who has heard Elton John's "Candle in the Wind 97" will recall.

♫ Little Queenie **BY CHUCK BERRY** (1959)

Love across a crowded soda pop—how many guys fell in love with a girl they first saw leaning on the record machine?

♫ God Save the Queen

BY THE SEX PISTOLS (1977)

Written in the run up to the Queen of England's Silver Jubilee festivities in 1977, and released just weeks before the big day, the Pistols' rousing condemnation does not actually diss Her Majesty in the slightest. It's people's interpretation of what she stands for that really gets singer Johnny Rotten's goat.

♫ Two Princes **BY THE SPIN DOCTORS** (1993)

One of those cute little numbers in which a Prince (real or otherwise) reminds his girl that it's not the amount of money in his wallet that matters, it's the amount of love in her heart. Or something like that.

♫ King of the Rumbling Spires

BY TYRANNOSAURUS REX (1969)

A solid slab of post-Tolkienesque mythology from one of the precious few songwriters who actually knew how to use such subjects wisely. Marc Bolan's best lyrics were incredibly evocative, immensely believable, and the mood of celebration here is so vivid as to be palpable.

♫ Prince Charming

BY ADAM AND THE ANTS (1981)

The life of the privileged dandy. At the time, so much was made of Adam's videos that the songs seemed somehow secondary. Time has proved that they weren't.

The Sex Pistols

WHO ME, BITTER? BITTERNESS, BETRAYAL, AND GETTING YOUR OWN BACK

Yes it's childish, yes it's pointless, and yes, there are so many better ways of using energy than sitting around bearing grudges and plotting revenge. But are they as much fun?

Probably not.

♫ Violet BY HOLE (1995)

Courtney Love spits out rage and devotion in equal parts. Written before husband Kurt Cobain's death, but released in its immediate aftermath, "Violet" is impossible to hear without applying your own interpretation to the lyric. Which is how all the best songs should sound.

♫ Dancing in the Dark BY BRUCE SPRINGSTEEN (1984)

When his manager asked him to write a hit single, Bruce Springsteen got mad. Very mad. So mad, in fact, that he went off and wrote one. Ha, that'll teach ya.

♫ Get Back BY THE BEATLES (1969)

Paul gets pointed to his increasingly artful bandmates—stop pretending you're something you're not.

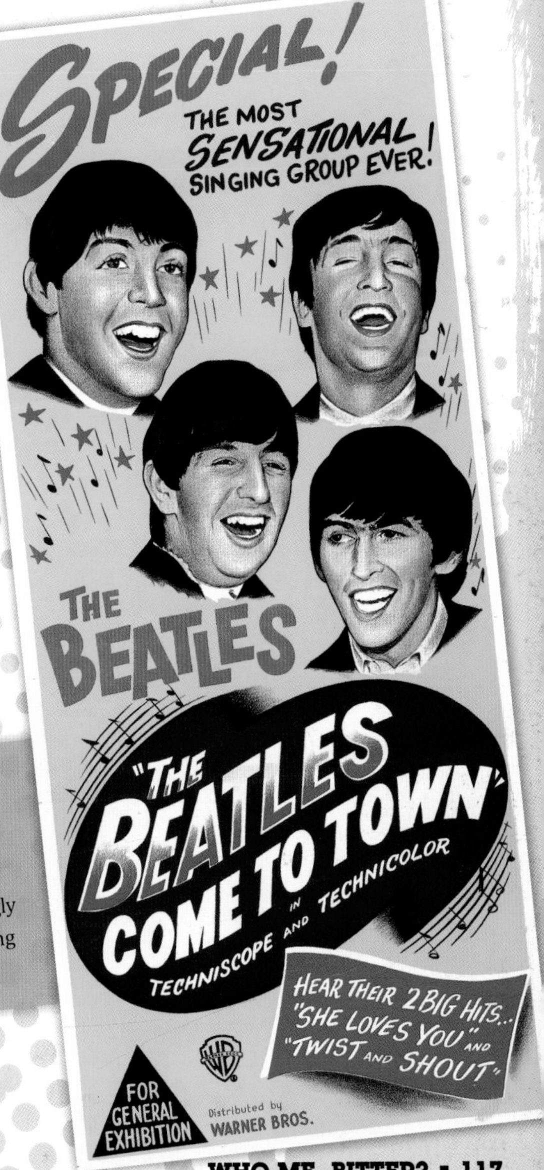

♫ Alternate Title BY THE MONKEES (1967)

The pre-fab four were in England when Mickey Dolenz overheard the phrase "randy scouse git" and, without inquiring what it means ("oversexed ass from Liverpool," or thereabouts) titled a new composition for it. More linguistically-minded heads prevailed before release, of course, but the raving rage of the chorus still makes you wonder who the luckless target of Dolenz's anger might have been.

♫ Positively Fourth Street BY BOB DYLAN (1965)

Dylan was already the master of the three-minute put-down when he delivered this nasty little notice, complete with one of the most damning lyrics anybody has ever set to music. I wish you could stand in my shoes, he sings, and that I could stand in yours. Because then you'd see what a drag it is to be you. Ouch.

♫ It's All Over Now, Baby Blue BY BOB DYLAN (1965)

Dylanologists have downed several rain forest's worth of paper trying to deduce towards whom this brutal farewell is addressed, but the fact is, Dylan was drawing towards closure in so many different relationships at this time that he could have been warning off anybody, or anything.

♫ I Don't Want to Know BY NILS LOFGREN (1975)

Less a revenge song than an ode to total indifference. He knows his girl is fooling around, he knows she has at least one other guy on the go. But you know what? He doesn't care.

♫ Say Hello, Wave Goodbye BY SOFT CELL (1982)

A brusque brush off set to a haunting (synthesized) woodwind line. A lot of people accused the synthipop bands of just singing along with a doorbell chime. This beauty proved that they could write songs as well.

♫ This Corrosion BY THE SISTERS OF MERCY (1987)

The break-up of the original Sisters of Mercy allowed a lot of bad feeling to spill out, in the pages of the music press and on vinyl. But personal vitriol has rarely sounded so vivacious.

♫ Seether BY VERUCA SALT (1994)

You know how sometimes, someone gets you so mad that you just want to punch them? That's what this song is about.

♫ When Do I Get to Sing 'My Way'? BY SPARKS (1994)

Sibling rivalry is always unpleasant—ask the Kinks and Oasis. But Ron and Russell Mael would seem to have extra special reason to hate each others' guts... one is good looking and sings like an angel; the other's stuck behind the keyboards and looks like Adolf Hitler. But they'd been in a band together for 25 years before this tell-all opus hit the streets (with a video to match the lyric as well), and surely the only solace was—they didn't really mean it. Did they?

♫ Tunnel of Love BY THE FUN BOY THREE (1983)

To paraphrase Edwin Starr—"marriage? HUH! What is it good for?" Quite a lot, if you happen to be a divorce lawyer. The twisted tale of the death of a teenaged marriage, wrung through Terry Hall's most soul-shattered vocal.

♫ In Bloom BY NIRVANA (1991)

Asked what this song was about, Cobain explained he was thinking about those songwriters who pen lyrics, but don't have a clue what the song is actually about. Ouch!

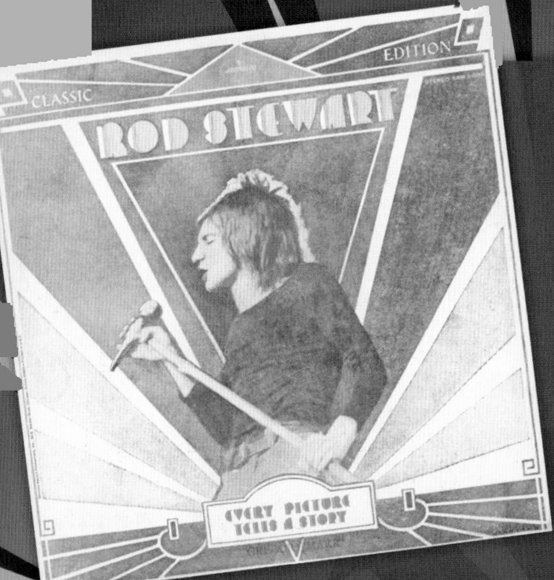

THE POWER OF POSITIVE THINKING

That's right. Look on the bright side of life. Keep your chin up. Worse things happen at sea. Well, it worked the last time I tried it....

♫ Reason to Believe **BY ROD STEWART** (1971)

A Tim Hardin song that might have been lost on the B-side of "Maggie May." So deejays played them both.

♫ I Still Haven't Found What I'm Looking For **BY U2** (1987)

Which, presumably, is why they shot the video on the streets of Las Vegas.

♫ Lust for Life **BY IGGY POP** (1977)

By 1977, Iggy Pop had convinced almost everyone who'd heard of him that he was hellbent on self-destruction, and his body packed the scars to prove it. But the hyperactive pulse of "Lust for Life" let us know what was really going on behind the broken glass and bleeding flesh.

♫ Lay Down (Candles in the Rain) **BY MELANIE** (1970)

"Lay Down" was written following Melanie's Woodstock performance in 1969. It rained throughout her set; then, when the downpour finally stopped, the audience began lighting candles.

♫ It's Alright Ma, I'm Only Bleeding BY BOB DYLAN (1965)

The title's ironic intent has not stopped a host of politicians from lifting lines from this song for their own purposes.

♫ You're So Vain BY CARLY SIMON (1972)

Are we the only people who feel this song lost a lot of its impact once Carly explained who it was really about (record label chief David Geffen), as opposed to whoever the last forty years of rumors suggested it was about (backing singer Mick Jagger, actor Warren Beatty....)?

♫ Hold Your Head Up BY ARGENT (1972)

A lurching, loose organ/chant work out that just happened to pack a killer chorus, "Hold Your Head Up" lives and dies around a mid-song split second of almost absolute deathly silence.

♫ My Life BY DIDO (1999)

"What I choose to do is of no concern to you and your friends." You can do, and say, so much with an opening line like that.

♫ It's My Life BY THE ANIMALS (1965)

So quit trying to tell me how to live it. There is no angrier declaration of independence than this.

♫ The Sounds of Silence BY SIMON & GARFUNKEL (1966)

Paul Simon once claimed it took him six months to write this song, one line a day. "The key to 'The Sound of Silence' is the simplicity of the melody and the words, which are youthful alienation. It's a young lyric, but not bad for a 21-year-old. It's not a sophisticated thought, but a thought that I gathered from some college reading material or something. It wasn't something that I was experiencing at some deep, profound level—nobody's listening to me, nobody's listening to anyone—it was a post-adolescent angst, but it had some level of truth to it and it resonated with millions of people. Largely because it had a simple and singable melody."

♫ Rebellion (Lies) BY ARCADE FIRE (2005)

"Ninety percent of what people are forced to listen to in a day is someone trying to force them to buy something that they don't need," composer Win Butler said of this song. "At a certain point you've got to say, 'shut up.' It's like someone poking you in the face all the time. You can just ignore it and try to go about your life in a certain way or say, 'stop hitting me.' You have to say, 'Stop! Stop! Stop hitting me. Stop pushing me.' I think that's rebellion.

♫ The River BY BRUCE SPRINGSTEEN (1980)

Written after his brother-in-law lost his construction job, Springsteen explained, "[this was] a breakthrough song for me. It was in the detail. One of the first of my story songs that eventually led to Nebraska."

♫ Come Back BY MIGHTY WAH (1984)

Pete Wylie's Wah were one of the highlights of the early 1980s post-punk scene, their arsenal bristling with self-affirming rockers and revolutionary ferment. Clashing the two together, "Come Back" reminds us never turn our backs on our dreams.

♫ My Hero BY THE FOO FIGHTERS (1998)

"My Hero," explained the band, ""was written as a celebration of the common man and his extraordinary potential." Which made it especially galling after John McCain adopted it as his campaign anthem during the 2008 Presidential battle. "To have it ... used in a manner that perverts the original sentiment of the lyric just tarnishes the song."

ROCK THE BOAT

Time was, a man wanted to escape from a doomed love affair, an abusive family, or the long arm of the law, he'd run away to sea. That option doesn't seem to be so available these days, because even the pirates have gone all high-tech, which means Big Brother is watching you everywhere. But the ocean remains a romantic escape and, although there's no bona fide sea shanties on our list, it still gives us plenty to sing about.

♫ Ride Captain Ride BY BLUES IMAGE (1970)

IN HIS OWN WORDS—MIKE PINERA (co-writer): "...We got to the end of the sessions, we only had another day in the studio, and the producer looked at me and said 'I've got to be honest here, you guys haven't come up with a hit single, or something that has the potential to be one, and this is your last day so I don't know if you can pull out a miracle, do you have anything else you can play me?' And I said oh yeah, I think I remember something, so I went and told the rest of the band what I'd just been told and our keyboard player, Skip, had this little chorus line he'd been playing with that went 'ride captain ride upon your mystery ship.... Dadada dadada.'

"That was all he had, but that inspired me and I went into a back room, I locked myself in and I just cleared my mind and all of a sudden the words and the melody started flowing all at the same time, I came out and went to the producer and said 'okay, you want to hear this?' And I started playing 'Ride Captain Ride' to him and he said 'oh my God, this is it, this is the one we've been waiting for.' It was done in fifteen minutes. We cut it right that day."

"Ride Captain Ride" climbed to #4 on the *Billboard* chart, but the story did not end there. Writing the opening verse, Pinera took a little inspiration from the keyboard he was sitting at, a Model 73 Rhodes Piano; "it had a big chrome emblem saying 'Model 73' and I saw the words 'seventy three' and what got me was the rhythm of the word, so the next thing I know, I'm singing 'seventy three men sailed out from San Francisco Bay....'

"Now, here is the weird thing that happened. It got released, it was in the Top Ten, #1 in a lot of regional markets, and my manager gets a call from the Pentagon, wanting to know how I, as the writer of those words, knew about the secret spy ship *USS Pueblo*. My manager goes 'what are you talking about? I don't think Mike knows anything about this stuff. Ask him about the latest Gibson guitar and he'll know, but he doesn't know anything about spy ships. Which I didn't.

"But it turned out that I had written a song about an incident that had not yet happened; that happened after the song was released; and here's what made it so freaky. There were seventy-three men who sailed out from San Francisco Bay on this secret spy mission that nobody was supposed to know about, and they got in trouble out there on the ocean, they were captured and taken prisoner.... As far as I was concerned, those lyrics were free form flow of consciousness stuff, but then you get to the third verse...

But no one heard them callin', no one came at all, 'Cause they were too busy watchin' those old raindrops fall

The radio guy from the *Pueblo* told me that when they were actually captured, it was during a massive storm and they couldn't get word out on the radio to say what was happening.

As a storm was blowin' out on the peaceful sea, Seventy-three men sailed off to history

"Anyway, all this stuff was happening and it coincided exactly with the words to 'Ride Captain Ride.' So the Pentagon thought 'this can't be a coincidence.' To this day, people come up to me after the show to say hi, and it turns out they're guys who were on the *Pueblo*, and they say 'thanks for writing that song about us.' And I have to tell them...."

♫ Submission BY THE SEX PISTOLS (1977)

A succession of aquatic puns and wordplays define the one song in the punk icons' arsenal that pointed the directions that they might have journeyed in next—had they not been holed beneath the waterline just three months after releasing it.

Creedence Clearwater Revival

♫ A Salty Dog BY PROCOL HARUM (1969)

A tale of an ancient mariner, all circling gulls, creaking masts and the forlorn knowledge that you'll probably never see home again. Composed with all the weary despair of a William Hope Hodgson thriller, an old time sailor's life is brought home with a resounding crash.

♫ Proud Mary BY CREEDENCE CLEARWATER REVIVAL (1969)

It's indicative of just how suspicious people can get that, when "Proud Mary" first set sail up the charts, a lot of folk thought that it was all about drugs—the line "keep on rolling" was to blame. In fact, it's the story of a Mississippi paddle steamer as she plies the waters from Memphis to New Orleans, a reminder of the days when the river was alive with traffic, and every smokestack told a tale.

♫ Life in Dark Water BY AL STEWART (1978)

Or, as one shark said to the other as a submarine passed by, "do you have a can opener?" As chilling and claustrophobic as its subject matter, a highlight of Stewart's *Time Passages* LP.

♫ Aqualung **BY JETHRO TULL** (1971)

Not, sadly, a song about the diver's greatest friend, but a lament for a man who sounds like he's wearing one. So it shouldn't really be in this section, should it?

♫ Nantucket Sleighride **BY MOUNTAIN** (1971)

Prefaced by a lilting minute of the instrumental "Taunta," but crossfaded to render the two inseparable, Mountain's mightiest moment is not merely the greatest song about whale hunting ever written (although it is). It also packs some of the most scintillating guitar-organ interplay this side of Vanilla Fudge.

♫ No-one Knows

BY THE QUEENS OF THE STONE AGE (2002)

A series of snapshots of a life that drifts forlornly by, climaxed by the startling image of dead lifeboats under the sun.

GIANT STEPS ARE WHAT YOU TAKE...

Do you know why madmen are called lunatics? Because their moods, it was once believed (and is still assumed) are affected by the moon. Which does make you wonder why man has always been so keen to go trampling all over its surface. After all, if it can drive you nuts from 238,857 miles away (that's the average... sometimes it's further), what's it going to do when you're actually walking on it?

The Moody Blues

♫ Pink Moon **BY NICK DRAKE** (1972)

A pink moon occurs during an eclipse; Drake took the title from a folklore dictionary he was browsing.

♫ Nights in White Satin

BY THE MOODY BLUES (1967)

Often regarded as the founding father of Prog Rock, the Moodies *Days of Future Passed*, from which this was taken, was originally conceived as a stereo demonstration album!

♫ Marquee Moon

BY TELEVISION (1977)

Eleven minutes of ricocheting angles, it's hard to say what the song's about, but you'll know how it makes you feel.

♫ Harvest Moon

BY NEIL YOUNG (1992)

The follow up, two decades on, to "Harvest."

♫ Moondance BY VAN MORRISION (1970)

Morrison wrote the song, originally, as a saxophone solo. "I used to play this sax number over and over, anytime I picked up my horn." It was only later that he add lyrics and further instrumentation.

♫ C Moon BY WINGS (1972)

Paul McCartney was listening to "Woolly Bully" one day, when he heard the expression L-7, meaning "square." C-Moon, he decided, would be the opposite equation.

♫ Because the Night BY PATTI SMITH (1978)

A Bruce Springsteen / Patti Smith cowrite. "Bruce gave me the music," Smith explained, "and it had some mumbling on it, and Bruce is a genius mumbler, like the sexiest mumbler I ever heard. I just listened to it, and the words just tumbled out of me. He wrote the tag 'because the night belongs to lovers,' which was in between the mumbling, he'd say that every once in a while. He said I didn't have to keep that bit, but I thought it was really nice. I always write the lyrics to my own songs, unless they're covers, but I respected his lyrics, and I thought it was a very nice sentiment, so I built the rest of the lyrics, which are obviously mine, around his sentiment."

♫ A Night In BY TINDERSTICKS (1995)

Britain's Tindersticks were crafted from the cloth of so many of rock's past introspectives that even their happiest songs sounded down. This one, though, nails the sound of solitude to everybody's wall.

I CAN SING A RAINBOW—
THE UNITED COLORS OF SONG

Red and yellow and pink and green orange and purple and blue.... Spot the odd one out.

♫ Famous Blue Raincoat BY LEONARD COHEN (1971)

"The problem with that song," Cohen bemoaned in 1994, "is that I've forgotten the actual triangle. Whether it was my own—of course, I always felt that there was an invisible male seducing the woman I was with, now whether this one was incarnate or merely imaginary I don't remember, I've always had the sense that either I've been that figure in relation to another couple or there'd been a figure like that in relation to my marriage.

"I don't quite remember but I did have this feeling that there was always a third party, sometimes me, sometimes another man, sometimes another woman. It was a song I've never been satisfied with. It's not that I've resisted an impressionistic approach to songwriting, but I've never felt that this one, that I really nailed the lyric. I'm ready to concede something to the mystery, but secretly I've always felt that there was something about the song that was unclear."

That may be true. But to several subsequent generations of listeners, the mystery is good enough.

Leonard Cohen

Silver Springs BY FLEETWOOD MAC (1977)

Incredibly released only on a B-side in 1977, this Stevie Nicks song swiftly revealed itself to be an awful lot of people's favorite.

Brown Eyed Girl

BY VAN MORRISON (1967)

Morrison originally wrote the song about an interracial relationship, with the title "Brown Skinned Girl." Aware that certain radio stations might not take kindly to the sentiment, he changed its title—presumably forgetting that they wouldn't much like the line about "making love in the green grass" either.

"More to the picture than meets the eye... Rock'n' Roll will ne
NEIL YOUNG
A CONCERT FANTASY
RUST NEVER SLEEPS
SEE IT IN RUST-O-VISION
DOLBY STEREO
SHAKEY PICTURES presents NEIL YOUNG & CRAZY HORSE
WITH A CAST OF THOUSANDS
AN INTERNATIONAL HARMONY RELEASE

Heart of Gold BY NEIL YOUNG (1972)

One of several songs Young wrote while recuperating from a back injury that left him unable to play electric guitar. He swiftly recovered—"This song put me in the middle of the road. Traveling there soon became a bore so I headed for the ditch."

Paint It Black BY THE ROLLING STONES (1966)

"That was the time of lots of acid," recalled Mick Jagger. "It has sitars on it. It's like the beginnings of miserable psychedelia. That's what the Rolling Stones started—maybe we should have a revival of that."

♫ A Whiter Shade of Pale BY PROCOL HARUM (1967)

According to Gary Brooker, who cowrote the song with Keith Reid, "I'd been listening to a lot of Classical music, and Jazz. Having played Rock and R&B for years, my vistas had opened up. When I met Keith, seeing his words, I thought, 'I'd like to write something to that.' They weren't obvious, but that doesn't matter. You don't have to know what he means, as long as you communicate an atmosphere. 'A Whiter Shade of Pale' seemed to be about two people, a relationship even. It's a memory. There was a leaving, and a sadness about it. To get the soul of those lyrics across vocally, to make people feel that, was quite an accomplishment. I remember the day it arrived: four very long stanzas, I thought, 'Here's something.'"

♫ White Light White Heat BY THE VELVET UNDERGROUND (1968)

The title track to the Velvet Underground's second album, an amphetamined rush that truly did blur at the sound of speed.

♫ Pretty In Pink BY THE PSYCHEDELIC FURS (1981)

IN THEIR OWN WORDS (John Ashton, guitarist): "We were just hanging out. I was playing the riff, Richard started singing, and there you have it. We wrote it in ten minutes."

♫ Blackberry Way BY THE MOVE (1968)

Composer Roy Wood never denied that "Blackberry Way" was his response to the Beatles' "Penny Lane." "We were all very influenced by what The Beatles were doing because they were the best songwriters around."

♫ Wear Your Love Like Heaven BY DONOVAN (1967)

What does God look like? Colors.

♫ Kodachrome BY PAUL SIMON (1975)

One of Paul Simon's most enduring songs was banned by the British BBC, for contravening their regulations regarding advertising in song.

WHAT'S THAT SMELL? IT'S HOT WAX, OF COURSE

Did you know that the nose is the most sensitive sense we have? Even more sensitive than the ears? Well, I hope you remember that, the next time you're listening to your Captain and Tenille albums.

♫ Smells Like Teen Spirit BY NIRVANA (1991)

The most significant song of the early 1990s, and the birth of the (shortlived) Grunge movement, "Smells Like Teen Spirit" developed out of the band's attempts to work out a cover of Boston's "More Than a Feeling" (122)

Nirvana

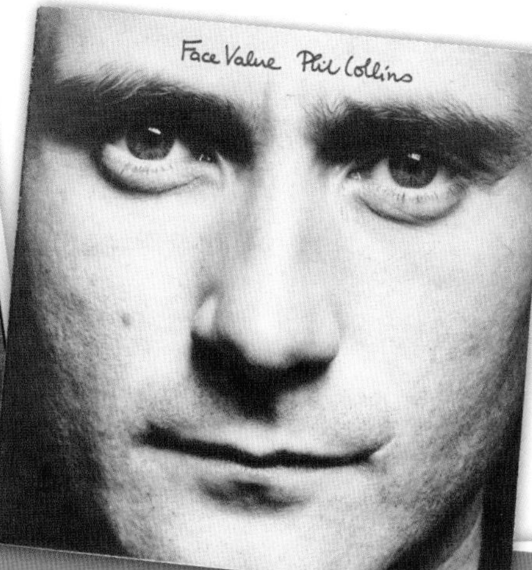

♫ In the Air Tonight BY PHIL COLLINS (1981)

Collins was still best known as the drummer with Genesis when he set his recent divorce and its dramas to music, in the form of his debut solo album. This was the first single ... and the first song written for the project, in fact. Percussive menace and a lyric that chills.

♫ The Air That I Breathe **BY THE HOLLIES** (1974)

The Hollies had more or less stopped having hits by 1974, just the occasional lower-rung entry that not many people would even remember. And then they came out with this, soaring guitars, yearning vocals, soul-baring lyrics… a blueprint, in fact, for half of U2's late 1980s career. Simply breathtaking!

♫ Something in the Air

BY THUNDERCLAP NEWMAN (1969)

The archetypal one hit wonders, Thunderclap Newman were brought together by the Who's Pete Townshend. He produced their records, he played bass on the single. And apparently, he shouted at them. According to songwriter Speedy Keen, "Something in the Air" was born out of Townshend bursting into an unproductive recording session, and shouting "fucking get it together!" Expletive deleted, Keen took the song from there.

♫ Life's a Gas **BY T REX** (1971)

From the epochal *Electric Warrior* album, a simple song of love and affirmation.

♫ Love Is Like Oxygen **BY THE SWEET** (1978)

IN THEIR OWN WORDS – BRIAN CONNOLLY (vocalist): "I love the arrangement on that song, the synthesisers and acoustic guitar passages. [It lets] us string out more instrumentally and show the musical side of the band."

IT'S ALL GREEK TO ME—SONGS OF FABLE AND MYTHOLOGY

One of the most common criticisms of early rock'n'roll was that it was simplistic; that a profound pop lyric was measured by the number of nonsensical grunts that could be fit into a verse; and that once past the insistence that "I love you, woo-wooo-wooo," the average rocker had the intellectual epth of a piece of very thin paper. Thankfully, opinions have moved on a lot since then, and these are a few of the songs that made a difference.

♫ Supper's Ready BY GENESIS (1972)

IN HIS OWN WORDS—STEVE HACKETT (guitarist): "'Supper's Ready' [was] conceivably the longest continuous piece of rock music that anyone had ever done at that point. There were a number of bands who were involved in long-form rock, Yes and King Crimson, ELP, but there was also a tremendous amount of improvisation involved in that. We worked on a piece that was 30 minutes long. And when we first wrote that, and performed it live, I really thought that the game was up and we'd be sussed for the imposters we were.

"Lyrically, you couldn't really pin it down. There was the gobbledygook factor and all the rest and, in the middle of this long piece, you had the occasional thing that were mini pop songs, like 'Willow Farm' ...which, funnily enough, was one of my favorites. That was one of the strongest segments, it was Beatlesque, very catchy, I thought that was the band playing at its best. Because it was pastiche, it was possible to do that with gusto in most situations.

"[But] I didn't think people would buy long form rock, and... I felt we'd outstayed our welcome by the time we were five minutes into that piece. [In fact], the reverse was true. We were hailed as beings from another realm, that managed to come up with this magic stuff, and so my instincts were entirely wrong."

Genesis

♫ Tarkus BY EMERSON, LAKE AND PALMER (1971)

Devouring one full side of the supergroup's second album, "Tarkus" follows the titular tank-like armadillo's battles with a succession of similarly mechanized mythical beasts—one of whom, the Manticore, would subsequently name the trio's own record label. In concert, incidentally, the "Battlefield" sequence of the multi-themed piece would often incorporate elements of "Epitaph" (249), the King Crimson song that vocalist Greg Lake also voiced.

♫ Isis BY BOB DYLAN (1975)

Ostensibly a pre-Spielberg take on archaeology, *Raiders of the Lost Mouth-Harp* if you will, although the average Dylanologist will offer up far more symbolic meanings than that.

♫ Tales of Brave Ulysses BY CREAM (1967)

Artist Martin Sharp had just returned from vacation when he bumped into his friend and neighbor Eric Clapton. He'd been to Formantera, in the Balearic Islands—the place where, according to legend, the Greek warrior Ulysses encountered the sirens, the sinister singing spirits who lure sailors to their doom.

"I've just written a song," Sharp announced.

"That's great," replied Eric. "I've just written some music."

The result was "Tales of Brave Ulysses."

♫ Achilles Last Stand BY LED ZEPPELIN (1976)

The echo that opened Zep's *Presence* album, inspired by Robert Plant's recent visit to Morocco, where the Atlas Mountains seem to hold up the sky. Jimmy Page has described it as his favorite Zeppelin song.

♫ The End BY THE DOORS (1967)

Oedipus wrecked—the first time Jim Morrison performed it on stage, during their first ever Hollywood residency, the Doors were banned from the club.

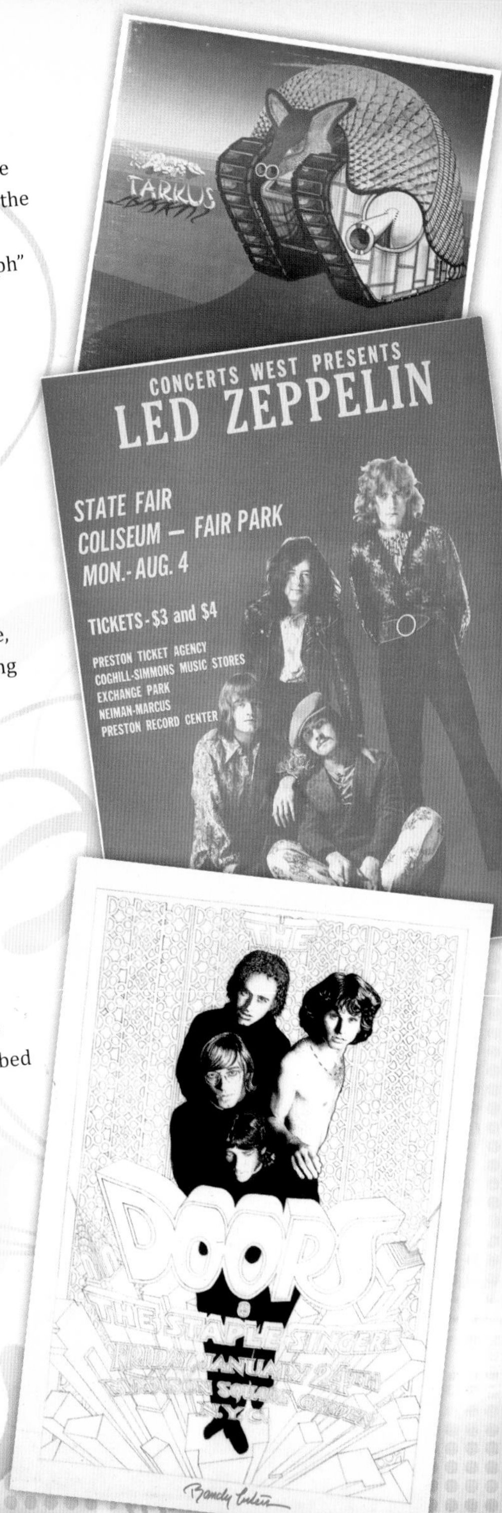

♫ Song to Comus BY COMUS (1970)

IN THEIR OWN WORDS – ROGER WOOTON (composer): It was based on the story of Comus from the *Masque of Comus* by John Milton. Actually I wrote the whole song in one afternoon on an acid trip. The whole concept of riffs, lyrics and ideas all came together in one intense LSD buzz. I remember it vividly. I was back at Eynsford (*the family home*) after leaving Perth Road (*Comus' communal house*). My mum was downstairs and I secretly dropped a tab out of sheer boredom really and "Song to Comus" just started.

BOBBIE WATSON (percussionist): I can just imagine his poor mother (a very nice lady by the way!) sitting downstairs, reading the paper, or cooking dinner, and hearing this frenzied, manic, rasping voice, screaming about rape and taking of virginity, emanating from the bedroom....

ROGER: If you listen to the lyrics you can hear that it was influenced by Diana [the opening cut on Comus' debut album, *First Utterance*]. It was the last song to be written for the album. I wouldn't return to drugs. I've done it and I no longer have the desire to take them. I prefer being more clear headed but I do find that the drug influence lingers on, which means I can still access that part of my mind and those sensations and write as if I was smashed!

GLENN GORING (guitarist): It's a very "colorful" song. It's earthy, rhythmically playful, and often visceral especially when Roger uses his chest as a drum. He always reminds me of some big hairy primate marking out his territory. I think, like a lot of the stuff we play, with "Song to Comus" you never know what's around the musical corner.

ANDY HELLABY (bassist): The song has a lot of carnal rhythms, grunting, and subject matter not usually discussed in polite society. Great prog material. How would I describe the song to people who've never heard it? Lyrically disgusting and musically amazing.

BOBBIE: It starts in a seemingly innocuous mode—"Bright the sunlight summer day, etc...." Then it has the feel of impending doom during the phrases "Comus glare, glare, glare, etc...., Comus bare, bare, bare, etc.... and then the frenzied build up to the rape scene, and the scream. The whole song has a disturbing, gleeful relish in acts of sexual pursuit and violence, and the way in which it's sung adds to this—the different timbres of the voice used in different parts of the song give a horrible, demonic edge to it.

I just think it is a well 'constructed' song, though Rog says it just all came together. The fact that 'it all just flowed' shows in the way it works as a song. I think what caught peoples' attention was that it has a compelling rhythm, which although it stops/starts/speeds up and down in typical prog fashion, basically runs through cohesively, and it has kind of two choruses (a feature of Roger's songwriting), so there is more than one 'hook' and there are parts of it that appeal to different peoples' taste. But basically I think it's the intensity, both in the music and the lyrics is what makes it work so strongly.

ROGER: Really weird and dark and with very violent lyrics. The most disturbing folk band I have ever heard.

♫ Song to the Siren

BY TIM BUCKLEY (1970)

As haunting as the mythical creatures that title it, "Song to the Siren" *will* shipwreck your heart.

♫ Pandora's Box

BY PROCOL HARUM (1975)

Pandora's box was the mythical casket from which all the evil in the world erupted, after it was opened by a curious Goddess. The song, somehow, retains a lot of the mystery that tempted Pandora in the first place.

A PAGE OUT OF HISTORY

"Why don't you turn off that noise and go and read a good history book instead?"

We are all familiar with Hollywood and television's attempts to dramatize great moments, and characters, from history, while the stage has been doing it for centuries. But rock'n'roll has also thrown its cap into the mind-enriching ring, and often with some spectacular results.

♫ Changing of the Guard **BY BOB DYLAN** (1978)

One of those wonderful slices of Dylanology whose meaning shifts from listener to listener. But the sense of high intrigue in a sun-drenched hacienda-style palace gives the song a costume drama mood, even if you can't put your finger on the when and where of it.

♫ Napoleon Bona-part One and Two **BY BUDGIE** (1975)

The punning title (something of a tradition for the Welsh metal trio) and the yearning quality of the opening verse disguises a riff you could flatten valleys with.

♫ Desperado **BY THE EAGLES** (1973)

It's rare that a great cowboy ballad escapes the clutches of the country crowd, but the Eagles knew a great piece of tumbleweed when they saw it.

♫ Soldier Blue **BY BUFFY SAINT MARIE** (1971)

Title song to one of the most compulsive (and, at the time, controversial) westerns ever made, the story of the stranded boy soldier and the kidnapped white woman also reminded us that there are two sides to every story, no matter what the old history books said.

After the Goldrush BY NEIL YOUNG (1970)

More a prayer for the future than a reflection on the madness that sent half of America hurtling westwards to drain mountain streams through little wire baskets, but the optimism of both cannot be mistaken.

Cortez the Killer BY NEIL YOUNG (1975)

It probably wouldn't have seemed so romantic at the time, but the arrival of the first white armies into what was then the New World has taken its place among the greatest legends of the modern age. Alongside Procol Harum's "Conquistador" (956), "Cortez" looks at the invasion from the locals' angle.

The Night They Drove Ol' Dixie Down BY THE BAND (1969)

The song of the South, circa 1864.

Immigrant Song BY LED ZEPPELIN (1970)

Another case of history softening what was once a brutal reality, but who can fail to be stirred by the vision of Norsemen sweeping down from the land of ice and snow?

Alley Oop BY THE HOLLYWOOD ARGYLES (1960)

With arch-prankster Kim Fowley at the helm, a tale of love and romance, Flintstone style. Watch that caveman go!

Indian Reservation BY PAUL REVERE AND THE RAIDERS (1971)

A lot more foreboding, lyrically, than the song's arrangement made it seem, the lament of the Cherokee nation.

Conquistador BY PROCOL HARUM (1967)

He thought he was so powerful in his armor, sword, and galleons. Now look at him, a heap of dust and rust.

Adam Raised a Cain BY BRUCE SPRINGSTEEN (1978)

An evocative slice of Biblical imagery carved out of the heartlands.

RAIN, RAIN, GO AWAY
(OR NOT, AS THE CASE MAY BE)

Let's talk about the weather again.

JAMES TAYLOR

♫ Fire and Rain **BY JAMES TAYLOR** (1970)

"The first verse," Taylor has explained, "is about my reactions to the death of a friend [Suzanne]. The second verse is about my arrival in this country with a monkey on my back, and there Jesus is an expression of my desperation in trying to get through the time when my body was aching and the time was at hand when I had to do it. And the third verse of that song refers to my recuperation in Austin Riggs [a rehab center in Massachusetts] which lasted about five months."

♫ It Might As Well Rain Until September

BY CAROLE KING (1962)

From one of America's finest ever songwriters, one of teendom's finest ever laments. Teenaged angst drowns out the summer time.

THE ROLLING STONES AMERICAN TOUR 1972

♫ Love Reign O'er Me

BY THE WHO (1973)

The final word in the band's 1973 *Quadrophenia* rock opera, hopes and a moped lying dashed on the rocks while the seagulls circle and the surf crashes down.

♫ Get Off of My Cloud

BY THE ROLLING STONES (1965)

A raucous dismissal of modern life in all its most annoying guises.

♫ No Rain BY BLIND MELON (1993)

Fronted by the effervescent Shannon Hoon (whose death in 1995 brought about the band's cruelly premature demise), Blind Melon's eponymous debut album had been out for two years before this was pulled as a single in late 1993… it topped charts worldwide, with a video that is oddly better remembered for its star, a little girl dressed as a bumble bee, than for the song itself. Oddly and unjustly. The song is a cloudless jewel.

♫ Change BY SPARKS (1985)

IN THEIR OWN WORDS—RUSSELL MAEL (vocalist): "It was one of those songs… you try to do stuff and you hope every time you sit down to come up with a new song, that you're going to do something special. And that's one of those times where there's something that really clicked, and when it clicks with us it does it both lyrically and musically. The lyrics are really strong, and then having the seventy-five different sections musically going on, it just really works in that particular song."

The Everly Brothers

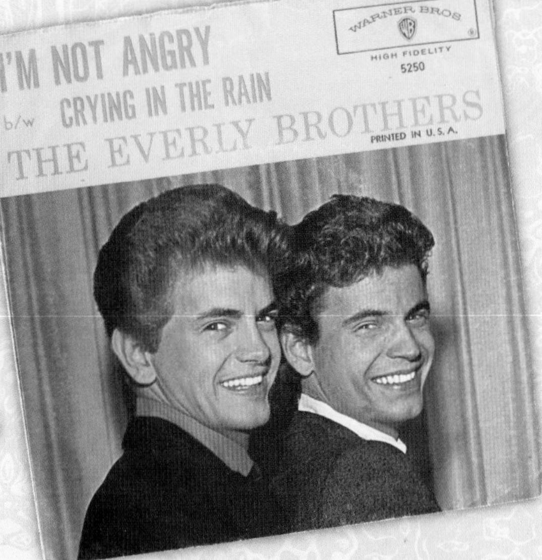

♫ Crying in the Rain BY THE EVERLY BROTHERS (1962)

Their first Brill Building hit (written by Carole King and Howard Greenfield) was their last before their military service.

SEX.... AND DRUGS...

According to the late, great Ian Dury, sex and drugs and rock and roll were all his brain and body needed. And judging from the number of songs to have discussed the subjects, he wasn't alone in that.

♫ Sex and Drugs and Rock and Roll

BY IAN DURY AND THE BLOCKHEADS (1977)

Dury was already well into his thirties, and generally regarded as a yesterday's man when he wrote this, the ultimate anthem of what makes music so magical. The year was 1977, and it seems impossible to believe that nobody had put the three things together beforehand. In song, at any rate.

So, without further ado...

SEX...

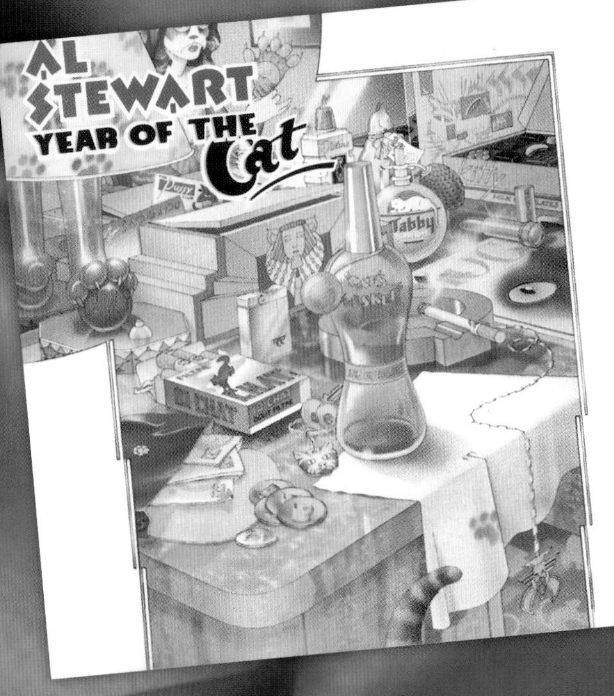

Year of the Cat BY AL STEWART (1976)

Al Stewart's breakthrough song (and album—the song also became the title track for his latest LP), "Year of the Cat" was almost a decade in the writing. Stewart originally wrote it in 1966, after attending a concert by comedian Tony Hancock. "He came on stage and he said 'I don't want to be here. I'm just totally pissed off with my life. I'm a complete loser, this is stupid. I don't know why I don't just end it all right here.' And they all laughed, because it was the character he played... this sort of down-and-out character. And I looked at him and I thought, Oh my god, He means it. This is for real." Two years later, Hancock would commit suicide.

"Foot of the Stage," as the song was originally called, was never recorded. But Stewart returned to the melody in 1975 (the Year of the Cat, according to the Vietnamese calendar), rescripting the song as a Casablanca encounter between an English tourist and a California girl. "He spends the night at her place and when he wakes up, the bus has gone and he's stranded. He just figures 'well, this isn't the way I'd planned my life, but I might as well stick around and make the best of it."

Satisfaction BY THE ROLLING STONES (1965)

Possibly the first song to reference menstruation ("she tells me come back... next week cos... I'm on a losing streak") on the radio.

Venus in Furs BY THE VELVET UNDERGROUND (1967)

Almost fifty years later, "Venus in Furs" is just a neat little song about kinky sex. But imagine how it sounded in 1966, in an age when tales like this weren't simply sold under the counter, the stores that sold them were on the top shelf as well.

♫ Tusk BY FLEETWOOD MAC (1979)

There's no polite way of putting this. It's a song about having an erection.

♫ Passion BY ROD STEWART (1980)

Neil Young once said that even the president of the United States must stand naked. Now Rod Stewart is insisting that he needs passion, too. The White House is getting raunchier by the decade.

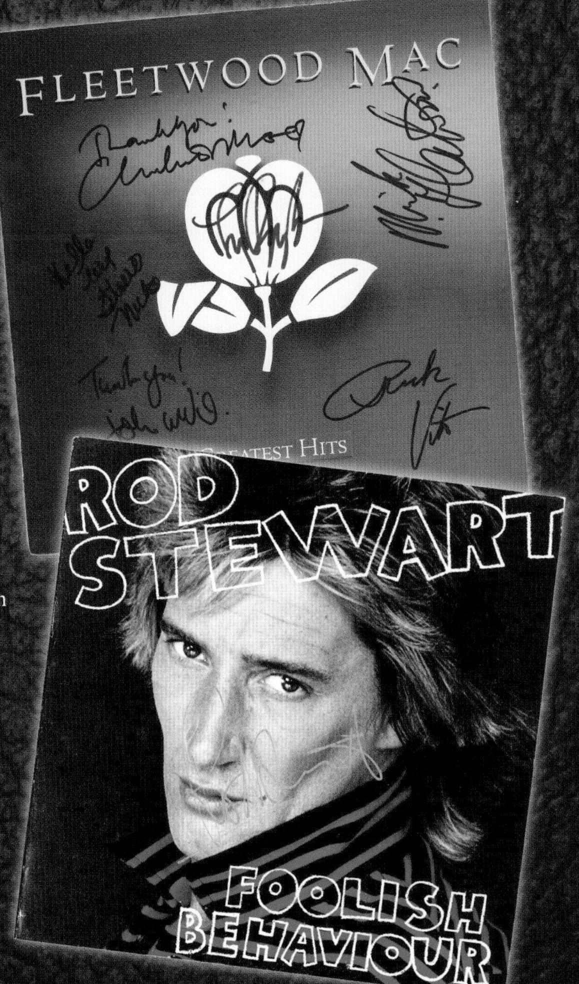

♫ Gimme Some Loving BY THE SPENCER DAVIS GROUP (1966)

You can't put it more plainly than that! The young Stevie Winwood at the helm of the last great beat group of the sixties.

♫ Stay with Me BY THE FACES (1971)

Rod Stewart and company rock out their memories of the morning after the one night stand before.

♫ Desire BY U2 (1988)

Not a band that one normally associates with raw sexual passion, but they don't keep too many secrets here.

♫ Sex and Candy BY MARCI PLAYGROUND (1997)

Well, if you can't have drugs and your iPod's gone missing...

♫ Love U More BY SUNSCREEM (1992)

A shopping list of impossible feats, none of which are really necessary.

AND DRUGS....

Don't bogart that joint. Man.

I'm Waiting for the Man **BY THE VELVET UNDERGROUND** (1967)

The intriguing thing is, at no point does Lou Reed ever explain *why* he's waiting, or what the man has. An unreleased David Bowie cover of this same song, dating from 1967, suggests this song should be placed in the section above, but it does fit better here.

Mother's Little Helper **BY THE ROLLING STONES** (1966)

From the mid-'60s days when a housewife only needed look depressed for her doctor to fill her up with tablets, a surprisingly mature slice of social commentary from the last people a lot of folk would have looked for such a thing.

You Can't Always Get What You Want **BY THE ROLLING STONES** (1969)

This sound piece of advice from Mom and Pop Stone seems to have been hijacked for so many other multimedia purposes that it's easy to forget that it's a song about trying to score in Swinging London... and check out the choirboys' pronunciation! Glarsss for glass, caarnt for can't... it's like *Masterpiece Theatre* for junkies.

Eight Miles High **BY THE BYRDS** (1966)

History remembers the Byrds for breaking through with a rocked-up version of Dylan's "Mr Tambourine Man." But it was this nugget of proto-psychedelia, all knowing grins and crafty winks, that truly set things rattling.

Heroin **BY THE VELVET UNDERGROUND** (1967)

"There's nothing wrong with writing a song about a bad trip," Velvet Underground drummer Maureen Tucker once said. No there isn't. Which is why Lou Reed used to tie off one arm and pantomime shooting himself up while he sang it.

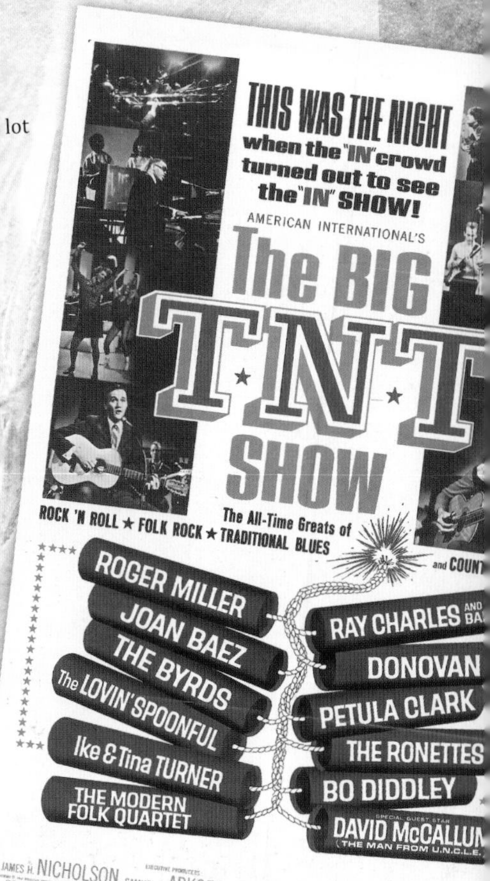

THIS WAS THE NIGHT
when the "IN" crowd
turned out to see
the "IN" SHOW!
AMERICAN INTERNATIONAL'S
The BIG
T·N·T
SHOW
The All-Time Greats of
ROCK 'N ROLL ★ FOLK ROCK ★ TRADITIONAL BLUES
ROGER MILLER
JOAN BAEZ
THE BYRDS
The LOVIN' SPOONFUL
Ike & Tina TURNER
THE MODERN FOLK QUARTET
RAY CHARLES
DONOVAN
PETULA CLARK
THE RONETTES
BO DIDDLEY
JAMES H. NICHOLSON, SAMUEL Z. ARKOFF & HENRY SAPERSTEIN · PHIL SPECTOR

♫ Ashes to Ashes BY DAVID BOWIE (1980)

In 1969, David Bowie introduced us to Major Tom, the lonely spaceman hero of his hit "Space Oddity" (448). A decade later, he told us how Tom filled his spare time.

♫ I Had Too Much to Dream Last Night BY THE ELECTRIC PRUNES (1967)

When you say "dream," what exactly do you really mean?

♫ My White Bicycle BY NAZARETH (1975)

Originally recorded by Tomorrow, the mode of transport is not necessarily a euphemism. But place yourself in the heart of Amsterdam, sampling legal spliff from a host of late night cafes, and it makes a lot of sense.

♫ Itchycoo Park BY SMALL FACES (1967)

The bulk of the Small Faces went on to become the Faces, while frontman Steve Marriot moved on to Humble Pie. But before all that, the quartet was responsible for some of the classiest pop of the late 1960s. And "Itchycoo Park" was the classiest of all, an acid trip set to some of the dreamiest music ever.

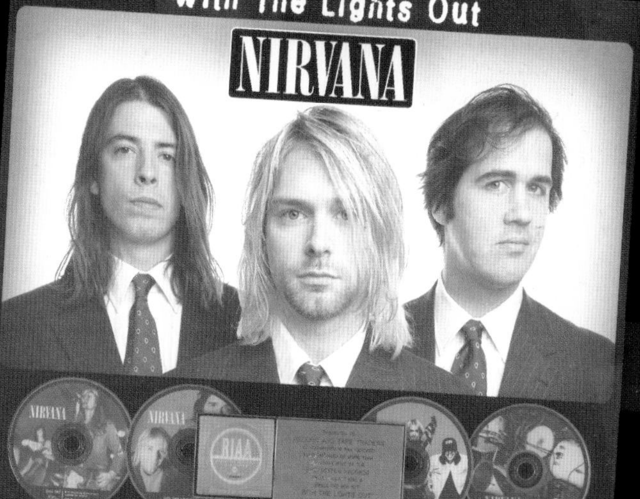

♫ Lithium BY NIRVANA (1991)

Lithium began its pharmaceutical life as a treatment for gout, in the 19th century. By the early 20th century, it was being given to patients suffering from mania, and in 1929, it was introduced as one of the key ingredients in a new hangover cure called Bib-Label Lithiated Lemon-Lime Soda—or 7-Up. It then became a dietary substitute for salt in patients suffering from heart conditions. An unsurprising rash of related deaths followed, leading to lithium being banned from sale in 1949, before being approved as a tranquilizer in 1970. The perfect subject for a song, then.

♫ Stoned Soul Picnic BY LAURA NYRO (1968)

"I think that's the best song about pot munchies ever. All her lyrics were very abstract, but the roots are obvious. The glorification of a psychedelic feeding frenzy!"—Alan Merrill, author of "I Love Rock'n'Roll" and the late Laura's favorite cousin.

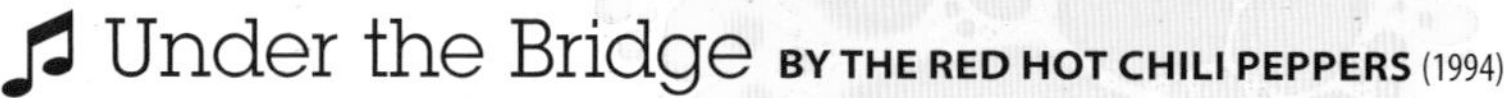

♫ Under the Bridge **BY THE RED HOT CHILI PEPPERS** (1994)

Bearing more of songwriter Anthony Kiedis' soul than ever before, "Under the Bridge" was "this really sad thing, sort of sensitive," recalling the hours he had spent downtown with the gangs, looking to buy the drugs that would help him erase another day from his diary—and which did, in fact, start life as a diary. "It was kind of an *a cappella* poem I would sing out of my notebook," he recalled. "It's about some hardcore self-destructive memories. But it's also about shedding the burden of those demons and knowing that there is always the possibility of emerging from that fucked-up space."

♫ Sister Morphine **BY THE ROLLING STONES** (1971)

Depending upon your state of mind, this is either the most terrifying anti-drug song in the world... or it isn't.

♫ The High Road **BY BROKEN BELLS** (2010)

You can take the title, and the metaphor strewn lyric, any way you like. But if you look at the way we've waged the war on drugs, and the absurd fixes that have tried to prevent people fixing, the epic, and much-anticipated combination of producer Danger Mouse and vocalist James Mercer definitely fits the bill.

♫ Brand New Key **BY MELANIE** (1972)

British comedy act the Wurzels scored a monster hit with this in 1975, rewiring Melanie's roller skates, etc, through a combine harvester. The original, however, has other forms of grass on its mind.

♫ Loaded **BY PRIMAL SCREAM** (1990)

Ignited by a sampled snippet of 50s-style anti-drug propaganda, "'Loaded' is a damned good approximation of how it feels to... er, have some fun?

♫ The Dope Show **BY MARILYN MANSON** (1998)

If ever there was reason to have a Glam Rock revival, this was it.

♫ Granny Takes a Trip **BY THE PURPLE GANG** (1967)

The song that gave its title to one of London's most happening sixties boutiques, and it ain't about no magical mystery tour. Or is it?

AND ROCK AND ROLL....

It has been said that a musician singing about rock'n'roll is a lot like a plumber singing about installing pipes, or an architect dancing to high rise shopping malls. Except it isn't. To sing about rock is to affirm your commitment to an artform that has the power to change worlds, alter perceptions, and instill belief in the callowest soul.

The only drawback is, it's hard to do it well.

Sultans of Swing BY DIRE STRAITS (1979)

Not content with singing about their job, Dire Straits compound the crime by singing about their workmates as well. And we all became sultans for a while.

Rock and Roll Music BY CHUCK BERRY (1957)

Even after all the years, the song that says it all.

Hey Hey My My BY NEIL YOUNG (1979)

Bookended by the acoustic "My My Hey Hey," Young's ruminations on the state of rock at the end of the 1970s were ineffably flavored by the impact of Punk Rock, but still this is Classic Rock in excelsis. And if you should ever tire of the song, listen to that guitar pitch instead.

Sweet Little Rock'n'Roller BY CHUCK BERRY (1958)

If you're gonna rock, you need someone to roll with.

Rock On BY DAVID ESSEX (1973)

The mood, the movement, the beat that can't still be stilled.

Move It BY CLIFF RICHARD AND THE SHADOWS (1958)

The birthplace of homegrown rock in the UK, the launching pad for the longest-lived superstar rock has ever seen and, like the best of Chuck Berry, a song whose uber-pure intent outweighs every other quality.

Golden Age of Rock'n'Roll BY MOTT THE HOOPLE (1974)

In concert, they kicked off this song with a verse from "American Pie"… "the day," Ian Hunter would croak, "the music died…. Or did it?" And "Golden Age" would explode, triumphant, defiant, immortal. Phenomenal.

God Gave Rock and Roll to You BY ARGENT (1973)

Cut at a time when an awful lot of religious organizations were getting very vocal about rock's evil influence, it was hard to tell just how tongue-in-cheek (or otherwise) this was. But it's equally difficult not to be stirred by it, either.

ONE MORE FOR THE ROAD—SONGS OF DRINK AND DRUNKENNESS

Drinking songs have a long and sometimes lewd tradition—many of our favorite folk songs started life as the laments of one drunken sot or another, and that's as true of the ones we still sing today, while sailing six sails to the wind, as those that are now recalled only by sober preservation societies. And why not? Getting drunk and singing loudly go together as well as any two pursuits that require only minimal co-ordination, and if you don't actually know all the words, then you should just sing them even louder. Nobody will mind, honestly.

♫ Tom Traubert's Blues (Four Sheets to the Wind in Copenhagen)

BY TOM WAITS (1976)

The title's Scandinavian but the refrain is pure Australia. Waits recalled, "well I met this girl named Matilda [in Sydney]. And uh, I had a little too much to drink that night. This is about throwing up in a foreign country."

♫ The Perfect Drug **BY NINE INCH NAILS** (1997)

From the greatest neo-nihilists of the Nineties, a love song to alcohol.

♫ Strange Brew **BY CREAM** (1967)

You know the one, it's the cheapest bottle at the liquor store.

♫ Alcohol **BY THE KINKS** (1972)

The cautionary tale of the well-to-do businessman, lured to the life of a lush by a floozy. Not a song to drown your sorrows to!

♫ Suffocate **BY GREEN DAY** (2002)

Life at the broken end of the bottle.

♫ I Want to See the Bright Lights Tonight

BY RICHARD AND LINDA THOMPSON (1974)

Former Fairport Convention guitarist Richard had already released one solo album when he and wife Linda pooled their talents as a duo that was greater than a band ten times their size. This was the title track to their first LP together, and sobriety has never felt so over-rated.

BABA LOVE COMPANY PRESENTS
England's No. 1 Concert Group

Cream

WAR... WHAT IS IT GOOD FOR?

WELL, THERE HAS TO BE SOMETHING, ELSE WE WOULDN'T FIGHT SO MANY

What if they started a war and nobody came? Then there'd be nobody there to sing about it. Anti-war songs make up one of the largest single canons in the rock'n'roll arsenal, with the vast majority additionally heralding from the Vietnam era, the decade-long struggle that not only changed the way we look at government, it also changed the way we looked at music. For the first time, rock had found a purpose, a single unifying cause that bound audiences more firmly than any political ideology could ever have hoped.

♫ Powderfinger BY NEIL YOUNG (1979)

With no suggestion of a point in either space or time, the saga of a young man protecting his family home from an invading gunboat is a timeless tale of doomed heroism. The song was originally written with Lynyrd Skynyrd in mind; they never recorded it, but Ronnie Van Zant was apparently buried in a Neil Young T-shirt.

♫ Life During Wartime BY TALKING HEADS (1979)

Listening to the Talking Heads, it's easier to equate them to a chemistry lesson than anything so mundane as music. Tunes to rattle test-tubes to. But the last days of civilization are utterly compulsive, and they're decidedly not like a disco.

♫ Invisible Sun BY THE POLICE (1981)

Beautifully non-specific, "Invisible Sun" decries violence, oppression, war, and just about everything else that was wrong with the world back then. Most of which has only gotten worse since then.

The Police

War Pigs BY BLACK SABBATH (1971)

Inspired by Vietnam, but looking back, too, over the centuries of conflict that had already occurred, the message of "War Pigs" was both chilling and simplistic. It is not the citizens of a nation that starts a war. It is the politicians who won't actually have to go out and fight it. "They," sang Ozzy, "leave that all to the poor."

Universal Soldier BY DONOVAN (1965)

And another reminder that no matter what uniform he wears, a soldier is just a soldier—following the same orders from the same generals as every other one.

Zombie BY THE CRANBERRIES (1994)

The struggle that the English press euphemistically called the Irish Troubles was nearing its end when this was released, after a quarter century of violence. But that didn't dent the power of the song.

Brothers in Arms BY DIRE STRAITS (1985)

An epic ode to solidarity, painted in both words and tone.

Volunteers BY JEFFERSON AIRPLANE (1969)

In 1967, it was the Airplane who turned around JFK's famous quote and demanded, "I'd rather know what my country can do for me." They have not changed their tune.

♫ Shots BY NEIL YOUNG (1981)

A tumultuous glimpse into the heart of revolution.

♫ I Feel Like I'm Fixin' to Die Rag

BY COUNTRY JOE AND THE FISH (1967)

Flippant enough to become a favorite campus singalong, but dark enough to taint even the most light-hearted get together, San Francisco's Fish celebrate the draft with jugband joy.

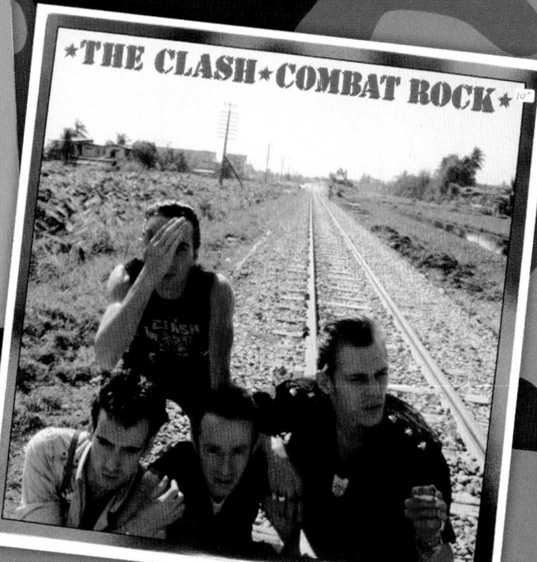

♫ Straight to Hell

BY THE CLASH (1982)

The invaders' presence in a war zone doesn't end when the occupying forces leave. The next generation remembers....

♫ Child in Time BY DEEP PURPLE (1970)

The most potent, and poignant of all British rock commentaries on the then on-going Vietnam War, "Child in Time" survived to become a private anthem for many of the underground opposition groups forged by the political turmoil of 1980-90s eastern Europe.

SHUT UP, CAN'T YOU SEE I'M ARGUING WITH YOU— THE PROTEST SINGER SHOUTS

As with so many other things, it was Bob Dylan who thrust protest music into the public eye, even though he simply followed in footsteps that had been worn down by centuries of folk singers. Apres lui, however, the deluge...

♫ Instant Karma **BY THE PLASTIC ONO BAND** (1970)

John and Yoko Lennon wrap one of their most caustic lyrics around one of their most buoyant melodies.

♫ American Woman **BY THE GUESS WHO** (1970)

As protest songs go, this one really did seem somewhat obtuse, and the lilting acoustic intro completely throws you for a loop. But then the riff comes in, and the anti-war dance starts here.

♫ Almost Cut My Hair **BY CROSBY STILLS NASH & YOUNG** (1970)

It's a little hard to take the line about freak flags seriously, but David Crosby's realization that a teenager growing his hair is committing a revolutionary act really did seem profound at the time.

Crosby Stills Nash & Young

Hey Mr Draft Board BY DAVID PEEL (1970)

From the crown prince of late sixties hairy hippydom, it's a simple statement, stated simply. Hey Mr Draft Board... I DON'T WANNA GO.

Alice's Restaurant BY ARLO GUTHRIE (1967)

An epic recounting of so many different strands that it's amazing that the son of protest legend Woody Guthrie only needed eighteen minutes in which to recount them. Still one of the single funniest songs of its era, it also pricks a lot of hypocritical bubbles, not least of all the discovery that a convicted litterbug might not be considered moral enough to napalm women and children.

Eve of Destruction

BY BARRY MCGUIRE (1965)

The protest boom was fading when P.F. Sloan penned "Eve of Destruction," but McGuire took it to number one regardless, as he rounded up absolutely everything that was wrong with the world... probably never even guessing that half a century on, the song still sounds frighteningly relevant.

I've Seen All Good People

BY YES (1971)

There's two sides to every battle, and both believe that they're right.

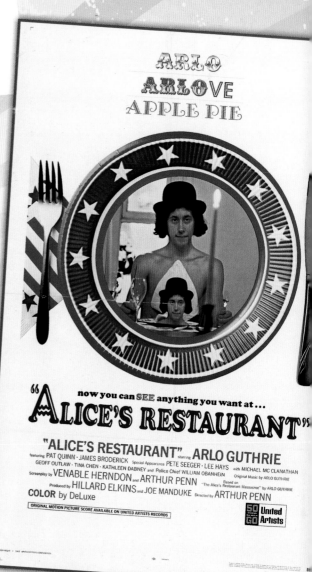

EIGHT DAYS A WEEK

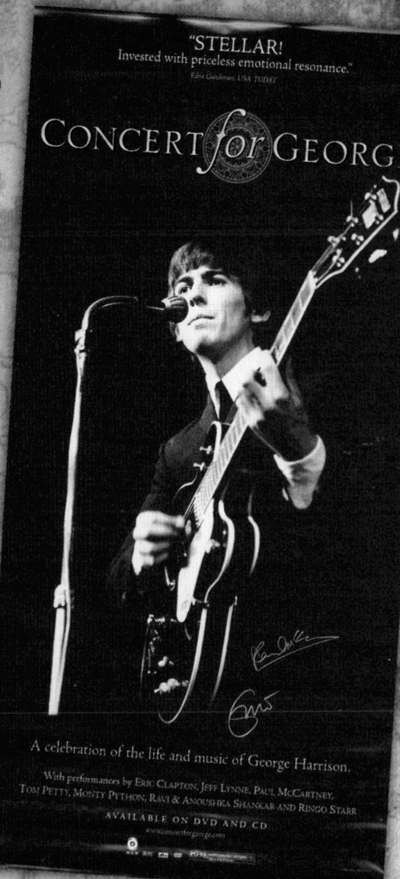

"STELLAR!
Invested with priceless emotional resonance."
CONCERT for GEORGE
A celebration of the life and music of George Harrison.
With performances by Eric Clapton, Jeff Lynne, Paul McCartney, Tom Petty, Monty Python, Ravi & Anoushka Shankar and Ringo Starr
AVAILABLE ON DVD AND CD

♫ Another Day BY PAUL MCCARTNEY (1971)

John Lennon may have mocked this song in his brutal How Do You Sleep?", but both melodically and lyrically, the tale of drudgery in "Another Day" is superior to any of the third-person observation songs ("Eleanor Rigby," "She's Leaving Home") for which McCartney is usually praised.

♫ All Day and All of the Night BY THE KINKS (1964)

Following up "You Really Got Me" (85) was never going to be easy, but the Dave Davies riff factory just shrugged and got on with it.

♫ Till the End of the Day BY THE KINKS (1965)

Another celebration of everyday life, another brain-jarring riff. What a magnificent band the Kinks were!

BILL GRAHAM PRESENTS
THE ROLLING STONES
OAKLAND STADIUM
NOVEMBER
4 & 5, 1989

♫ Eight Days a Week BY THE BEATLES (1965)

Paul McCartney was on his way to John Lennon's house when he asked his chauffeur what sort of week he was having. "I usually drove myself there, but the chauffeur drove me out that day and I said, 'How've you been?'—'Oh working hard,' he said, 'working eight days a week.'"

♫ Saturday Night BY THE BAY CITY ROLLERS (1975)

At the peak of their powers, the Tartan Terrors were as big as the Beatles, but without the longevity. All apart from this paean to the weekend, that is.

♫ Ruby Tuesday BY THE ROLLING STONES (1967)

Keith Richards recalled writing this about girlfriend Linda Keith. "I don't know, she had pissed off somewhere. It was very mournful, very, VERY Ruby Tuesday and it was a Tuesday."

DANNY ADLER'S TOP FIVE

Cincinnati born and bred, Danny Adler first came to American notice as the hot young guitarist in Elephant's Memory. He didn't stick there long, though, quitting after just one single ("Skyscraper Commando") and relocating to the U.K. in the early 1970s. There he launched Roogalator, kings of the London Pub Rock scene, and purveyors of some of the greatest rocking funk blues hybrids that pre-Punk Britain ever heard—including the immortal "Cincinnati Fatback" (649). Since then, on either side of returning to America, Adler has played with stars as far apart as reggae icon Niney, Charlie Watts, Jack Bruce, and Bo Diddley, while unleashing a never-ending stream of delirious solo albums.

♫ Feel Fine BY THE BEATLES (1964)

"It's Friday afternoon and she says "yes." Crystalline winter sunshine guitars, a marshmallow pillow of vocal harmony, contrasting relaxed raw Lennon. Ringo's incredible on this; I read in a period interview that he'd been listening to jazzers Chico Hamilton and Yusef Lateef. Like the Byrds mixing in John Coltrane and Ravi Shankar in "Eight Miles High," or Elvis blending Bill Monroe (bluegrass), Les Paul (jazz) and Arthur "Big Boy" Crudup (blues). To evolve and fight air pollution, we need to listen with big ears.

"PS: The Beatles did so many things before anybody else, that it's hard to believe Paul McCartney was the first bassist ever to lean his instrument up against an amplifier. Because he wasn't. But he was the first to insist the resultant feedback was then included on the record."

♫ It's Only Love BY THE BEATLES (1965)

"When it comes to love songs of the more tender variety (at which the Beatles excelled), I was tempted to choose either "Every Little Thing" or "In My Life." However, in the end I selected this *Help* highlight, because to me it's a much more profound love song than "Yesterday" (from the same LP). The kicker to some of the greatest ballads is that apparently perhaps-sarcastic offhanded remark that veils a very powerful emotion with humor. Making it all the more poignant. It's an effect that I've tried to evoke in my own ballads ("Dirty Old Men Need Loving"), but here are the masters."

♫ Bo Diddley BY BO DIDDLEY (1955)

"A totem of funk groove and trance, this record—like James Brown's "Cold Sweat" of 1967—changed the way we walk."

♫ You Can't Judge a Book By a Cover BY BO DIDDLEY (1965)

"Although Willie Dixon, the great blues composer ("Hoochie Coochie Man") wrote this, it was Bo's super rock'n'roll delivery and sensuously confident humor that sailed it through the goalposts. It's also quite a strong subliminal civil rights message, delivered at a very delicate time. A true plea for universality. And Big Fun."

♫ Opal BY SYD BARRETT (1969)

"When it comers to ballads and sharing the most delicate, tender feelings with a listener, it's hard to top this one. Syd's lyrics paint vivid landscapes of summer comfort, peace, isolation, and anxiety. And then he simply turns and faces us with the full and honest, totally frank, statement—that he really does want to connect, but he's slowly drifting out of reach."

LET'S GET TOGETHER AGAIN— SONGS OF REUNION

We said it before and we'll say it again. The best poart of breaking up is when you're making up. So put away those (depending on your age) Leonard Cohen / Cure / Coldplay records and put on a happy face.

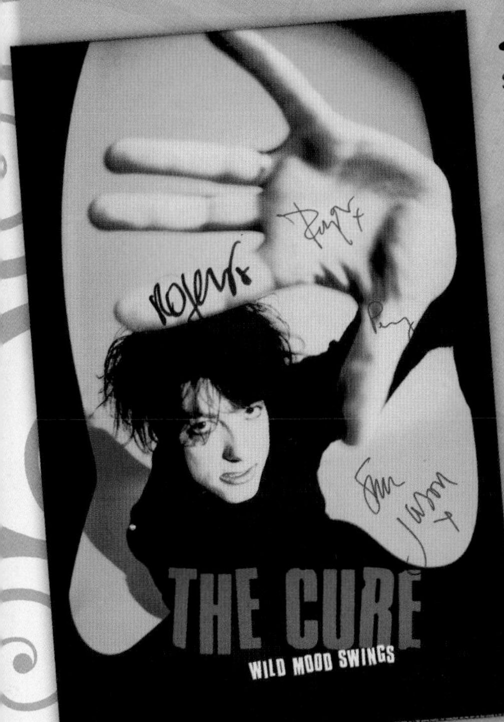

A Night Like This BY THE CURE (1985)

Stepping sharply away from the Gothic Rock tag that hung round their neck in the earliest years, Robert Smith and the Cure look at love and declare, just like the song says, that it's just the most gorgeously stupid thing…

Let's Hang On BY THE FOUR SEASONS (1965)

A reminder, in the heat of a blazing argument, that the grass is not always greener on the other side of the turnpike.

Rikki Don't Lose That Number BY STEELY DAN (1974)

Because she might not write it down for you again. Steely Dan are alternately loved or hated for the sheer perfection of their musical creations. But sometimes, they really did hit the nail on the head.

Love Will Come Through BY TRAVIS (2003)

A song, says author Francis Healy, "about love, not in the classic context of that sort of Hollywood love, you know the one that you see in the pictures "I love you/I love you too" and it's not like that. It's love that you have with your mum and your dad and your friends and stuff, love that equals hope in the face of everything, the love that conquers all, and its dedicated to that love."

Breakdown BY TOM PETTY AND THE HEARTBREAKERS (1977)

More than three decades on from release, it's still difficult to fault Tom Petty's debut album. "American Girl" is the undisputed jewel, of course. But "Breakdown" reminds us that persistence is a virtue, and that's a lesson that can never be repeated too often.

Tom Petty & The Heartbreakers

When We Meet Again BY NICOLE REYNOLDS (2010)

From Reynold's 2007 CD This Arduous Alchemy, a song of almost unbearable hyper sexuality… anticipation that's well worth waiting for.

WHILE MY GUITAR... SIX STRINGS UNLEASHED

One of the many arguments that threatened to transform this book into a battleground of Somme-like proportions was—what about those songs that are better regarded as instrumental showcases, than for whatever lyrics or sentiments they might embody?

Well, what about them? They're still great songs, as I discovered when I saw Lynyrd Skynyrd play, back in the early 1990s. The guitar monitor cut out at the beginning of "Free Bird," but half the audience was still playing ghost guitar, and it still got the greatest roar of the evening. And why? Because some songs are just wonderful, whatever instrument they may or may not be played on.

♫ While My Guitar Gently Weeps BY THE BEATLES (1968)

Recalling this most delicately moving of all his Beatle contributions, George Harrison mourned, "the [others] were not interested in it at all." He alone seemed convinced that "it was a nice song," but take after take passed by, and the performance was nowhere near completion. "The next day I was with Eric [Clapton], and I was going into the session, and I said 'we're going to do this song, come on and play on it'."

Clapton was horrified at the suggestion. "I can't do that. Nobody ever plays on the Beatles' records." But Harrison was adamant. "I said 'Look, it's my song and I want you to play on it.' So Eric came in…"

Clapton, studio engineer Brian Gibson told Beatles historian Mark Lewisohn, was "very quiet, [he] just got on and played. I remember [him] telling George that Cream's approach to recording would be rehearse, rehearse, rehearse, spending very little time in the studio itself, whereas the Beatles' approach seemed to be record, record, record and then eventually get the right one." According to the Abbey Road studio's own session log, 'While My Guitar Gently Weeps' ran to 44 separate takes, although Clapton was involved with only one, take 25.

♫ Elemental Child BY TYRANNOSAURUS REX (1970)

Indelibly marking the moment when Marc Bolan left behind his former acoustic folk leanings, to give birth to Glam Rock at the dawn of the 1970s.

♫ Layla BY DEREK & THE DOMINOS (1970)

Packing perhaps the most impassioned vocal of Eric Clapton's entire career, but driven by the twin guitar attack of Clapton and friend Duane Allman, the title track from the one and only album by this exercise in anonymity was a straightforward love song for girlfriend (later wife) Patti Boyd. The title was borrowed from the epic Persian poem "The Story of Layla."

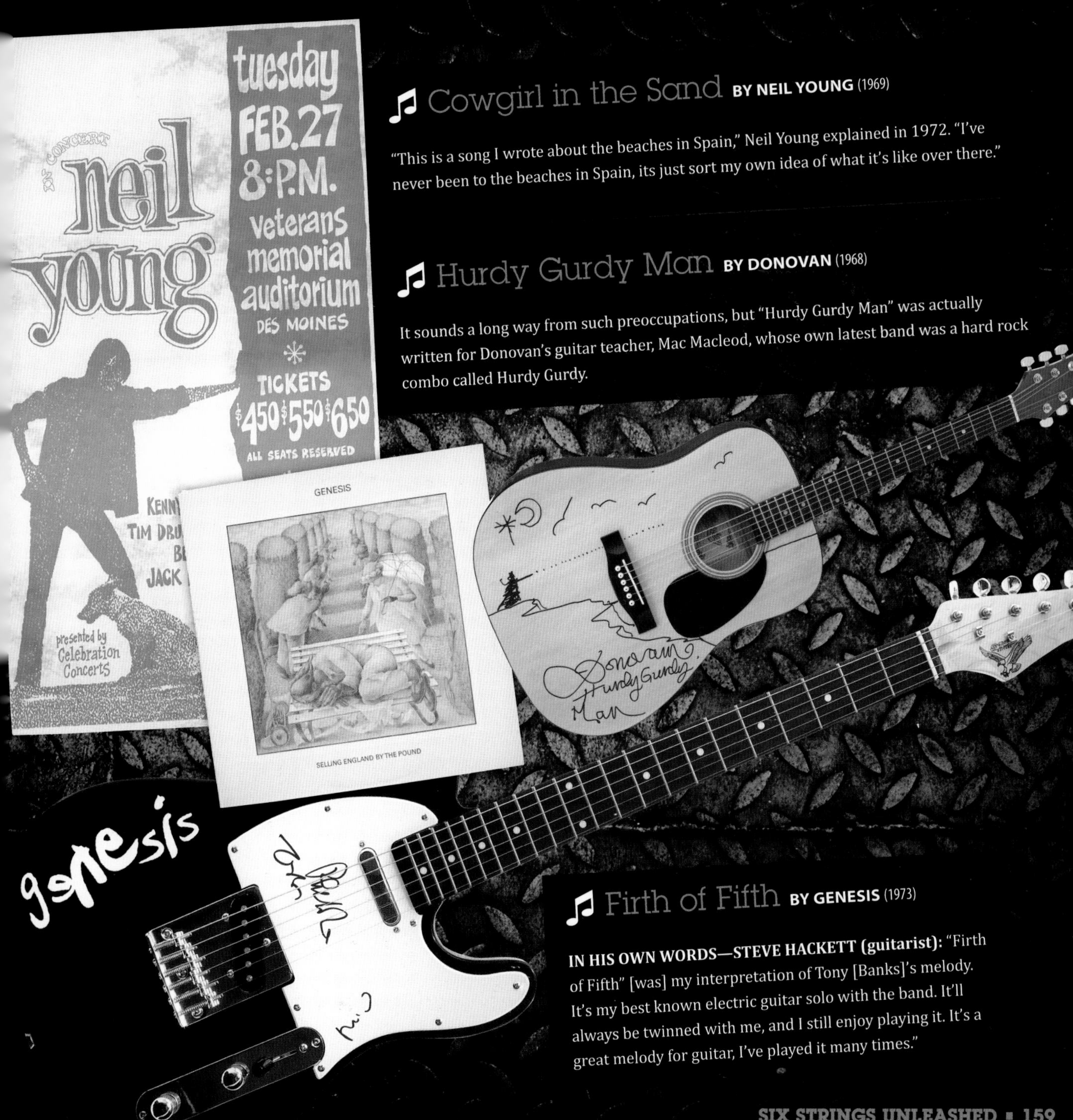

♫ Cowgirl in the Sand **BY NEIL YOUNG** (1969)

"This is a song I wrote about the beaches in Spain," Neil Young explained in 1972. "I've never been to the beaches in Spain, its just sort my own idea of what it's like over there."

♫ Hurdy Gurdy Man **BY DONOVAN** (1968)

It sounds a long way from such preoccupations, but "Hurdy Gurdy Man" was actually written for Donovan's guitar teacher, Mac Macleod, whose own latest band was a hard rock combo called Hurdy Gurdy.

♫ Firth of Fifth **BY GENESIS** (1973)

IN HIS OWN WORDS—STEVE HACKETT (guitarist): "Firth of Fifth" [was] my interpretation of Tony [Banks]'s melody. It's my best known electric guitar solo with the band. It'll always be twinned with me, and I still enjoy playing it. It's a great melody for guitar, I've played it many times."

MAKING WAVES—ROCKING THE RADIO

In the red corner, Jagadish Chandra Bose. In the white corner, Guglielmo Marconi. In the blue corner, Alexander Stepanovich Popov. And in the green corner, Nikola Tesla. One of these men probably invented the radio. But it could as easily have been somebody else.

♫ Radio Activity BY KRAFTWERK (1975)

IN HIS OWN WORDS—WOLFGANG FLUR (Performer): "'Radio Activity' had nothing to do with atoms, which is a popular misconception I am always trying to correct. That was a joke, a pun. We were talking about the radio activity of broadcasting. While we were touring America in 1975, the radio stations from town to town, that was new to us, that was very interesting. Everywhere we went, new radio stations, we liked that idea very much, and the chorus of 'Radio Activity,' 'radioactivity is in the air for you and me,' that was what that was about."

♫ Capital Radio BY THE CLASH (1977)

Written after London's local station, Capital Radio, instituted a policy of not playing Punk Rock in 1977—a policy that was hastily withdrawn once the UK charts began filling up with the stuff.

♫ Radio Free Europe BY REM (1981)

Hey boys, what's your first single about? Oh, Cold war politicking....

♫ Radio Radio

BY ELVIS COSTELLO AND THE ATTRACTIONS (1978)

One of the most dismissive songs ever written about what was, in the pre-MTV era, the single most important marketing tool any artist could have—and an especially effective one as well, given the medium's propensity for playing *any* song that mentioned its name in the chorus.

Panic BY THE SMITHS (1986)

You probably couldn't get away with a song like this any longer. Imagine, a room full of schoolchildren singing "hang the DJ, hang the DJ"…. Somebody would complain.

On the Radio BY CHEAP TRICK (1978)

The sad thing is, this is one of the Cheap Trick songs that you probably don't hear on the radio!

Radio Radio Radio BY RANCID (1994)

Savage singalong punk rock from California's answer to the Clash.

CALIFORNIA UBER ALLES

California is the fifth oldest European place name in America. It is the third largest state in the union, and the most populous as well. Maybe that's why so many people write songs about it.

♫ Hotel California **BY THE EAGLES** (1977)

One of the band's most thoughtful efforts, "Hotel California" imbibes the titular state with the same dramatic foreboding that you feel when you think about the passengers boarding the *Titanic*.

♫ California Girls **BY THE BEACH BOYS** (1965)

The song that confirmed California (two girls, cars, soda pops etc for every boy) in the pop consciousness forever.

♫ Promised Land **BY JOHNNY ALLEN** (1964)

One of the great (if not the greatest) road songs ever, written by Chuck Berry in 1964 but given its definitive slant by Cajun rocker Allen in 1971. Go west, young man!

♫ California Dreaming **BY THE MAMAS & THE PAPAS** (1966)

The quintessential West Coast harmonies, drenching and determined. There's no place like home—especially when the weather sucks. John Phillips wrote from the heart, too; he was in New York pining through a chilly East Coast winter when he and wife Michelle wrote it; and while Barry McGuire recorded a fine version soon after, it was the Phillips' own group, the Mamas and the Papas, that truly brought the lyric home.

♫ Californication **BY THE RED HOT CHILI PEPPERS** (2000)

Believe it or not, there was a time when California in general, and LA/Hollywood in general, was cultural shorthand for all that was phony and plastic about society. These days, declare the Peppers, it's hard to tell it apart from anyplace else.

♫ California Uber Alles **BY THE DEAD KENNEDYS** (1979)

What, the Kennedys ask, would life be like if Governor Jerry Brown became the President of the United States? A lot like this.

SAVING THE PLANET, ONE SONG AT A TIME

♫ San Francisco Nights BY ERIC BURDON AND THE ANIMALS (1967)

Englishman Burdon reflects on the utopia he seems to have found on the west coast of America.

♫ Never Turn Your Back on Mother Earth BY SPARKS (1974)

IN HIS OWN WORDS—RON MAEL (composer): "[The song came to me] fully formed. I never even had to go to the piano for that one."

♫ I Want to Kill You BY DAVID PEEL (1970)

One of the earliest overtly ecologically minded rockers, Peel's diatribe of murderous intent could be directed at anyone or anything, but finally sets its targets on air pollution.

♫ Let's Make the Water Turn Black BY THE MOTHERS OF INVENTION (1968)

Not, sadly, a song about oil, but still worth thinking about in that context, next time you drive through the Louisiana Delta.

♫ The Last Resort BY THE EAGLES (1977)

An updating, in a way, of "Big Yellow Taxi" (594) but even more weary and despairing. "Some rich men came and raped the land. Nobody caught them." Yeah, it's called a free market economy.

EARTHQUAKES, FLOODS, BODIES IN THE MUD....

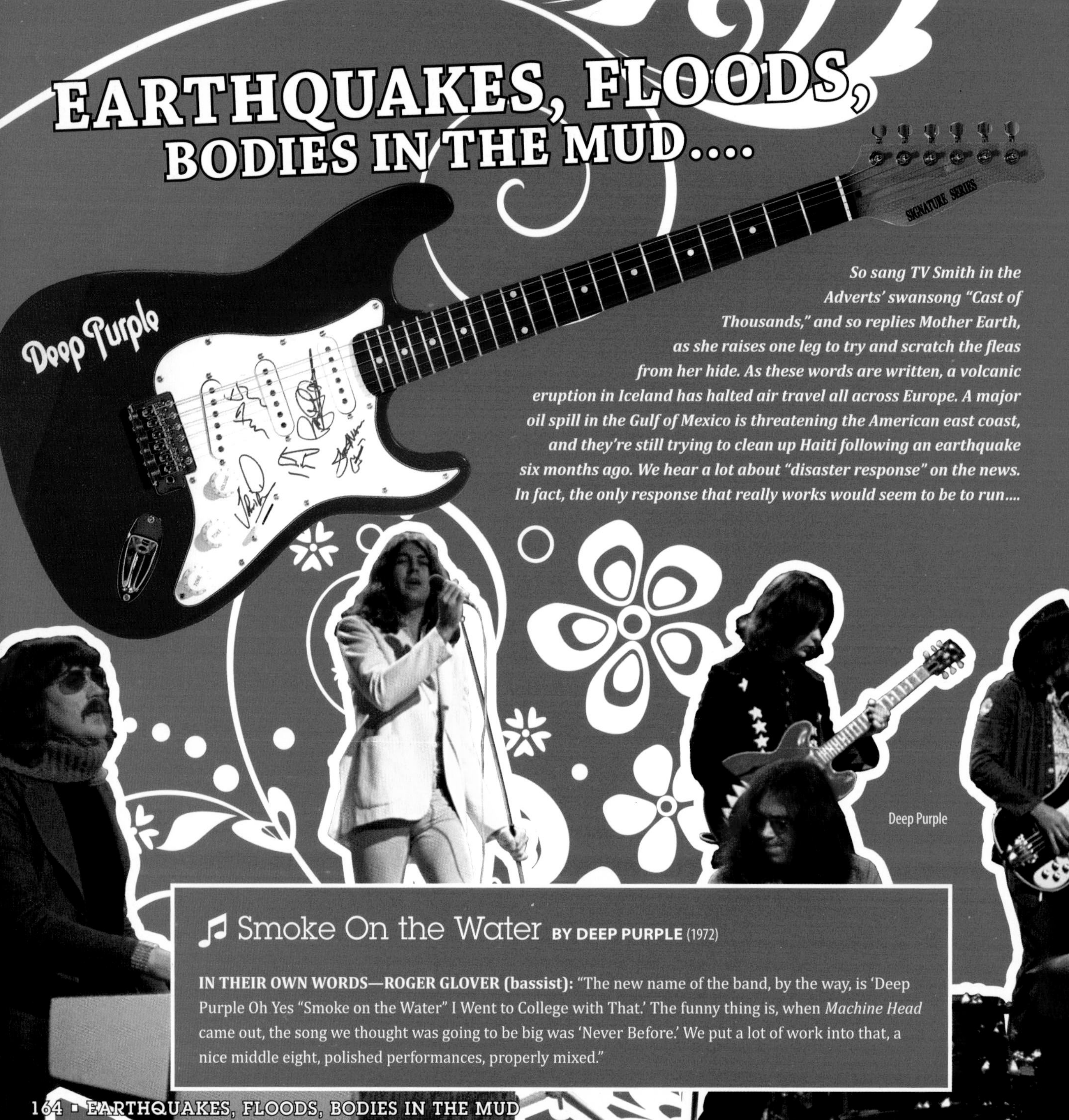

So sang TV Smith in the Adverts' swansong "Cast of Thousands," and so replies Mother Earth, as she raises one leg to try and scratch the fleas from her hide. As these words are written, a volcanic eruption in Iceland has halted air travel all across Europe. A major oil spill in the Gulf of Mexico is threatening the American east coast, and they're still trying to clean up Haiti following an earthquake six months ago. We hear a lot about "disaster response" on the news. In fact, the only response that really works would seem to be to run....

Deep Purple

♫ Smoke On the Water BY DEEP PURPLE (1972)

IN THEIR OWN WORDS—ROGER GLOVER (bassist): "The new name of the band, by the way, is 'Deep Purple Oh Yes "Smoke on the Water" I Went to College with That.' The funny thing is, when *Machine Head* came out, the song we thought was going to be big was 'Never Before.' We put a lot of work into that, a nice middle eight, polished performances, properly mixed."

♫ Bad Moon Rising BY CREEDENCE CLEARWATER REVIVAL (1969)

The end of the world set to music. It is every horror film you've ever seen, and every nightmare you've ever had. It echoes through the soundtrack of *An American Werewolf in London*, and it works there; it rebounds through *Twilight Zone* (the movie, not the vastly superior TV show) and *Shaun of the Dead*, and wrapped up the first season of *Supernatural*. And it works there as well.

♫ New York Mining Disaster 1941 BY THE BEE GEES (1967)

There never was a New York mining disaster in 1941, but if there had been, here's some captured conversation from two of the entombed survivors.

♫ Atlantis BY DONOVAN (1968)

The archetypal classical disaster, translated into the kind of love song that Neil Young would borrow during "Cortez the Killer" (266).

♫ It's The End of the World As We Know It BY REM (1991)

Or, one of those days when anything that can go wrong *does* go wrong. On the grandest scale imaginable.

♫ Tupelo BY NICK CAVE AND THE BAD SEEDS (1985)

IN HIS OWN WORDS—NICK CAVE (composer): "'Tupelo' is a huge nod to John Lee Hooker [whose song of the same title and mood recounted the flood that struck Tupelo in the early 1930s], drawing together different lyrical elements. I just kind of tossed everything in there. I was reading a lot of Faulkner and these southern American writers and all that stuff had a huge impact."

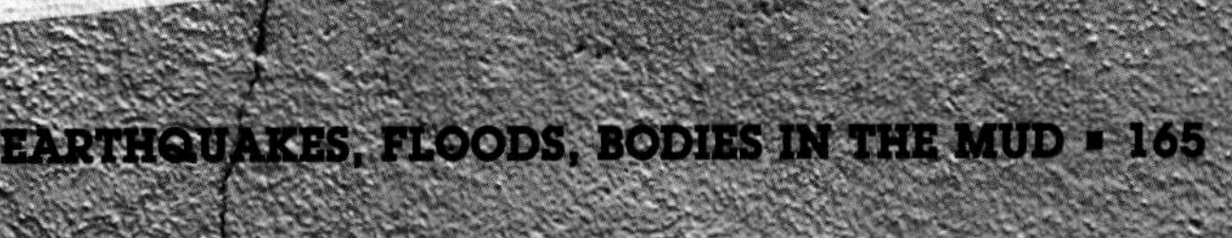

IVAN KRAL'S TOP FIVE

Co-writer of "Dancing Barefoot" (609), Ivan Kral was born in Prague, the capital of what is now the Czech Republic, but which was then the Iron Curtain nation of Czechoslovakia. He arrived in New York City in 1966, three years after his journalist father, Karel Král, was appointed a translator at the United Nations. Ivan's pianist mother Otylie traveled with her husband; Ivan and brother Pavel joined them once their education was complete, and were plunged immediately into a whole new learning experience.

Ivan had already tasted fame in Czechoslovakia, as a member of the teenaged rock band Saze. "Pierrot" topped the Czech charts in 1966, shortly before Kral left the country. Now he was working in the mailroom at businessman Allen Klein's ABKCo empire, where the affairs of state revolved around the latest happenings in the world of the Beatles and the Rolling Stones; and spending his free time haunting the clubs and nightspots of New York City. He ran through a handful of small bands, then formed Luger in 1972, a tight and glamorous outfit who were constantly being tipped for big things. They never reached them and in 1974, he joined then infant Blondie, before being recruited to the Patti Smith Group.

An intrinsic part of that band until its breakup in 1980, Kral went on to work with Iggy Pop, before launching a solo career both in the U.S. and, following the collapse of the Iron Curtain, back in his homeland. Aside from Patti Smith, his songs have also been recorded by David Bowie, U2, the Mission, John Waite, and Simple Minds, together with Czech artists Dan Barta, Lucie, Aneta Langerova, Jiri Suchy, Jaromir Klempir, and Pavel Bobek.

Away from his musical accomplishments, he is also an acclaimed film maker.

♫ Love Me Tender **BY ELVIS PRESLEY** (1956)

♫ Lucille **BY LITTLE RICHARD** (1957)

♫ Johnny B Goode
BY CHUCK BERRY (1958)

♫ Brown Sugar
BY THE ROLLING STONES (1971)

♫ I Just Wanna Make Love to You
BY THE ROLLING STONES (1964)

LEAVING ON A JET PLANE

Air travel, we are told, is the safest mode of transport there is. And the fact that the attendant statistics are usually only trotted out after a plane has gone down should not deter us from flying. Ask these people!

♫ This Flight Tonight BY JONI MITCHELL (1971)

Ah, the freedom of the skies. Unfortunately, this was written in the days before safety regulations, security precautions, and corporate greed transformed air travel into the battery hen-like experience that it has become. In the days when it was actually an enjoyable experience....

♫ Expecting to Fly BY BUFFALO SPRINGFIELD (1968)

One more Neil Young classic from his first days in California. Or another day in the departure lounge.

♫ Ebony Eyes BY THE EVERLY BROTHERS (1961)

Don and Phil had been covering love in all its guises since they cut their first record together. But "Ebony Eyes" was the most heartbreaking of them all, a young man waiting for his girl's plane to arrive when a voice comes over the PA system....

Ooops. This flight didn't make it.

Buffalo Springfield

Jet BY PAUL MCCARTNEY AND WINGS (1974)

Taken from the career-best Band On The Run, 1973's "Jet" was not really a song about a plane per se. But it's a high-flying rocker regardless.

Talking Airplane Disaster Blues

BY PHIL OCHS (1964)

Although the late Phil Ochs is remembered for any number of musical qualities, his Talking Blues had a passion that few, if any, other exponents of that art form could deliver, all the more so since he frequently laced them with devilish humor and knowing irony. "I heard Bob Dylan say, 'you gotta take a train… nothin' ever happens to trains at all. There was just one accident he could recall. A plane crashed into it…."

ME-262 BY THE BLUE OYSTER CULT (1974)

Immortalizing one of the first jet fighter planes ever to get off the ground, a World War Two Messerschmidt that could have changed the course of history.

NO WORDS—INSTRUMENTAL CLASSICS

Where licks speak louder than lyrics.

♫ Hocus Pocus BY FOCUS (1971)

Manic guitars, frenzied percussion and a guy on keyboards yodeling. It might sound weird on paper but, truly, it becomes one of the most exhilarating combinations imaginable.

♫ Echoes BY PINK FLOYD (1971)

It's not strictly an instrumental, because there's all that business about "overhead the albatross" going on early in the piece. But the bulk, the heart and the intent of this lengthy journey is the melody, tone, and texture that have established it among Pink Floyd's most genuinely lasting works.

♫ Jessica BY THE ALLMAN BROTHERS (1973)

A jaunty instrumental with just a dash of southern fire, "Jessica" probably means more to British readers than American—it was theme music to radio D.J. Nicky Horne's show in the '70s, and to BBC TV's *Top Gear* today. It is also utterly compulsive.

♫ Song for Guy BY ELTON JOHN (1978)

"As I was writing this song one Sunday," recalled Elton, "I imagined myself floating into space and looking down at my own body. I was imagining myself dying. Morbidly obsessed with these thoughts, I wrote this song about death. The next day I was told that Guy (Burchett), our 17-year-old messenger boy, had been tragically killed on his motorcycle the day before. Guy died on the day I wrote this song."

Apache BY THE SHADOWS (1960)

Jørgen Ingmann and His Guitar scored the American hit version in 1961, but it was the Shadows, hitherto best known as Cliff Richard's backing band, who truly brought life to this brooding guitar instrumental; and, in the process, inspired every aspiring young musician of the age to form his own beat band.

Pipeline BY THE CHANTAYS (1963)

The sound of surfing USA… in pastime parlance, a pipeline is when the crest of the wave goes over the surfer and crashes down in front of him, to leave him in the center of what could be described as a pipe made from water.

Walk Don't Run BY THE VENTURES (1960)

But you do run when you hear it… to turn up the volume and grab your air guitar. The Pink Fairies, curiously, later added a few verses to the original instrumental experience, but the riff remains the rocking soul of the ensuing picnic.

Soul Sacrifice BY SANTANA (1969)

A lot of music can claim to be the definitive sound of the Woodstock Festival. But if any single piece truly captures the abandon, electricity, and eclectic joy of that odd weekend, this is it.

Sylvia BY FOCUS (1972)

Quite simply, gorgeous. And heartbreaking.

Samba Pa Ti BY SANTANA (1974)

The title translates as "Samba For You," and Jose Feliciano added lyrics to Santana's *Abraxas* original.

THANK CHRIST FOR THE BOMB

Looking back on his childhood, British author and political commentator Francis Wheen recalled hearing, for the first time, the Groundhogs' "Thank Christ for the Bomb," the title track to their latest LP. "My politics at the time were inchoate... but I was enough of a hippy... to know that the Bomb was a bummer man. It amused and puzzled me that three hairy scruffs in an electric blues band were singing in praise of nuclear deterrence and the policy of Mutually Assured Destruction."

But even the most avowed peacenik must concede, the policy did work. It must have—how else to explain how we've not been obliterated ten times over by the procession of lunatics who've ruled the world for the last fifty years?

Morrissey

♫ Every Day Is Like Sunday BY MORRISSEY (1988)

Less a warning about the terrors of the bomb, than the heartfelt wish that someone would just drop the thing, to alleviate the tedium of waiting for it to happen.

♫ Breathing BY KATE BUSH (1980)

The nuclear winter, from the perspective of an unborn child.

♫ Tomahawk Cruise BY TV SMITH'S EXPLORERS (1980)

IN HIS OWN WORDS—TV SMITH (composer): It was around the time the U.S. was pushing to install a nuclear missile in England, as a stepping stone to bomb Russia. They needed agreement from the natives, of course, which meant a propaganda campaign in the media to convince us how much threat we were under from the evil East. Unsurprisingly, the politicians were all for it, but the public was proving harder to convince. At the time I was thinking, just the name of the missile—Tomahawk Cruise—was part of the attempt to persuade us. Has there ever been a sexier, more stirring name for something designed for mass slaughter? How could we resist something so evocatively titled that it almost seemed to have its own personality. But strip away the name and you see something created by mere men, no different from us—and our opinion that we didn't want this missile was just as valid as their opinion that we should have it. You choose!

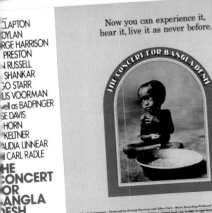

Now you can experience it,
hear it, live it as never before.
THE CONCERT FOR BANGLA DESH

♫ A Hard Rain's A Gonna Fall BY BOB DYLAN (1963)

Written around the time of the Cuban Missile Crisis, a very real fear laid out in very chilling terms.

ALL ABOARD! ROCKIN' THE RAILS

The United States were built by the railroads, pushing out into the wide open spaces on the other side of nowhere, to eventually link two coasts with one artery that carried life to every quarter. And it doesn't matter how far and fast other forms of transport travel, there is still something heroic and romantic about taking the train, knowing just how many historic footsteps you are following in. No wonder there's so many songs about the subject!

♫ Freight Train BY CHAS MCDEVITT SKIFFLE GROUP FEATURING NANCY WHISKEY (1957)

Chas and Nancy emerged from Britain's so-influential Skiffle scene, and rapidly became one of the entire movement's most beloved acts. This, their greatest hit, reminds is that the rails don't always carry you somewhere new. Sometimes they carry your loved ones far away, as well.

BILL GRAHAM PRESENTS IN SAN FRANCISCO
EXCEPT SUNDAY
JETHRO TULL
FAIRPORT CONVENTION
SALT 'N PEPPER ~ CLOUDS
LIGHTS BY LITTLE PRINCESS 109
APRIL 30 MAY 1-2-3 FILLMORE WEST

♫ Up the Junction BY SQUEEZE (1979)

A 1960s kitchen sink drama set to music by London's finest purveyors of inner city grit, the opening verse and the final line place the action near one of the city's busiest railway interchanges, Clapham Junction.

♫ Locomotive Breath BY JETHRO TULL (1971)

So many nuances, so little time. Tull really never stood still long enough for anybody to get a bead on them, for better or worse. But the day radio stopped playing one side or other of *Aqualung* was the moment that the dynamic "Locomotive Breath" swept forth to prove what a dramatic proposition Ian Anderson and his merry men could be when they felt like it.

♫ City of New Orleans BY ARLO GUTHRIE (1972)

You can hear this Steve Goodman song a thousand times, and the chorus will still get you every time. "Good morning, America, how are ya?"

♫ Homeward Bound BY SIMON & GARFUNKEL (1966)

Railroad stations can be busy places. They can also be among the loneliest in the world.

Neil Young

♫ Trans-Europe Express BY KRAFTWERK (1977)

IN HIS OWN WORDS—WOLFGANG FLUR (Performer): "The Kinks have something special, they are very special, and they use very English pop melody lines, which was always in them. I think Kraftwerk had the same thing. There is something you cannot put your finger on, which is very English, in the Kinks' music, which I could not do, which is their own style. There was something very German, but equally indefinable, on 'Trans Europe Express'."

♫ Southern Pacific BY NEIL YOUNG (1981)

A lament for the lost days when the railroads ruled America, set (of course) to a truly locomotivating rhythm.

♫ Runaway Train BY SOUL ASYLUM (1993)

Love seen through the prism of the engine driver's cab.

SCHOOL'S OUT FOREVER!!!!

♫ School's Out BY ALICE COOPER (1972)

IN HIS OWN WORDS—NEAL SMITH (drummer, cowriter): "With the success of the singles 'I'm Eighteen' off *Love It to Death* and 'Under My Wheels' off the *Killer* album we were climbing the charts all through the heartland of the USA. Unfortunately and unbelievably we were still not able to crack the Big Apple on the east coast or LA on the west coast. We were being rejected by the two largest music markets in America. The *powers that be* thought after two hit records Alice Cooper was just a fluke. The music world also thought we had a theatrical rock show that overshadowed our questionable musical abilities. We desperately wanted to write a rock anthem that not only would not only get airplay in the US, but also in England and Europe as well. When it came down to crunch time our lead guitarist the late Glen Buxton, came up with the intro rock 'n guitar riff for the ages and 'School's Out' was born. It was one of the most successful collaborations written by all five members of the band. And the rest as they say was rock'n'roll history. We got the national and international airplay we were looking for, only we never dreamt it would continue into the next millennium. RIP/GB!

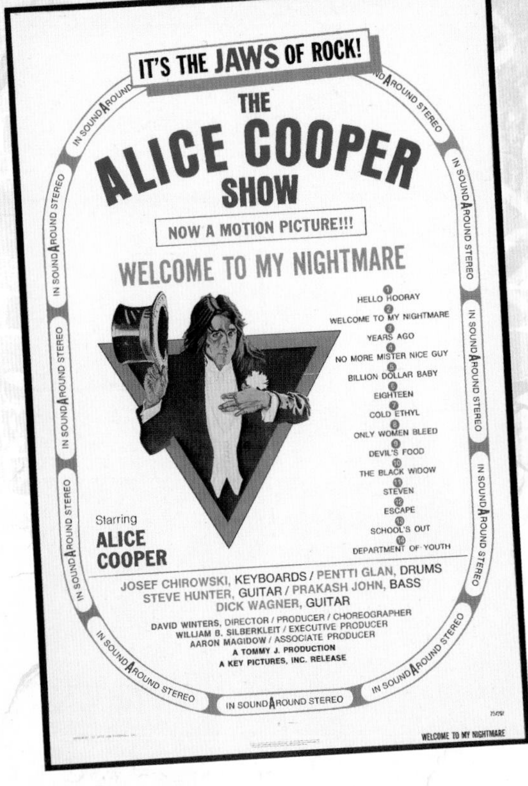

IT'S THE JAWS OF ROCK!
THE ALICE COOPER SHOW
NOW A MOTION PICTURE!!!
WELCOME TO MY NIGHTMARE
HELLO HOORAY
WELCOME TO MY NIGHTMARE
YEARS AGO
NO MORE MISTER NICE GUY
BILLION DOLLAR BABY
EIGHTEEN
COLD ETHYL
ONLY WOMEN BLEED
DEVIL'S FOOD
THE BLACK WIDOW
STEVEN
ESCAPE
SCHOOL'S OUT
DEPARTMENT OF YOUTH
Starring ALICE COOPER
JOSEF CHIROWSKI, KEYBOARDS / PENTTI GLAN, DRUMS
STEVE HUNTER, GUITAR / PRAKASH JOHN, BASS
DICK WAGNER, GUITAR
DAVID WINTERS, DIRECTOR / PRODUCER / CHOREOGRAPHER
WILLIAM B. SILBERKLEIT / EXECUTIVE PRODUCER
AARON MAGIDOW / ASSOCIATE PRODUCER
A TOMMY J. PRODUCTION
A KEY PICTURES, INC. RELEASE
IN SOUNDAROUND STEREO
WELCOME TO MY NIGHTMARE

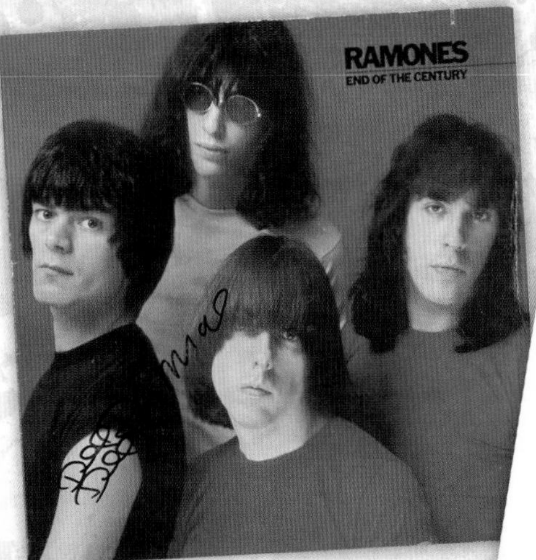

♫ Rock'n'Roll High School BY THE RAMONES (1979)

Now, that's more like it.
If school had been like this,
we'd never have left.

I Don't Like Mondays **BY THE BOOMTOWN RATS** (1979)

Bob Geldof was doing a radio interview in Atlanta, Georgia, when news came over the telex of a school shooting in San Diego, in which sixteen year old Brenda Ann Spencer killed two adults and injured eight children and a police officer because, she said, "I don't like Mondays."

"I read [the story] as it came out," Geldof recalled. "Not liking Mondays as a reason for doing somebody in, is a bit strange. I was thinking about it on the way back to the hotel, and I just said 'Silicone (*sic*) chip inside her head had switched to overload'. I wrote that down. And the journalists interviewing her said, 'Tell me why?' It was such a senseless act. It was the perfect senseless act and this was the perfect senseless reason for doing it. So perhaps I wrote the perfect senseless song to illustrate it. It wasn't an attempt to exploit tragedy."

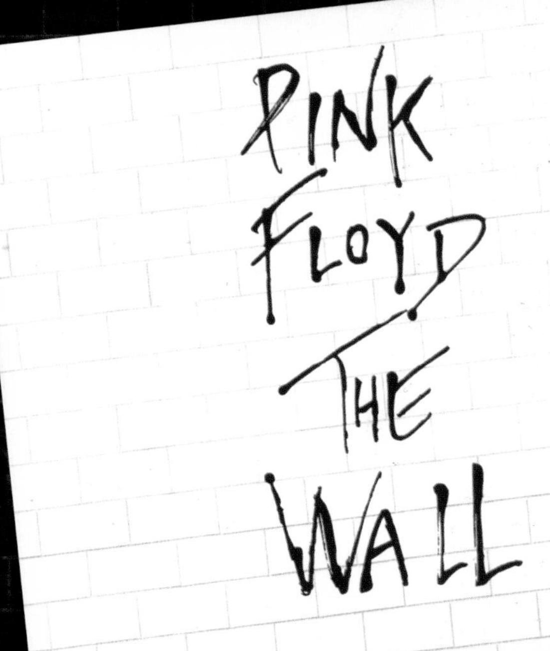

Freshmen **BY THE VERVE PIPE** (1997)

Written after his girlfriend had an abortion, "Freshmen," said composer Brian Vander Ark, was inspired after he rented the movie *The Freshmen* (starring Marlon Brando and Matthew Broderick). "The case was just sitting there the next morning and I found myself staring at it. Then I realized that we are all freshmen at some point in our life—why not write a song for all of us?

Another Brick in the Wall
BY THE PINK FLOYD (1979)

From Floyd's 1979 *The Wall* album, a taste of juvenile rebellion that has been granted adds subversion by having a bunch of school kids sing the refrain.

Good Morning Little Schoolgirl **BY THE YARDBIRDS** (1964)

And the less said about this, the better.

NOSTALGIA AIN'T WHAT IT USED TO BE

More Than A Feeling BY BOSTON (1976)

The lyric is little more than another blast of nostalgia for the memories invoked by an oldie on the radio. But what was the record they were singing about? It was "More Than a Feeling," self-referential, self-reverential and utterly self-perpetrating.

Drive In Saturday BY DAVID BOWIE (1973)

Visualizing a future in which sex is dead and we all live in Astrodomes, Bowie sits gazing at old photographs of Mick Jagger and Twiggy, and wondering whether the Sixties really were all they were cracked up to be.

Night Moves BY BOB SEGER (1976)

Lurching from Motor City Madman to Detroit's answer to Van Morrison, with a touch of the Springsteens thrown into the street balladry, Seger nevertheless nails the nostalgic teen anthem bang between the eyes.

Bob Seger & The Silver Bullet Band
NIGHT MOVES

Boston

Come Dancing BY THE KINKS (1983)

Looking back on your teens from a position in the region of parenthood.

You Can't Put Your Arms Around A Memory BY JOHNNY THUNDERS (1978)

So don't try, cautions the former New York Doll. The late Johnny Thunders' career is best remembered for the rockers and the drugs. But the highlight of his So Alone solo album has nothing to do with either.

When We Were Fab BY GEORGE HARRISON (1988)

The Quiet Beatle remembers the days when… well, like the song says… they were fab.

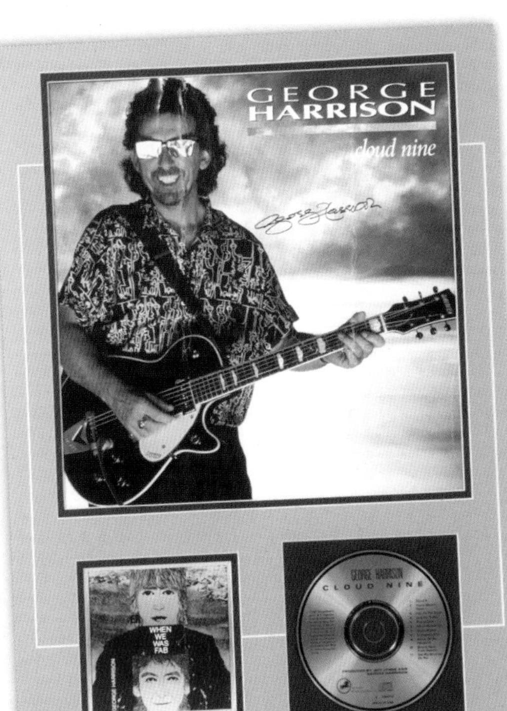

The First of May BY THE BEE GEES (1969)

When we were small and Christmas trees were tall… have the agonies of adulthood ever been painted so bleakly?

Village Green BY THE KINKS (1968)

Ray Davies is the master of the bittersweet reflection, and this ode to lost youth, and the sheer lack of complications that a past life once rejoiced in, wraps both of those flavors in one.

New Ways Are Best BY TV SMITH (1981)

Well, they are, aren't they? Smith had just broken up his TV Smith's Explorers when he penned this scathing assault on the modern world's insistence on updating absolutely everything, regardless of whether it needs improving, and it seems incredible to remember that it would be close to a decade before he released it. But the words were no less apposite at the end of the Eighties than they were at the beginning… proof, therefore, that some things don't change.

WHEN I PAINT MY MASTERPIECE

It was Brian Eno who once said that writing about music is like dancing about architecture. By which token, singing about art is probably like ... well, you can probably make your own analogy there. But the two really aren't that incompatible; the best songs are akin to a beautiful painting, and the greatest paintings are melodies as image. Plus, the lives of great painters have already filled a small library's worth of books. It's only right that they fill a few sides of vinyl, too.

♫ Pablo Picasso BY THE MODERN LOVERS (1976)

Painter, draughtsman, sculptor, Cubist... Pablo Picasso was a lot of things. But, insisted Bostonian Jonathan Richman, he never got called an asshole. The fates conspired hard against this song—Richman wrote it in the early 1970s, and recorded it for his first album in 1973. But the oil shortage of the day did more than create lines at gas stations. It also caused record companies to start slashing their vinyl production, canceling albums and dropping acts, and the Modern Lovers were just one of the casualties. It would be 1975 before "Pablo Picasso" saw daylight, in the hands of that doomed album's producer, John Cale—he covered it for his *Helen of Troy* album, which meant that, by the time the original finally made it out the following year, a lot of people already knew the words. They still do.

♫ Virginia Plain BY ROXY MUSIC (1972)

Named for a stylish cigarette ad, and Warhol's Baby Jane, the original "Virginia Plain" was a picture Ferry painted in 1964. By summer, 1972, it was a space-age rockabilly anthem. "The song came together quickly," guitarist Phil Manzanera, recalled. "We started with chords, no top-lines or anything. Bryan wrote the top-line without anybody having any idea what the song was about." He also admits that he has never been able to duplicate the solo that explodes from the middle of the song; "I just went 'blam!'"

♫ Matchstalk Men and Matchstick Cats and Dogs BY BRIAN & MICHAEL (1978)

Dedicated to L.S. Lowry (1887-1976), the English painter whose work focused almost exclusively on the sights and scenes of his native Lancashire, vividly populated indeed by matchstalk men and matchstick cats and dogs. Early critics characterized his work as primitive and naïve (but only if they were feeling generous), and he did have a very idiosyncratic style. But admirers of his work saw past the sticks and stalks and today, Lowry's work evokes a slice of northern English working class life that history has otherwise completely forgotten.

♫ Vincent BY DON MCLEAN (1972)

Ask most people what they know about Vincent Van Gogh and they'll mumble something about him cutting off his ear, and then point to that picture of the sunflowers that seems to have been reproduced in every thrift store in the land. Delve deeper into his life, however, and he might well have invented the tortured artist syndrome, as this song—McLean's follow-up to "American Pie" (43)—reminds us.

♫ Andy Warhol BY DAVID BOWIE (1971)

David Bowie was in fits of nervousness the day he met Andy Warhol for the first time. He had so much he wanted to ask Warhol, or say to him, and he'd lost every single word. Instead, the diminutive blonde man stood surveying him without, apparently, even the slightest intention of breaking the silence. Bowie small-talked his love of Syd Barrett and his shock at the cost of LP records in New York City; Warhol nodded in response. Bowie performed a little mime, expressing his admiration for Warhol by dragging his beating heart out of his chest. Warhol smiled wanly. Occasionally he would whisper something to one of his companions. But finally, he spoke.

"What pretty shoes."

Bowie was staggered. "It was my shoes that got him. That's where we found something to talk about. They were these little yellow things with a strap across them, like girls' shoes. He absolutely adored them."

"Thank you. I got them…"—mortified, Bowie found himself standing before the man he believed to be the most significant artist of the century, prattling on about how he bought a pair of shoes. And Warhol was just lapping it up. He produced a Polaroid camera and began photographing the shoes, while Bowie died another thousand deaths. He had to break the spell cast by his footwear.

"I've written a song about you… for you," he said softly. "It's called 'Andy Warhol.' Would you like to hear it?" In his hand he clutched an acetate of the song, pressed for this very opportunity and, without waiting for Warhol to reply, he cast around for a record player, only to discover that the agonies he'd suffered while they all stood in silence were nothing to the pains he felt as his ode to Andy spun on the turntable, and every eye in the room now lit onto his.

The track finished. There was silence. According to Tony Zanetta, "Warhol didn't know what to say, so he said nothing." In fact, Warhol was feeling a little hurt. He had forever been conscious of his looks, had battled eternally to keep Andrew Warhola, the shy, short-sighted, thin-haired albino from Pittsburgh as far from the public gaze as he could. Now here was this Englishman telling the world that Andy Warhol looks a scream. A scream?

Bowie looked on in horror. If the ground could have opened up and swallowed him, he'd have welcomed it. "He hated it. Loathed it. He went 'oh, uh-huh, okay...' then just walked away. I was left there. Somebody came over and said, 'gee, Andy hated it'."

"Sorry, it was meant to be a compliment."

"Yeah, but you said things about him looking weird. Don't you know that Andy has such a thing about how he looks? He's got a skin disease and he really thinks that people kind of see that."

Horror piled onto Bowie's embarrassment. "I was like, 'oh, no.' It didn't go down very well."

Silence reigned again, punctuated only by the whispered conversation that Defries and Morrissey were now winding down. It was time to leave. Warhol's final words to Bowie as they left were, "goodbye. You have such nice shoes."

IN PRAISE OF OLDER WOMEN (AND MEN)

♫ Maggie May BY ROD STEWART (1971)

"Wake Up Maggie!" That opening line gets you every time, dragging you into a ballad that is half-confessional and half-drunken boasting, the younger man ensnared by a woman twice his age, and seduced so hard that he might not ever get away. It's a love song, to be sure, but not one that you would ever want to be on the receiving end of.

♫ A Touch of Grey BY THE GRATEFUL DEAD (1987)

The Dead's first and only hit single arrived at a time when the title was more than a little accurate.

♫ Mrs Robinson BY SIMON & GARFUNKEL (1968)

It's the movie, *The Graduate*, rather than the lyric that places this song in its best known context—Paul Simon later revealed its original title was "Mrs Roosevelt."

♫ Don't Forget to Dance BY THE KINKS (1983)

As Ray Davies aged, so did the characters he sympathized with—and the "nice bit of old" who dances through this song is a well-observed case in point.

♫ Hey Nineteen BY STEELY DAN (1980)

The perils of dating someone thirty years younger than you. She won't know who Aretha Franklin is.

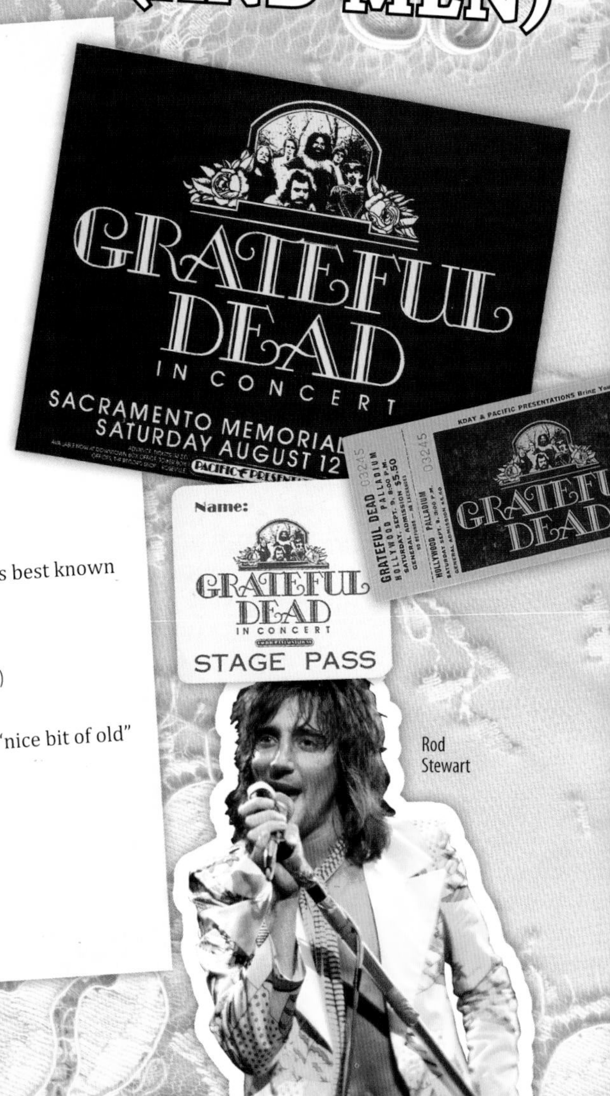

Rod Stewart

ANDREW LOOG OLDHAM'S TOP FIVE

He discovered the Rolling Stones, launched Marianne Faithfull, and blueprinted the model for every independent U.K. record label of the past 45 years. He produced, arranged, or otherwise contributed to some of the greatest music of the sixties, including no less than TWELVE of the songs in our Top Thousand (#74, 121, 224, 332, 350, 390, 410, 620, 714, 766, 825, 942), and has published two of the most successful, and widely read memoirs of the rock'n'roll era, Stoned and 2Stoned (a third volume, Stone Free, is imminent). He is Andrew Loog Oldham and, without him, a lot of the music in this book would probably never have happened.

♫ Be Bop A Lula BY GENE VINCENT (1956)

"The Marat Sade black leathered pill'n grease seating pimp of pop."

♫ Maybe Baby BY BUDDY HOLLY AND THE CRICKETS (1958)

"The sex, the slow foreplay, the innuendo, the track, the vocals, the absolute magic."

♫ I Want You, I Need You, I Love You BY ELVIS PRESLEY (1956)

"The king said it all, the words that we didn't know how to say. A total emote."

♫ 20 Flight Rock BY EDDIE COCHRAN (1958)

"Attitude, beat generation nonchalance, belligerence and long range fire."

♫ I'm Ready BY FATS DOMINO (1959)

"Our Liberace of rythmn'n'hope. The shuffle, the nuance, the style, the shine above the swamp."

MURDER MOST FOUL

Among the multitude of charges that were leveled at rock'n'roll during its earliest flowering, the suggestion that it encouraged criminal behavior was one of the most pronounced. But what, in those far off days of innocence, would that behavior have really amounted to—a fake ID, a borrowed car, a stolen kiss? Far worse things happened in other genres—opera, for instance, country and jazz [see sidebar], and would continue to do so, for a few years to come. But rock would get a taste for blood in the end and, while nobody has yet surpassed Nick Cave and the Bad Seeds' **Murder Ballads** *extravaganza... an album jam-packed with blood, gore, and gristle... there's a killer compilation just dying to be made.*

The Ax-Man Loved Hot Jazz

On the morning of May 22, 1918, police were called to a home in one of New Orleans' poorer quarters, to be confronted by the bodies of a local baker, Joseph Maggio, and his wife, Catherine, lying brutally hacked on their blood-soaked double bed. A panel had been carefully chiseled out of the back door, a bloody axe stood in the bathtub. And that was the end of the clues.

A month later, a local grocer Louis Bossumer and his common-law wife, Annie Harriet Lowe, were attacked but, miraculously, not killed. In August, a woman named Mrs. Edward Schneider awoke just as the axeman swung his weapon—she, too, survived the assault. But a few nights later, the killer returned to his murderous ways with the slaying of a grocer, Joseph Romano.

Hysteria swept the city. The only things the police had to go on was, all the victims were Italian, all worked either as a grocer or a baker, and all the murders appeared to have been committed by a character whom the New Orleans Times-Picayune described as "the greatest bogeyman that New Orleans has ever known."

And a bogeyman is precisely what he was. With no clue as to who, or even what, he was, the Axeman took on every conceivable shade of identity.

He was the London Ripper, emerging from his blood-stained retirement to revel again in the gore of the innocent! He was a madman, escaped from one of the state's lunatic asylums, or maybe he'd never even been placed into one. He was God's punishment on a sinful city—although even the religiosos were hard-pressed to explain why the Lord would be conducting a vendetta against the grocery community. He was any of so many past victims of New Orleans' lawlessness, or maybe one of its perpetrators—a pirate, a rapist, a murderer, a thug.

Whatever he was, the city panicked. Across town, families divided their nights into hours-long segments, and took turns to stand guard while the other members slept. Shotgun sales soared, and armed citizens walked the streets day and night, eyes peeled for anyone who fit the admittedly vague descriptions offered by the survivors of the Mysterious Axeman's wrath and, as the year rolled on, it appeared as though the Mysterious Axeman had vanished as suddenly as he had arrived. Into the new year and he remained a memory. Life returned to normal, sleep patterns went back to how they used to be. And then, the Mysterious Axeman reappeared in Gretna, and the city trembled again. Except now, the terror was about to take on a new dimension. Not only was he, as the local newspaper spat, "a bloodthirsty maniac, filled with a passion for human slaughter." He also loved jazz, and he promised to spare the city its bloodiest night ever if the city in turn would do one thing for him. In a letter to the local press, he pledged, "Every person shall be spared in whose home a jazz band is in full swing.... If everyone has a jazz band going, well, then, so much the better for you people."

The following Tuesday, the entire city poured out to accede to the Axeman's wishes. Restaurants, clubs and niteries the entire city over were packed with dancers and musicians. Private parties were arranged, and opened to all-comers, each of them determined to "jazz it up." There was not a musician in New Orleans or beyond who did not have at least one booking for the night, and many had several, racing from house to house to club to bar, their instrument in hand, to help protect the city from the Axeman's curse.

There was even a song composed to mark the occasion, "The Mysterious Axeman's Jazz," and the sheet music sold as quickly as it could be printed. More than any other single piece of music performed that night, "The Mysterious Axeman's Jazz" rang out over the entire city.

The Axeman was true to his word; he did not return that night. But he would be back in August, and again in October, to butcher a grocer with such horrifying stealth that the dead man's wife and six children, asleep in the next room, were not even aware of the killing until morning.

And then the Axeman did depart, but why—nobody knows. Perhaps he died, perhaps he simply tired of the slaughter. Perhaps he moved away. One thing is for certain, though. He has never been forgotten.

♫ Midnight Rambler BY THE ROLLING STONES (1969)

Based on the exploits of the Boston Strangler, "Midnight Rambler" merges fact with art in its spoken midsection, as Mick Jagger recites excerpts from the original Strangler's own confession.

♫ Stagger Lee BY NICK CAVE AND THE BAD SEEDS (1996)

"'Stagger Lee' appeals to me simply because so many people have recorded it," Nick Cave explained in 1996. "The reason we did it... was that there is already a tradition. We're kind of adding to that. The final act of brutality, where the great Stagger Lee blows the head off Billy . . . while he is committing fellatio [was] especially attractive. I like the way the simple, almost naive traditional murder ballad has gradually become a vehicle that can happily accommodate the most twisted acts of deranged machismo. Just like Stag Lee himself, there seems to be no limits to how evil this song can become."

♫ Watching the Detectives BY ELVIS COSTELLO AND THE ATTRACTIONS (1977)

A 1950s B-movie cop show set to a sultry reggae-ish beat, all itchy fingers and lake-dragging angst. Listen to it by the light of a flickering neon sign.

♫ Shoot-Out At the Fantasy Factory BY TRAFFIC (1973)

Another Hollywood-esque theme builds around the epic tale of the bad boy knifeman being pursued to his logical end.

♫ Psycho Killer BY TALKING HEADS (1977)

A nervous jerky shuffle and a lyric ripped from your nightmares, delivered with all the agitation of a boxful of startled insects.

♫ Alive BY PEARL JAM (1992)

Among the manifold interpretations of this song, several of which have been coined by lyricist Eddie Vedder, the pervading belief that it is at least partly inspired by a California serial killer, the so-called Night Stalker, is one of the most powerful.

♫ Jack The Ripper BY MORRISSEY (1994)

IN HIS OWN WORDS—BOZ BOORER (co-writer): "Jack the Ripper" has a special place with me as it was the first song of mine that Morrissey wrote [lyrics] to. It had a basic "Mambo Sun" [T Rex] groove, and we recorded it at Abbey Road Studio Three with Mick Ronson. The flanger sound came from the Boss se50 and Alain Whyte played the slide guitar. The live version evolved into a better arrangement, and we were still playing it until recently."

Pearl Jam

♫ Delilah BY TOM JONES (1968)

Probably the archetypal murder ballad, the betrayed lover taking revenge in the most pointed way he can think of.

♫ Amos Moses BY THE SENSATIONAL ALEX HARVEY BAND (1976)

Amos Moses, says the song, was a Cajun, the son of Doc Milsap and his pretty wife Hannah, and if you dig into the old Louisiana state documents, there *was* a Mose Milsap whose birth was registered in an undetermined part of the state in 1884. More than that, though, the historical record keeps silent, and so it should. Jerry Reed laughed at the suggestion that Amos Moses was anything more than a figment of his imagination. Maybe he had heard something long ago that set his mind running in that direction, but it was just as likely that he hadn't. "So you just go look for him anyway. If he didn't exist, then there's still plenty like him."

♫ Jenny Was a Friend of Mine BY THE KILLERS (2004)

Part of the band's so-called Murder Trilogy, vocalist Brandon Flowers explained, "we had the verse forever, and we knew in our hearts that it was good. But we wondered if we'd ever get past that verse. And then the day came where (bassist) Mark (Stoermer) started playing the chorus. And it could have been anybody. Because we're able to work together like that it helps us to avoid being stuck a lot of the time."

♫ This Town Ain't Big Enough for Both of Us BY SPARKS (1974)

IN THEIR OWN WORDS—MARTIN GORDON (bassist): "When Ron [composer Mael] brought in 'This Town Ain't Big Enough for Both of Us,', the chords were scribbled down, and we all began to construct parts to play. I heard something revolving around the D/A chord movement, and began to play the riff with which the song opened. Adrian expanded it with a change every second repetition, and it worked very well. I threw some offbeat bass and drum punctuations, straight out of the Yes canon, or so I imagined, and when the rehearsal finished, Ron said to me 'It's funny, I hadn't heard that riff as a part at all....'"

♫ Worcester City BY ELIZA CARTHY (2002)

Decrying Ms. Carthy's reputation as a folk artiste, and this hoary old ballad's historical place in the repertoire of 19th century singer Joseph Taylor, Eliza breathed 21st century life into what was already a timeless song. "In the story," Carthy laughed, "I think that if I was her I'd have clocked him and tried to get back to his house and the antidote, rather than giving him the satisfaction of dying in his arms... might not have been as good a story, but Steven Spielberg might have been with me.

ON THE BEACH—SUN, SAND, SEA, AND SONG

Fourth of July, Asbury Park (Sandy) BY BRUCE SPRINGSTEEN (1973)

Evoking memories that are practically a shared East Coast experience, the Boss remembers days of boardwalks gone by.

Peaches BY THE STRANGLERS (1977)

Gleefully growling on the sunburned sands, the Strangers watch the girls and miss their charabanc home.

Surf's Up BY THE BEACH BOYS (1971)

Originally recorded for the legendarily shelved *Smile* album in 1966, "Surf's Up" was reprieved five years later for the LP of the same name. Brian Wilson cowrote it with Van Dyke Parks, and later remarked, "the lyrics for 'Surf's Up' were very Van Dyke; only he could have done that—only Van Dyke could have written those lyrics. We wrote that at my Chickering piano, I think, in my sandbox and it took us about an hour at most to write the whole thing. We wrote it pretty fast; it all happened like it should."

Remember (Walking in the Sand) BY THE SHANGRI-LAS (1964)

The first song that producer Shadow Morton wrote for the Brill Building, and the first he produced with the Shangri-Las, "Remember" was originally over seven minutes long, before being cut down and faded at a little over two.

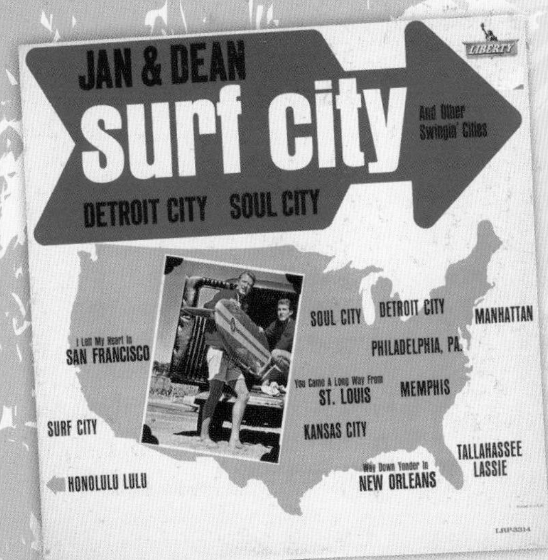

Surf City BY JAN AND DEAN (1963)

When Brian Wilson handed his friends Jan Berry and Dean Torrance an unfinished song he was writing, he could never have imagined that "Goody Connie Won't You Come Back Home" could ever become a surfing anthem. But it did!

On the Beach BY NEIL YOUNG (1974)

One of Young's most spectrally beautiful songs (from an album, also titled *On the Beach*, that is full of the things), this is the beach as a place of solitude and contemplation. Which, after all the excitement elsewhere, is probably a good thing.

MIKI BERENYI'S TOP FIVE

Miki Berenyi formed Lush in 1988 with Emma Anderson, Steve Rippon, and the late Chris Acland. The band released four excellent albums between 1990 and 1996—"Ciao" (754) spun off their last, the effervescent pop of* Lovelife*. The band broke up in 1998, following drummer Acland's suicide, and Berenyi left the music industry for a career in publishing. Asked about her old fans' demand for her to return, she responded "I guess it's flattering that anybody gives a shit. Not sure how enthusiastic the support would be if they realized that bringing back Miki Berenyi would deliver a 40-year-old office employee with graying hair who's still struggling to shift the weight from her last pregnancy."

♫ Nite Klub **BY THE SPECIALS** (1979)

"What dancing in clubs really feels like. And it makes you want to dance too!"

♫ Dreaming **BY BLONDIE** (1979)

"Bursting with energy and joy—what falling in love feels like!"

♫ 16 Again **BY THE BUZZCOCKS** (1978)

"My idea of the perfect pop song."

♫ Mad Eyed Screamer **BY THE CREATURES** (1981)

"Drums and vocals. It's all you need."

♫ Rowche Rumble **BY THE FALL** (1979)

"Like an angry tramp shouting at the traffic. Brilliant!"

Blondie

BUDDY, CAN YOU SPARE THE TIME?

Time, David Bowie once declared, "flexes like a whore." Peter Hammill called it a thief. It can certainly steal a woman's beauty, add the Rolling Stones, and it's like a clock in Boy George's heart. Outside of love and death, in fact, there have probably been more songs written about time, its passage and its power, than any other subject you can think of. Because, like love and death, it's something that no amount of success or money can buy you any more of.

♫ 25 or 6 to 4 BY CHICAGO (1970)

"The song is about writing a song. It's not mystical," explained songwriter Robert Lamm, with even the title reduced to something considerably more prosaic than many people surmised. "It's just a reference to the time of day"—twenty five-or-six minutes to four.

♫ Rock Around the Clock BY BILL HALEY & THE COMETS

Musical archaeologists can talk your arms off listing all the songs that rocked before "Rock...." But in terms of giving the kids of the day something new to get excited about, and kickstarting a few cute ideas into mainstream awareness, "Rock Around the Clock" remains rock'n'roll Year Zero.

♫ Time BY PINK FLOYD (1973)

Seriously, think too hard about the lyrics to this one and you might as well end it all now.

♫ Clocks BY COLDPLAY (2002)

All those damned missed opportunities really begin to pile up after a while.

♫ Born Too Late BY THE PONI TAILS (1958)

Once you hit your thirties or so, you really do stop worrying about a few years worth of age difference. In your teens, on the other hand, it's another matter entirely.

♫ 10:15 SATURDAY Night BY THE CURE (1979)

Another night at home with your cloying claustrophobia, listening to the tap drip… drip… dripping.

♫ Hold the Line BY TOTO (1979)

In other words, hang on and stop trying to force things. Time takes time.

♫ Eminence Front BY THE WHO (1982)

The last great song of the Who's career, five long years after drummer Keith Moon's death should have laid the band to rest, "Eminence Front" is vocalist Pete Townshend himself finally admitting that it's time to say goodbye.

The Who

REMEMBERING BUDDY HOLLY

Buddy may not have been the first rock'n'roll superstar... Elvis, Jerry Lee, Little Richard and so on all beat him to that punch. But he was the first modern superstar, a self-contained writing, singing, playing machine who upped the ante even further by becoming the first rocker who really didn't* look *like a rocker. Even more important, though, was the fact that he really did write rock songs. They weren't blues, they weren't country, they weren't R&B. They didn't rely on an updated arrangement to give them that rock and roll sound. They just* were *rock, and although Buddy didn't live to see his legacy come to life (aged just 22, he perished in a plane crash on February 3, 1959), he remained the most successful, and consistent, white singer-songwriter of his generation.

The music you'll love forever.
The man you'll never forget.
The movie you must not miss.
THE Buddy Holly STORY
COLUMBIA PICTURES PRESENTS
AN INNOVISIONS-ECA PRODUCTION
THE BUDDY HOLLY STORY starring GARY BUSEY
also starring DON STROUD · CHARLES MARTIN SMITH
Produced by FRED BAUER
Screenplay by ROBERT GITTLER

THE MUSIC

- That'll Be the Day (1956)
- It's So Easy (1959)
- Not Fade Away (1957)
- Oh Boy (1957)
- Peggy Sue (1957)

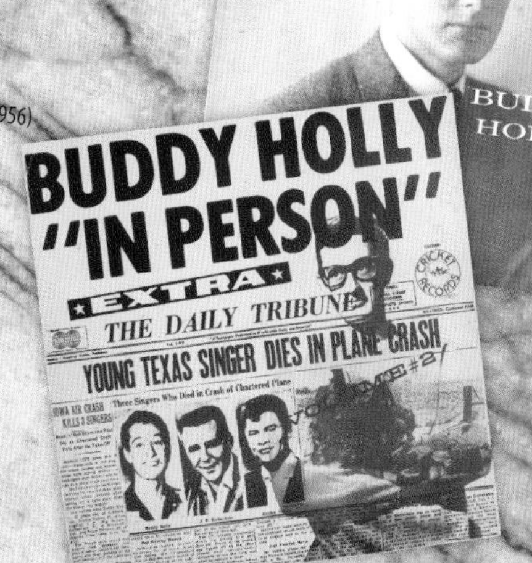

BUDDY HOLLY
BUDDY HOLLY "IN PERSON"
EXTRA
THE DAILY TRIBUNE
YOUNG TEXAS SINGER DIES IN PLANE CRASH

- It Doesn't Matter Anymore (1959)
- Everyday (1957)
- Rave On (1958)

THE MEMORIES

BUFFIN (drummer, Mott the Hoople): "Buddy Holly...WOW! Holly was a huge influence on the youth of the day in the UK. From film and audio clips I have seen and heard, he and the Crickets were pretty wild, live on stage—and in backstage parties afterwards, allegedly.

"Start with The Beatles, whose first acetate and lo-fi reel-to-reel recordings featured Holly songs, or their own early attempts at songwriting, which were heavily Holly-influenced. His U.K. tour in the late 1950s galvanized thousands of British youths to buy (usually unplayable) guitars, strumming to Buddy's tunes. Back then, the UK government did not allow such fripperies as electric guitars to be imported from the U.S.A., land of the Fender, Gretsch, Rickenbacker and Gibson guitars. U.K. law only allowed imports from Germany (Hofner and Framus) or Scandinavia (Kay and Hagstrom guitars). Bill Wyman used a Framus bass and McCartney still uses his foul-sounding Hofner bass. Mott's Overend Watts owned a Hofner Colorama guitar in the 1960s. Not names, nor instruments, that set the soul aflame with desire!

"Buddy Holly began the smuggled-in Fender Stratocaster "epidemic" in the U.K. His songs were tuneful, with simple chords which were relatively easy to learn and play along with. He also proved that wearing very heavy, old spectacles didn't mean you could not be a bona fide Rock'n'Roll Star, much to the relief of thousands of short-sighted wannabes.

"Also, the way his songs were constructed and arranged was a template for Merseybeat and many other beats for years after his demise—and the Crickets were a fine example of a backing band, who were great musicians—an example which was another template for many groups to come.

"I was around nine years old, when the news of Buddy Holly, Big Bopper and Ricky Valens dying in an aeroplane wreck came through. My father, who was a rock'n'roll fan, had just bought us a good quality radiogram and I had been playing some Holly and Presley 78s. 45s took quite awhile to reach the U.K. For weeks I was scared that the ghost of Buddy Holly would "get me" for playing his music. Dumb Kid! The press and TV reaction to the deaths of these young rock stars was enormous in the UK, and there was a huge wave of sympathy and sense of loss, particularly amongst the ardent young Bespectacled Holly fans, my friend John Farr being one of them. There was even a discussion about the matter that took over the whole of one music lesson at school in that bleak time. Even the teacher, who was a classical music person, knew something of Buddy Holly.

"Buddy Holly was as vital to the young, white youth music of the 50s and very early sixties as were the Beatles to the early Sixties into 1970s.

"The members of Mott the Hoople, particularly Mick Ralphs, Ian Hunter, Watts and myself, all grew up with Holly's music in our ears and never forgot him or his far-ranging influence, certainly on young, white kids from the Western hemisphere looking to make a name in the music biz, or just looking to have fun playing Buddy's songs with their friends for sheer pleasure and relaxation. Mott the Hoople's use of (a slice of) "American Pie" was a humble homage to Buddy Holly and his ill-starred companions."

MICK FARREN (author, journalist, musician):

"1: The Ray-Ban nerd who made rock accessible to those of us less blessed and God-like in looks and voice than Elvis.

"2: The first white boy to put a Stratocaster on an album cover.

"3: Virtuoso guitarist in rock's first power trio. Eric Clapton has confessed that Holly was his first influence, long before Elmore James, BB King etc. (See 1)

"4: The first rock star to die so visibly. Made us teens ponder mortality for the first time since James Dean.

"5: As it turned out, Buddy was a recording/composing genius who, had he lived, could have perhaps been Phil Spector or Frank Zappa. We'll never know."

PETER NOONE (vocalist, Hermans Hermits): "I was, like most lovers of American rockabilly (I think we called it rock'n'roll, but we also called Memphis and Sam Cooke rock'n'roll) one of the kids on my block who could sing and play Buddy Holly's total collection and was called upon regularly to do so. The Hermits were originally called Pete Novac and the Heartbeats, the Heartbeats so-called after a Buddy song.

"Every single person I knew who was a musician knew every one of Buddy and the Crickets' names, and who had done what and who was pissed off not to be on the New York Buddy Holly sessions, which still rate as the most interesting and possibly most brilliant performances (strings on "Raining in My Heart" etc) until the Beatles (also inspired by Holly and the Crickets) recorded *Revolver.*

"His death was a shock to all of his followers, but sort of set the stage for others to learn about who and what he was. I regularly listen to Buddy and the Crickets. They influenced Herman the most, and he was the man."

SUZI QUATRO (vocalist, bassist): "Buddy Holly was a one off. He had a unique downstroke style of playing guitar, and bridged nicely the gap between country and rock'n'roll. And, most important… his songwriting. I always wonder where the music industry would be today if he had lived. Such a lot of great music in such a short life. I can't wait to get to Heaven and meet all my favorite people. It will be one helluva jam session."

CHAD STUART (one half of Chad and Jeremy): "Buddy was significant for four reasons in my book:

"1: He made it okay to wear glasses. This was a huge step forward. Before that, we were all condemned to the nether regions of uncoolness with epithets like "four eyes" hung around our necks.

"2: For me, he was the missing link between skiffle music and rock'n'roll. He took the same old primary chords as "Cumberland Gap" or "Rock Island Line" and made them cool somehow.

"3: He used violins and nobody laughed.

"4: He died a premature and tragic death. This ensured his place in rock'n'roll heaven."

THE TRIBUTES

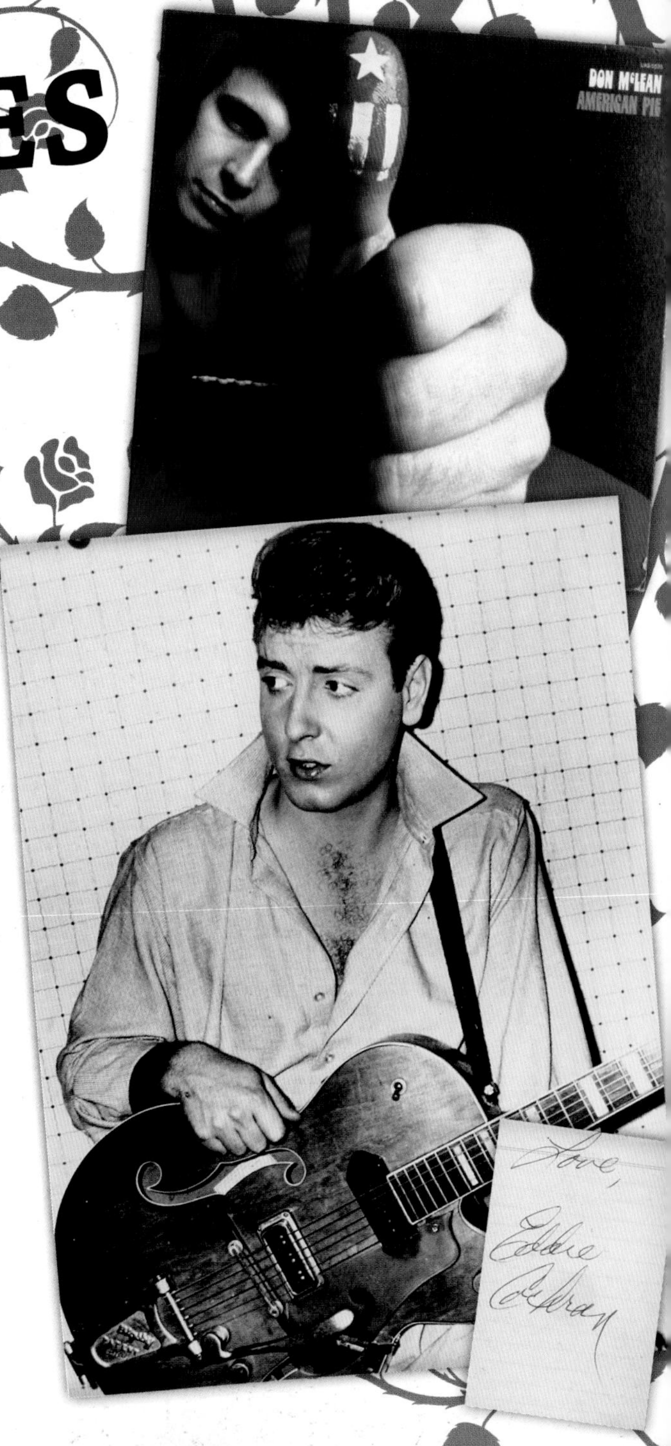

♫ American Pie BY DON MCLEAN (1972)

Too long in its original form for a single, "American Pie" was sliced in two for 45 release, but radio delighted in airing the full version regardless. The title song of McLean's second album, "American Pie" tells the tale of America's musical life from the death of Buddy Holly ("the day the music died") to the murder of Meredith Hunter at Altamont in December 1969; a tumultuous decade that ends with McLean already mourning the music's loss of innocence.

♫ Three Stars BY EDDIE COCHRAN (1959)

Written and recorded in instant tribute to Holly, the Big Bopper and Ritchie Valens, "Three Stars" was the first rock song to pay tribute to fallen comrades—although, given some of the horrors that succeeded it (Danny Mirror's "I Remember Elvis Presley" strikes a particularly grisly chord in the memory), that may not necessarily be a good thing.

♫ Buddy Holly BY WEEZER (1995)

It's probably impossible to think of this song without remembering the *Happy Days*-themed video that accompanied it to world domination, but it reminded us that almost forty years after Holly's death, his example still lived strong.

FIRE ESCAPE IN THE SKY—THE ART OF JACQUES BREL

Aux Suivantes (English Title: Next)

BY THE SENSATIONAL ALEX HARVEY BAND (1972)

The brutal memories of a young army recruit, and Harvey's version, caught on SAHB's *Next* album, remains the most powerful of all Brel covers.

La Mort (English Title: My Death)

BY DAVID BOWIE (1972)

A song not of morbidity but of absolute love and hope. Bowie took to performing "My Death" in the late 1960s, retaining it in his live show until 1972, when it became a key element in his *Ziggy Stardust* concept.

Ne Me Quitte Pas (English Title: If You Go Away)

BY MARC AND THE MAMBAS (1982)

Brel's most oft-covered song, at least in English translation, is a portrait of absolute devastation, as seen through the eyes of a man who's waiting for it to happen. Marc Almond cut it for his first non-Soft Cell album, the first in the long series of Brel covers that have entered his repertoire.

Jackie **BY SCOTT WALKER** (1967)

A riotous slice of debauchery, the fantasies of a man who wishes that he didn't have to dream with his hands. Marc Almond (again) probably cut the version that leans most closely to the lyric's actual intent, a flash slash of electrifying disco. But Walker's version wins through because of the sheer gravity of the performance.

SONGS OF OLD LONDON TOWN

It's strange; songwriters, especially English songwriters, frequently complain that their native placenames simply don't sound as good in song as American ones. The Beatles would much rather have sung about Kansas City than Tunbridge Wells; Route 66 feels a lot more romantic than the M13; and, of course, New York was so good they named it twice, but try singing the same thing about Manchester.

But England is *poetic, and its capital, London, has lent itself to so many songs that maybe we simply forget that you don't have to have a Stateside zipcode to enfold the world in a tangible glamor. And besides, they named Walla Walla twice as well, but you don't hear Frank Sinatra telling us that.*

ckvn and medium rare presents
KINKS
STALLION THUMBROCK • GARDENS AUDITORIUM • NOVEMBER 20 • 6:30 – 10:30
tickets: 3.50 adv. 4.50 door at bay • creative sound by commercial electronics

♫ Waterloo Sunset BY THE KINKS (1967)

Terry is actor Terence Stamp, Julie is actress Julie Christie, but the song was originally titled "Liverpool Sunset," before Davies relocated it to London's Waterloo Station.

♫ White Man in Hammersmith Palais BY THE CLASH (1978)

Written by Joe Strummer, after attending a reggae show at the venue of that name, and feeling as though he really were the only…

♫ Soho Square BY KIRSTY MACCOLL (1994)

In August 2001, eight months after she was killed by a drunken speedboater, Kirsty MacColl was remembered with a commemorative bench in London's Soho Square—the same inner city space that she immortalized in this song. Chris Winwood, one of the organizers behind the project, explained, "Kirsty MacColl once sang about Soho Square: with pigeons shivering in naked trees, it's a sad place. There's an empty bench in Kirsty's Soho Square, if we'd have come, we'd have found her there."

Baker Street **BY GERRY RAFFERTY** (1978)

One of the few songs (or anything else, for that matter) that manages to talk about Baker Street without mentioning Sherlock Holmes.

Down in the Tube Station at Midnight **BY THE JAM** (1978)

Chillingly first person, a mugging on a London subway station.

I Don't Want to Go to Chelsea

BY ELVIS COSTELLO AND THE ATTRACTIONS (1978)

A miraculous mash of high fashion, low life, lunacy and lechery—just like Chelsea itself.

Werewolves of London

BY WARREN ZEVON (1978)

Classic Zevon, as lighthearted as you like, but riddled with menace regardless.

Big Black Smoke **BY THE KINKS** (1965)

The lure of the bright lights and big city, and the perils that await when you get there.

THE BESTIARY OF BEAT—ROCK GOES TO THE ZOO

From the Crickets and the Beatles to Crazy Elephant and the Byrds, rock has never been shy about looking to the animal kingdom for inspiration. No surprise there... the Animals were so named because that's how their audience viewed them, as animals. The Monkees admitted that they monkeyed around, and the Dixie Chicks were chicks from Dixie. Easy.

Songs follow the same kind of logic; when the Cure sing of "Lovecats" you can imagine the cute little kittens even if you've never seen the video. Maybe the lyrics are sometimes allegorical... nobody really thinks the Sweet were chasing after a bushy-tailed chicken-eater, or that Anne and Nancy Wilson were in love with a great big fish. But they capture an image regardless.

♫ Octopus BY SYD BARRETT (1969)

Barrett was two years and one solo album out of Pink Floyd when he recorded this, a cataclysm of images that tumble over one another in their race to reach the end. Deeply mystifying, utterly evocative, and as multi-tentacled as any mystery could be.

♫ Wild Horses BY THE ROLLING STONES (1971)

The origin of the phrase "wild horses couldn't drag me away" is lost in literary antiquity. But nobody made better use of it than Mick Jagger, as he contemplated then-girlfriend Marianne Faithfull....

♫ White Rabbit BY JEFFERSON AIRPLANE (1967)

Lifting Lewis Carroll's Alice out of the rabbit hole and into the heart of psychedelia, one of the crucial sounds of the late '60s freak scene, with one of the most intriguing lyrics.

♫ Wild Thing BY THE TROGGS (1966)

Wild thing? I think you mooooooooooooooooooove me.

♫ Welcome to the Jungle

BY GUNS 'N' ROSES (1987)

A glimpse into the sometimes nightmare of modern urban life, where even the wildest beasts are uncaged.

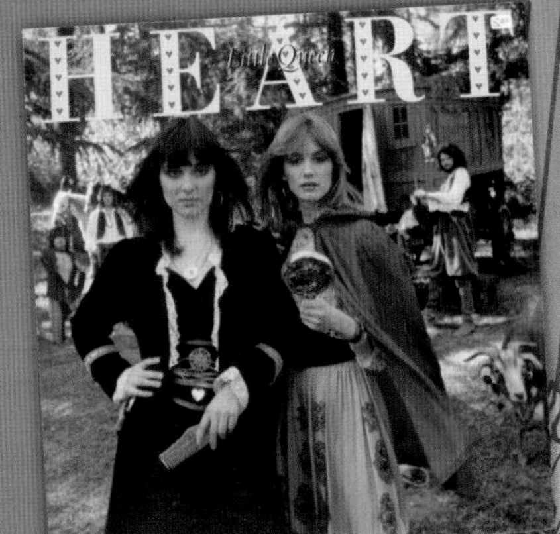

♫ Barracuda

BY HEART (1977)

There are twenty-seven different known species of barracuda, some of which can grow up to six feet long. They have razor-sharp teeth, a voracious appetite, and a riff that is half heart attack, half Led Zeppelin's "Immigrant Song." Heart have never sounded so hungry.

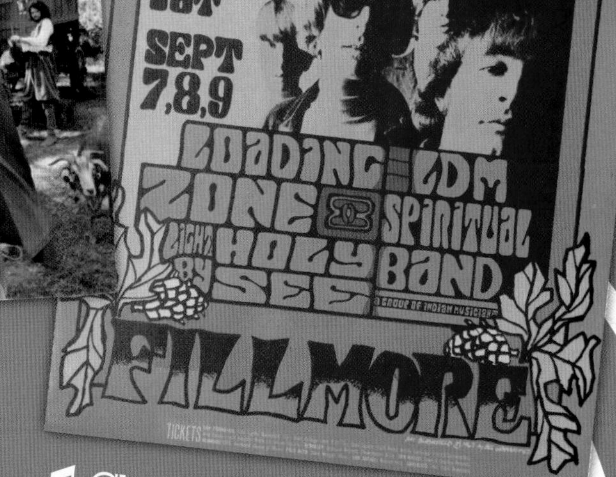

♫ Soft Wolf Tread **BY GRANT LEE BUFFALO** (1993)

A song about a wolf. Softly treading. Poised and poetic, but with teeth in the tail.

♫ Chestnut Mare **BY THE BYRDS** (1970)

Roger McGuinn takes a ride.

♫ Rock Lobster **BY THE B-52S** (1978)

A maniacal day at the shore, playing I-Spy with some of the sea's wackier denizens.

♫ Porpoise Song **BY THE MONKEES** (1968)

The last great hurrah of the Monkees' pure pop factory, a dreamy Goffin-King number that may have been influenced by the Beatles' dips into the psychedelic grab-bag, but which actually mastered the masters with lyric, pacing, and most of all, mood. And why are the porpoises saying goodbye?

Guns 'N' Roses

Fox on the Run **BY THE SWEET** (1975)

Originally conceived as an album track, and a piece of last minute filler at that, "Fox on the Run" became one of the Sweet's biggest selling records ever, after their label demanded they release a new single, and no-one could think of anything else. Swiftly shortened and completely rerecorded, it emerged so distinctive that it was *impossible* to believe that, says bassist Steve Priest, "when we first wrote it sounded exactly like David Bowie's 'Rebel Rebel'. (181)"

Bat Out of Hell **BY MEATLOAF** (1978)

"Bat Out of Hell" was originally written for a projected updating of the Peter Pan saga, *Neverland*, while composer Jim Steinman and singer Meatloaf were touring with the National Lampoon. From such unlikely origins, a legend was born.

Sheep **BY PINK FLOYD** (1977)

The follow-up to Floyd's *Wish You Were Here* album, *Animals* was a menagerie in miniature. But neither the pigs nor the dogs could hold a candle to the raving and babbling sheep.

Lovecats **BY THE CURE** (1983)

The song, explained composer Robert Smith, was inspired by a line in a book he was reading, where a sackful of kittens is thrown into the sea. But the song quickly escaped that ghastly imagery, to become one of the most wonderfully, wonderfully, wonderfully, wonderfully pretty hits of the 1980s.

Monkey Gone to Heaven **BY THE PIXIES** (1989)

The song really doesn't have anything to do with monkeys. But what a great title, and an intriguing number regardless.

PARLEZ VOUS FRANCAIS (AND OTHER FOREIGN TONGUES)

It is one of the great conceits of rock'n'roll that it only works well in English. Other tongues may try, but with the exception of Nena and the Singing Nun, who can name a single foreign language mega hit, or a minor one, come to that? Well, here's a few. Almost.

♫ Bohemian Rhapsody **BY QUEEN** (1975)

Three weeks in the studio and over 200 vocal overdubs were required to bring Freddie Mercury's operatic vision to life, and it would be difficult to think of a more *un*single-like single to release by a band that was still only just breaking even, critically and commercially. But "Bohemian Rhapsody" went on to top the U.K. chart for six weeks in 1975, and for another five in the wake of Freddie Mercury's death in 1991. The odd thing is, no matter how easy it is to describe the song as a mini-opera, the segment in question lasts just a minute. The balladic outro is almost as long.

♫ What Have They Done to My Song, Ma **BY MELANIE** (1971)

The peril of putting your songs out to be covered. With a verse in French, just in case.

Queen

♫ Don't Let Me Be Misunderstood **BY THE ANIMALS** (1965)

Always carry a phrase book on vacation.

The Animals

♫ C'est La Vie **BY EMERSON LAKE & PALMER**

A shimmering ballad from ELP's *Works* album, Lake's worn out lover might be reduced to linguistic cliché, but he does sound like he means it.

Emerson Lake & Palmer

Joan Jett

♫ Jennifer Juniper BY DONOVAN (1968)

We're not certain whether even a French speaker would recognize the final verse as actually being their language, but the lyric itself insists the song "just came along," and like so many simple things, it's irresistible.

♫ Je T'Aime (Moi Non Plus)

BY SERGE GAINSBOURG AND JANE BIRKEN (1969)

The popular legend was that the pair—French singer Gainsbourg and English actress Birken—taped themselves making love, then set it all to music. It's not true, but why spoil a great story (and a completely unexpected U.K. chart topper) with reality?

♫ Broken English

BY MARIANNE FAITHFULL (1979)

No linguistic gymnastics here, but the essence of the song highlights the importance of speaking the right language to your audience.

♫ Reconnez Cherie

BY WRECKLESS ERIC (1978)

Looking back at art school days, with a singalong chorus in French.

♫ The French Song BY JOAN JETT (1983)

A gorgeous romp that was matched by a video of similar proportions. Sadly, you wouldn't have seen it on TV; as producer Kenny Laguna remarked, "MTV wasn't keen on a song about sex between three people"—or, as the song says, *J'aime faire l'amour sur tout a trois*. "I love to make love, especially with three." The French translation was provided by Jett's guitar tech, Mike Winter—five years before, he'd been a member of one of the biggest French punk bands of all, Shakin' Street.

THE LOOK OF LOVE (PART TWO)

Falling in love again... and again... and again...

Diamonds and Rust BY JOAN BAEZ (1975)

La belle Baez's most haunting lyric, about a love affair that seems to have haunted her since it ended. It's no secret that the autobiography dates back to her early sixties romance with Dylan, nor that the lyric is aimed directly, and almost prohibitively privately in his direction. But that hasn't stopped people as far afield as Judas Priest and Blackmore's Night from covering it.

Abandoned Love BY BOB DYLAN (1975)

Unavailable for almost a decade and a half after it was recorded during the sessions for Dylan's *Desire* album, a tale of lost love shot through scenes from everyday life.

No Matter What BY BADFINGER (1970)

One of those songs that grabs you from the off, by appearing to begin in mid verse. Badfinger were often described as the new Beatles, and this song proves that wasn't a put down.

Everything I Own BY BREAD (1972)

Again, the sentiment is so simple that there's really nothing else to say.

♫ Wonderful Tonight BY ERIC CLAPTON (1977)

It's been played so often that it's practically a cliché today. But still, Slowhand's account of watching his lady love get dressed for the evening became the slowdance anthem that the '70s were waiting for.

♫ You Can Make Me Dance, Sing or Anything BY THE FACES (1974)

It's the end of the evening and you're drunk as a skunk. What else are you going to say to your lover?

♫ You Ain't Seen Nothing Yet BY BACHMAN TURNER OVERDRIVE (1974)

The Who had already delivered the last w-w-w-word in stuttering, but the Canadian B.T.O. updated it for the hard rock age. Coupling it with that riff was a stroke of absolute genius.

♫ Can't Get Enough BY BAD COMPANY (1974)

A solid return to vocalist Paul Rodgers' Free-filled past, after even he had veered away from its most earthy joys, "Can't Get Enough" wasn't quite a rewrite of "Alright Now" (70).

But the riff was almost as brutal, the solo was almost as breathtaking, and the song remains a kick-ass reminder of all the promise that Bad Company evinced when they first appeared.

♫ All I Have to Do Is Dream BY THE EVERLY BROTHERS (1958)

Just so long as you don't do it in the cinema! (see 367)

Ever Fallen In Love BY THE BUZZCOCKS (1978)

Shedding the final vestiges of their artpunk origins, Buzzcocks previewed their second album with what became their obsession, Shelley's hot pop hotline to the lovelorn teenage psyche. He later admitted the ability to change was what stopped him quitting the band—"Ever Fallen in Love" was actually the answer to having fallen out of it.

To Know Him Is to Love Him BY THE TEDDY BEARS (1958)

Phil Spector adapted the title "To Know Him Is to Love Him" from his father's gravestone, *To Know Him Was to Love Him*. But the simple change in tense transformed the words from elegy to eulogy, from pain to panegyric. From the moment he completed "To Know Him Is to Love Him," he knew it was destined for greatness; and the first time he heard Annette Kleinbard sing it, he was convinced it could be even bigger than that, although she wasn't so sure, the first time she heard it. Spector called her up to sing it down the telephone. "It sounded awful! He may be the world's greatest producer, but he does not have the world's greatest voice! And he said, 'Be here tomorrow, we have to rehearse it.' I said, 'But then I have to take a bus.' He said, 'Fine, then take a bus.' So I took a bus. I think we rehearsed it in Marshall Lieb's garage, if I'm not mistaken, because Phil's mother... wouldn't allow us to rehearse at the house."

Atomic BY BLONDIE (1980)

Tender, sexy and tuneful, "Atomic" had it all.

Coz I Luv You BY SLADE (1971)

The English rockers' first number one may have meant nothing in America, but the stomping beat and the ethereal violin were simply the icing on top of the cocktail. Very few people would dare rhyme "laugh at you" with "boo hoo hoo." Slade did, and they made it work.

I Got You Babe BY SONNY AND CHER (1965)

Veering into protest song territory, two mid-sixties long hairs shrug away the world's antipathy by reminding one another, it doesn't matter what anyone else says about the length of their hair or the cut of their clothes. They have each other and that's all that matters.

A Certain Girl BY THE YARDBIRDS (1964)

A blues standard rearranged for the beat generation, a simple call and response restated as defiance.

Stand By Me BY JOHN LENNON (1961)

Lennon recut "Stand by Me" for his *Rock'n'Roll* album and, in the process, breathed fresh life into a song that a lot of people had forgotten. How on earth they managed to do that is another matter entirely, because it grabs you from the opening line.

WHY DON'T YOU WRITE ME (OR CALL OR VISIT OR E-MAIL OR ANYTHING)?

Ever since the Marvelettes sat waiting for the mailman ("Please Mr Postman"), or Elvis sat dreading his inevitable return ("Return to Sender"), we've been singing along with the U.S.P.S. And a lot of other means of communication, too. Postcards and parcels, phone calls, and Morse Code... there's even a great song about semaphore signals. So, cut yourself off from your loved one for a while, and see how long it is before you start humming a tune....

Oh, and one honorable omission from way down Nashville country. "Hello This Is Joanie (The Telephone Answering Machine Song)" by Paul Evans... you want to know why your baby isn't picking up her messages? Because she's dead. The devil may have all the best songs, but Country & Western has the sickest ideas.

The Birthplace of Abba

Grown men claim they quake at its name. Responsible adults believe they would rather die than suffer through an entire performance. And self-declared serious music lovers will feign fits of violent vomiting at the very thought of this loathsome abomination. It is the Eurovision Song Contest, and for 44 years—since its inception in the postwar bewilderment of a suddenly pacifist Europe—the annual quest to find a Song For Europe has kept alive more traditional continental enmities than all the politics, religions, and American Presidents in the world.

Some fifty nations now compete for the prize, but the Greeks always vote for the Cypriots, and never give points to the Turks. The Germans vote for the Turks every time, but rarely have time for the Brits, and though the U.K. will always give high marks to Malta (one of the last colonies they have left, after all), 1,000 years of hating the French will never be quenched by a simple pop song. The former Communist states always vote for each other, but seldom for anyone else; and Israel, not actually being a part of Europe, simply distributes her favors to everybody, in the hope that no-one will notice she's there. Then, with another mid May evening of song, dance, and telephone balloting wrapped up, everyone goes home to sharpen their pens for the next year.

Eurovision was born in 1956, part of the same tide of well-intentioned idealism which simultaneously spawned the European Community (for the best countries on the continent) and soccer's European Cup (for the best teams). The Swiss won the first competition; the Dutch and the French shared the next four between them; and it would be a full eleven years before anybody anyone actually remembers walked off with the coveted Grand Prix—barefoot songstress Sandy Shaw, whose "Puppet on a String" not only beat off such spirited competitors as Monaco's Minnie Barelli and the Spaniard Raphael, it also set the musical precedent for which Eurovision would be forever renowned.

Given the wide range of styles, fashions, and cultures that comprise Europe, the idea of one song actually being the "best" is of course a preposterous one. A brilliant Bavarian oom-pah number will never translate into the bouzouki-sodden extremes of the Greek musical mind, while even the French don't really like the sound of accordions.

The most successful Eurovision songs, then, had always been those which placed the least alien strain upon its audience's ears, but "Puppet" lowered the common denominator so far that even today, it rings out of jukeboxes from Lake Geneva to the Finland Station. At the time, it swept Europe like a medieval plague, and when battle was joined the following year, the sonic consequences were apparent from the moment the qualifying rounds began. Every song sounded like "Puppet on a String."

There was a time, through the 1960s and 1970s, when the opening rounds of the competition were almost as avidly followed as the finals themselves. Every spring, the organizing committee in each country (usually the main television network) invites songwriters to contribute possible entries. An internal panel whittles these down to a final handful, which are then aired on a popular variety show, where a public vote decides the winning song—with occasionally wry results.

In 1987, Israel's Minister of Culture threatened to resign after his countrymen elected a pair of Blues Brothers lookalikes, The Lazy Bums, to represent the country; eleven years later, half the Government went similarly ballistic when the people's choice turned out to be a nightclub transvestite named Dana International. But while the Israel Broadcasting Authority merely smirked, "we checked the body of the song, not the body of the singer," still they had the last laugh. Dana won the competition by a mile.

Red faces erupted across Cyprus, meanwhile, the year (1988) when somebody realized that the country's chosen entry was actually the same song they'd entered a few years before. And then, of course, there's the sad tale of aspiring Swedish songwriters Benny Andersson and Bjorn Ulvaeus, whose luck was so atrocious that they not only fell in the qualifiers three times running, but Benny's girlfriend, Frida, was a two-time loser as well.

Of course, they would win the whole shebang in 1974, when "Waterloo" (sung in English by Swedes about a Frenchman in Belgium—how much more international can one song get?), but the bitter taste of past failures is not something one forgets... as Cliff Richard (52, 466, 712, 717, 990), second in 1968 and again in 1973, admits. Even today, Richard says that when the Spanish entry, "La La La," beat his hotly tipped "Congratulations" to the finish, "I was the first to rush up and shake [winning singer] Massiel warmly... by the throat."

ABBA (865), Sandy Shaw and Cliff, of course, are by no means the only star performers to have taken up arms in the name of European pop's most cherished institution. Scots R&B shouter Lulu, the Brotherhood of Man, disco sensations Silver Convention, Patrick Juvet and Baccara, Russian duo Tatu (874), even Les Miserables diva Francis Ruffelle, have all combined careers as chart-toppers with stabs at Eurovision immortality, while no less a titan than Celine Dion represented Switzerland in 1988, and won the hearts of the Eurocrowd a full decade before she sank the Titanic. And before anybody screams foul, Eurovision rules demand only that the song was written by a national of the country it represents. It can be sung by whoever you like—which is how Australians Olivia Newton John and Johnny Logan gave their all for Britain and Ireland respectively, and Belgian powerpop sensation Plastic Bertrand turned out for Luxembourg.

All of which should also remind us that behind the popular image of mawkish nonsense and singalong bing-a-bongery for which the Contest is renowned, it has attracted some of the hardest hitting acts in the world—a world, that is, which exists utterly separate from the Anglocentricities of what we traditionally call rock and pop; a world, too, in which reputations count for naught, hype is immaterial, and the only thing that matters is the song. Which is a good thing, right?

So, when grown men start quaking, adults start dying, and serious music fans begin barfing theatrically... well, like a few of the Contest's most memorable songs say, diggi-loo-diggi-ley ding-a-dong bang-a-bang to the lot of them.

♫ The Letter BY THE BOXTOPS (1967)

Statistically, more songs rely on the mails to bring bad news than good. But the late Alex Chilton growls his way through one of the exceptions that not only prove the rule, they remind us why we even bothered opening letters.

♫ Answering Machine BY THE REPLACEMENTS (1984)

It's a simple question. How can you say goodnight to an answering machine?

♫ Badge BY CREAM (1969)

Not quite a letter, an e-mail or whatever, but when George Harrison gathered up a bunch of the things he'd talked to Ringo about, then set them all to music, still there was a wonderfully telephonic sense to it all.

♫ Somebody To Shove BY SOUL ASYLUM (1993)

Frustration and longing ooze from every groove.

♫ Memphis, Tennessee **BY CHUCK BERRY** (1959)

Long distance information gets its moment in the musical sun.

♫ Standing Outside a Broken Phone Booth With Money in My Hand **BY THE PRIMITIVE RADIO GODS** (1996)

Don't you *hate* it when that happens?

♫ Metal Guru **BY T REX** (1972)

All alone without a telephone. But that was in the days before telemarketers got our number. Nowadays such solitude doesn't sound so bad.

♫ Everyone Says Hi **BY DAVID BOWIE** (2002)

An astonishing song, all the more so since we'd more or less stopped looking to David Bowie for genius by the dawn of the 21st century. Melancholy, almost tearful, a farewell despite the optimism that sneaks in around the edges ("you can always come home… I'd like to get a letter"), "Everyone Says 'Hi'" is lush, gorgeous, framed within a string of thoughts and remarks that read like postcards—old-time postcards, the 50s' seaside comic ones that are evoked even further by the doo-wop backing that lopes into earshot every so often; and, crowning the masterpiece, a compelling fade that namechecks everyone who *does* say hi… the girl next door, the guy upstairs, your mum and dad, your big fat dog….

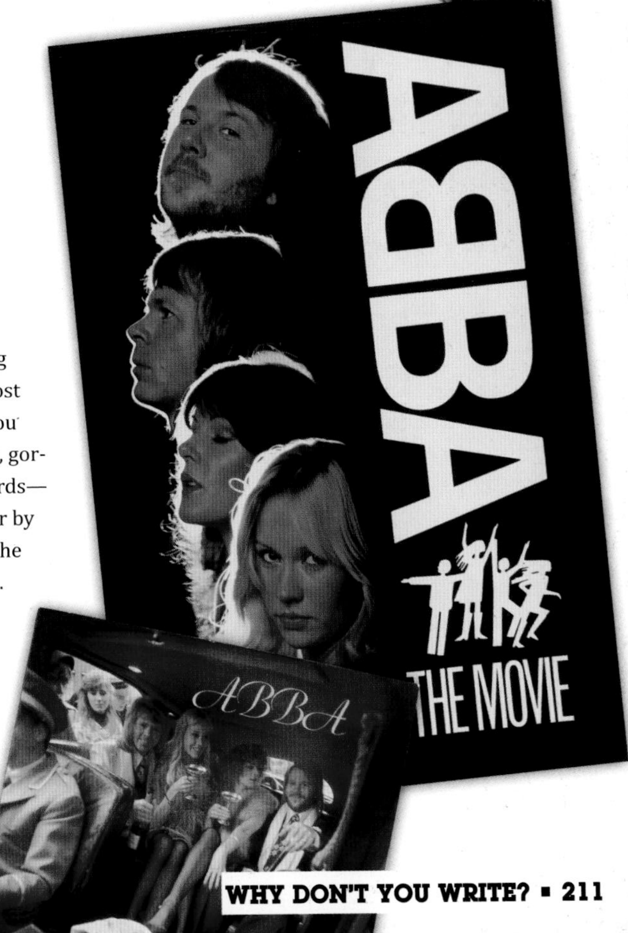

♫ SOS **BY ABBA** (1975)

Dot dot dot, dash dash dash, dot dot dot. The international distress call.

All the Things She Said BY TATU (2003)

Amid all the media-generated fuss surrounding the are-they-lesbians-or-aren't-they controversy generated by the Russian duo's stage act and video, it was easy to overlook the fact that this is a great song, about the need to open all lines of communication.

Communication Breakdown BY LED ZEPPELIN (1969)

Or, what happens when everybody stops listening...

Semaphore Signals BY WRECKLESS ERIC (1977)

In the days before all mod cons came to fill our lives with the constant chatter of total strangers, a young man had to be inventive if he wanted to contact his sweetheart. Standing on a hillside waving a couple of flags was certainly one way of going about it.

Telephone Line BY THE ELECTRIC LIGHT ORCHESTRA (1977)

Having already serenaded us with the tones of "Ma Ma Belle," E.L.O. followed up with a reminder of just how *lonely* the sound of an unanswered telephone could be. Of course, now that everyone carries cellphones everywhere, this song sounds hopelessly old-fashioned.

ALL THE FUN OF THE FAIR

There was a time, through the 1950s, 1960s, even the 1970s, when the fairground was one of the key arenas for hearing great rock'n'roll—check out David Essex's 1973 movie That'll Be the Day *for the most nostalgic recollection of those halcyon days, but you probably have your own memories already. But it ain't all dodgems, rollercoasters and the house of fun. There's dark doings behind the carnival lights, and sinister shapes in the shadows. Just be grateful there's not any clowns as well.*

♫ Helter Skelter **BY THE BEATLES** (1968)

How an innocent English fairground ride was translated, in the mind of Manson, to a clarion call to mass murder is one of those things we might never truly understand. But listening to the Beatles' own interpretation, the slashing guitars and screaming vocals, maybe it's not such a leap after all.

♫ The Carny **BY NICK CAVE AND THE BAD SEEDS** (1986)

One of Nick Cave's most beautifully dark and despairing compositions, "The Carny" is both a personal lament for a single human being, and a keening farewell to a way of life. "It's a major, deep work," says guitarist Mick Harvey. Musically, the band echoed a carnival calliope, but one that was galloping both behind and ahead of itself. "There was a template laid out for the song with a click track. What became interesting is that all the sections were different lengths, completely by accident. They were not meant to be, but some of them are fourteen bars and some of them are eleven, all completely inconsistent. So that meant that all the instrumental passages, the vibraphones and piano interiors, became irregular. The melody had an intentional length, but then there would be an extra bar."

And around that bar, the buzzards flew, picking the flesh off the rain sodden corpse, conjured up by German-born guitarist Blixa Bargeld after Nick Cave had left the studio one night. "I came back the next day and Blixa had put his guitar on it," says Cave. "I hadn't really sung on it yet. I just sat in an armchair with all these verses and notes and stuff, and we constructed the music from a very rough perspective. Blixa had come in and done this really beautiful guitar which sounded like a dying horse…and he said, 'well the song's about a fucking dying horse, isn't it?'" At the song's climax, the absent Carny's horse, Sorrow, is laid to rest before the circling buzzards.

Nick Cave and The Bad Seeds

♫ Wishing Well BY FREE (1972)

A song of loss and regret, written for errant Free guitarist Paul Kossoff, and treated to one of Paul Rodgers' most effective ever vocals.

♫ Roundabout BY YES (1972)

The Hollies' "On a Carousel" sums this ride up best, but Yes have rarely sounded finer than they do on this epic.

♫ Cathy's Clown BY THE EVERLY BROTHERS (1960)

I said there were no clowns. Sorry, I lied.

♫ Hypnotized BY FLEETWOOD MAC (1974)

From that odd era that lurks between the Peter Green led blues, and the Buckingham-Nicks flavored pop, a magnificent Bob Welch composition that looks at love through the eyes of the Mystifying Mesmero.

♫ Blinded by the Light BY BRUCE SPRINGSTEEN (1973)

Arguably, Manfred Mann did it better, but the Boss knows Asbury Park like the back of his hand.

♫ Spinning Wheel **BY BLOOD SWEAT AND TEARS** (1969)

A song of hope and redemption, writer David Clayton Thomas drawing on fairground imagery (“ride a painted pony, let the spinning wheel spin”) as a reminder that no matter how awful the ride is, at some point it will stop.

♫ Pinball Wizard **BY THE WHO** (1969)

Visually it’s hard to disassociate *Tommy*’s greatest hit from the scene in the movie, with the hyper-platformed Elton John leading the band through a manic reconstruction of the deaf, dumb and blind boy’s most potent anthem. But musically, the original is still the one that matters.

♫ Nature’s Way **BY SPIRIT** (1970)

Life is a zoo, and then the bears eat you.

♫ The Carnival Is Over **BY THE SEEKERS** (1965)

A glorious piece of maudlin mournfulness, performed by British Invaders who weren’t actually British… like the Easybeats (whose “Friday on My Mind” is also immaculate), the Seekers hailed from Australia.

BOZ BOORER'S TOP FOUR

Throughout the 1980s, and his early twenties, guitarist Boz Boorer was best known as one of the shining lights of British rockabilly—he led the Polecats to a clutch of hits at the beginning of the decade, and continued in that vein once he left the group. In 1991, he joined Morrissey's band as guitarist, band leader, and occasional co-writer:"Jack the Ripper" (475) and "Speedway" (607) are both Morrissey-Boorer compositions.

♫ Fireball BY DEEP PURPLE (1971)

One of the last numbers to be recorded for the album of the same name, "Fireball" was a supersonic rocker whose so-distinctive opening moments included a roar that could indeed be a passing fireball. How disappointing it was, years later, to discover that, far from pointing a microphone at the mysteries of the heavens, engineer Martin Birch simply recorded the studio air conditioning clicking on.

♫ Nobody's Fault But Mine BY LED ZEPPELIN (1976)

A traditional blues first recorded by Blind Willie Johnson, then heavily revised for Zeppelin's *Presence* LP.

♫ I'm Going Home BY TEN YEARS AFTER (1968)

Immortalized by the marathon workout that was caught by the *Woodstock* cameras, the epitome of the late Sixties British Blues boom.

♫ The Rocker BY AC/DC (1975)

Even if you have never heard of AC/DC, and don't have a clue what rock'n'roll is, the title still says it all.

ARE YOU STILL HERE? MORE GREAT BREAK-UP SONGS

Because there's an awful lot of them around.

You Keep Me Hanging On BY THE VANILLA FUDGE (1967)

Drawing the Supremes classic out to preposterous lengths, and then imbibing it with kaleidoscopic moods, the Fudge spread the drama so liberally across the grooves that the song is practically a soap opera. The inescapable blueprint for every Prog band of the next two or three years, it proved an albatross for the Fudge (who never scaled such peaks again), but was the self-confessed launching pad for the early Deep Purple.

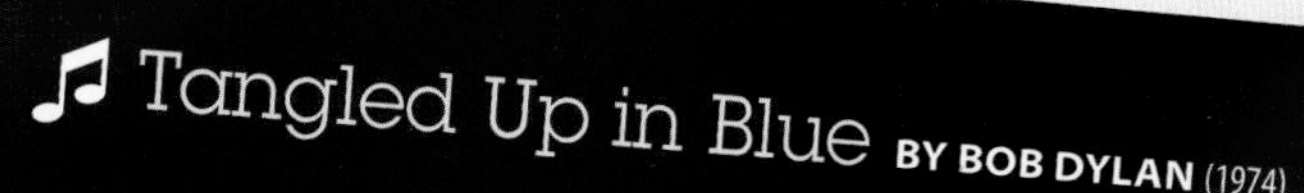

Tangled Up in Blue BY BOB DYLAN (1974)

Dylan once said he wrote the song after spending a weekend listening to Joni Mitchell's *Blue* album, which might well be true. A triumphant, if occasionally opaque opening to the otherwise-less-than-exuberant *Blood on the Tracks*, "Tangled Up in Blue" features what is simultaneously one of Dylan's most perfectly realized lyrics, and the one that he seems the least happy with—at least to judge by the number of times he's changed it in concert.

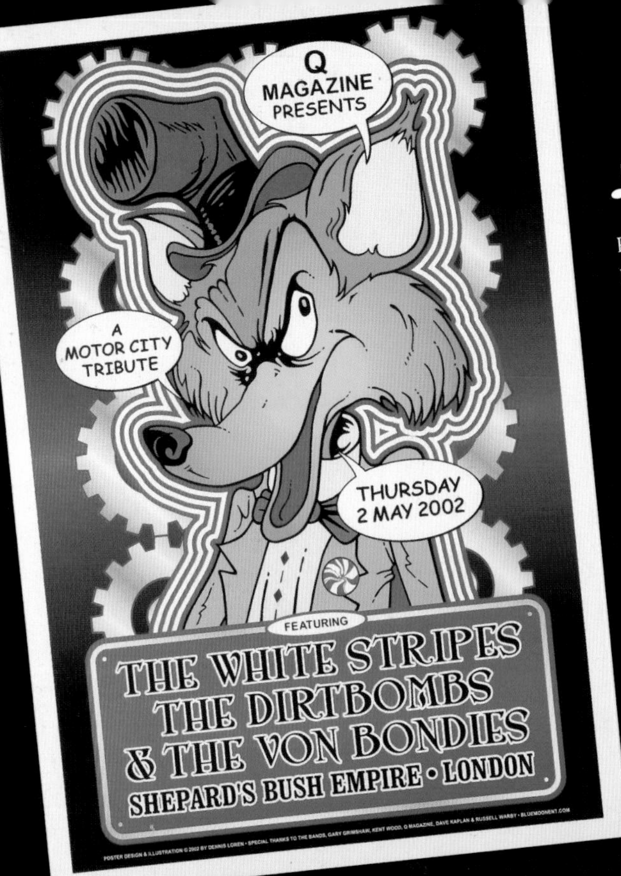

♫ Hello It's Me BY TODD RUNDGREN (1972)

Rundgren thought "I Saw the Light" would be his first big hit. Instead it was this rerecording of a song he first cut with the Nazz.

♫ I Don't Want to Talk About It

BY ROD STEWART (1977)

A gorgeous song nevertheless grabbed a slice of unexpected immortality when, in the week of the Queen of England's Silver Jubilee in 1977, it remained at #1 on the U.K. chart despite being soundly outsold by the Sex Pistols' "God Save the Queen" (592). The punks smelled a fix-up; the royalists simply shrugged.

♫ Haitian Divorce BY STEELY DAN (1976)

Precision-built funk from the California duo's 1976 The Royal Scam LP, the story of love gone bad and goodbye.

♫ Fell in Love with a Girl

BY THE WHITE STRIPES (2002)

ack and ex-wife Meg White bestrode early Noughties American rock like no duo before or after, with their third album White Blood Cells pushing them even further ahead. "Fell in Love with a Girl" arrived with a LEGO animation video, and a lot of people remember that. But more folk remember the song.

♫ Maybe BY THE CHANTELS (1958)

One of those songs that gnaws into your brains, whether you like it or not. Because most of us have been to the place that it maps out. Maybe? Or maybe not.

No Regrets BY THE WALKER BROTHERS (1976)

You can break your heart to this darkly sonorous version of the Tom Rush chest-beater.

Without You BY NILSSON (1972)

If it's overwrought emotion you're looking for, the late Nilsson Schmillson serves it up with tears to spare.

Fifty Ways to Leave Your Lover BY PAUL SIMON (1976)

Think of a name, and Simon will come up with a ruse to rhyme with it. Just flush him away, May...

Your Woman BY WHITE TOWN (1997)

Ever fallen in love with someone you shouldn't have?

Ex-Girlfriend BY NO DOUBT (2000)

Gwen Stefani and co emerged on the back of America's mid-1990s fixation with punk-flavored ska, but did so, too, with a sharp eye for pop that transcended the most generous boundaries. Here, Stefani gets to grips with life after the luster has faded.

ROCK ME AT THE BALLPARK, BABY

Few events raise our passions higher than a sporting contest. No matter what the event... yes, even bowling aficionados get excited... sports can divide families, ignite wars, and bring total strangers together with the kind of rapport that even lovers would be hard pressed to emulate.

Of course, the same can be said for pop music and, over the years, innumerable attempts have been made to blend the excitement of sport with the effervescence of rock—and vice versa. Rod Stewart was a promising soccer player long before he started singing, and he isn't the only one. Talking of soccer, however, reminds us of one area of recorded endeavor that few people reading this book are probably aware of, for which, they may believe, they ought to be grateful. Check out the accompanying sidebar, if you dare.

Sing A Song Of Soccer

You probably think songs about soccer are a peculiarly European pursuit, and you'd be wrong.

You probably think (to paraphrase Brian Eno) that singing about soccer is a lot like dancing about architecture. You'd be wrong.

And you probably think that 99 percent of records written, recorded, and sung about soccer are all but unlistenable. You'd be... well, in this instance, you'd be correct. Writing in his Odd Man Out autobiography, Scottish soccer ace Brian McClair shuddered, "it is traditional for [soccer] records to be awful." He is correct, and what's more, it's a tradition that, in Britain, stretches back to the 1930s, when music hall songbird Gracie Fields recorded the first one, immortalizing her hometown team of Rochdale.

In the decades that followed, more soccer songs followed and, by the early 1970s, they were even making the U.K. charts—hitherto, they were curios for the faithful fans, or a way of squeezing a last lump of publicity out of a dying career. (In 1966, several years after his last hit single, skiffle superman Lonnie Donegan recorded "World Cup Willie," to mark the arrival of the World Cup tournament in England; it went nowhere.)

In 1970, however, the England players themselves were dragged into a studio (none too willingly, judging by period footage) to record "Back Home," a plaintive ditty demanding that their home fans support them while they were in

Mexico for that year's World Cup. The record went to #1, England was eliminated in the quarter finals, and since that time, neither the quality of songs nor the quality of the players have improved very much.

But the quality of performers has. Rod Stewart fans, for example, will at least be aware of their hero's periodic pairings with the Scotland team, to record such one-off crackers as 1978's "Ole Ola" (absent, interestingly, from EVERY Rod hits record ever issued, despite being a bigger hit than almost every new single he's released since then) and "Purple Heather" (embarrassingly ditto). There's also a lipsmacking version of Jimi Hendrix's "Angel," Rod duetting with soccer maestro Denis Law.

In 1996, the Lightning Seeds linked with the England team to record another #1 hit; and two years later, a remix of the same combination topped the chart again, while the charts behind it ached to the unholy union of England, Ian McCulloch, and the Spice Girls. That same year, Del Amitri flew the flag for Scotland; Jean Michel Jarre touted official themes for both France and Japan; and Sly and Robbie (of course) came up with Jamaica's.

But if fans of the musicians appreciate such unusual (and generally unrepeatable) couplings, the players are less certain. Brian McClair, again, recalls a conversation he had with another player, Bryan Robson, about England's 1990 record.

Robson: "We've just made a record for the England World Cup Squad with some blokes called New Order."

McClair: "You'll have a #1 there, no problem."

Robson: "Never, no way! There's no way that rubbish is going to get to #1."

Of course it did, and it stayed there for a month, while New Order's own Bernard Sumner admits that his band recorded "World in Motion" only because "it was such an unexpected thing for us to be doing. But we wanted to bring some respectability to a disgraced musical genre."

And disgraced it has been, not only in Britain, but in virtually every other soccer playing country in the world. Including the United States. Back in 1990, while they should have been getting ready for that year's World Cup, Team U.S.A. was instead coaxed into a recording studio to tape a World Cup rap record which was truly so appalling that even the game's governing body, the United States Soccer Federation, disowned it.

It was screened once on the cable sports channel Prime Sports Network, at halftime during one of the team's pre-tournament friendlies, and was never heard of again... indeed, not only was it never given a full release, it didn't even get a full airing on the television. Halfway through, the song faded out and the program went to commercial. And the commercial was preferable.

♫ The Boxer BY SIMON & GARFUNKEL (1970)

"The Boxer" was Paul Simon's riposte to the increasingly harsh press that he and partner Art were receiving at the time. "I think the song was about me: everybody's beating me up, and I'm telling you now I'm going to go away if you don't stop. For the first few years, it was just pure praise. It took two or three years for people to realize that we weren't strange creatures that emerged from England but just two guys from Queens who used to sing rock'n'roll. And maybe we weren't real folkies at all! Maybe we weren't even hippies!"

♫ Paradise by the Dashboard Light BY MEATLOAF (1978)

The ultimate Loaf song, the ultimate teenage passion drama, love and lies and promises made in the heat of the night, with the car radio blaring a ball game, and the youngsters getting very hot (him) and very bothered (her) in the front seats. Sheer sweaty perfection.

♫ Boxers BY MORRISSEY (1995)

Until as late as the 1970s, amateur boxing was very much a part of the east London landscape, and this gem recaptures all the sweat and turmoil associated with it.

♫ Centerfield BY JOHN FOGERTY (1985)

Up there with "Talkin' Baseball" and "Take Me Out to the Ballgame," the National Anthem of the national pastime.

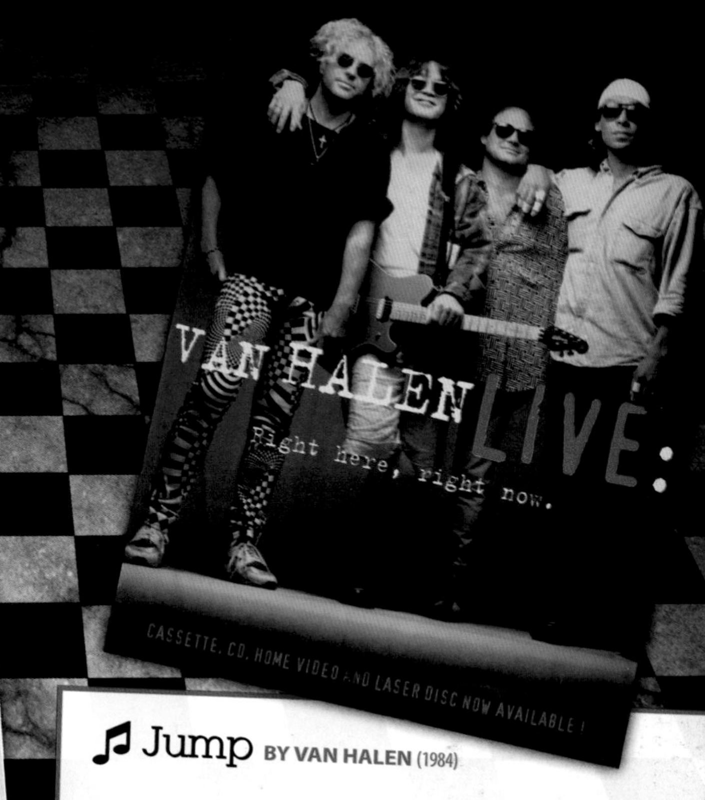

♫ Jump BY VAN HALEN (1984)

Lyrically, it's probably not much to write home about, just a succession of increasingly volatile exhortations that leave the protagonist resigned to jumping… where, or off what, we don't know. Musically, however, it's an Olympic event set to music, with a riff so raw that you can't help but obey.

♫ Hurricane BY BOB DYLAN (1975)

The story of "Hurricane" Ruben Carter, the boxer who was tried and convicted of murder in the midst of a rising career.

RICH MAN, POOR MAN

The Prince and the Pauper, Lady Chatterley's Lover, Mrs Brown… "a posh bit of totty and a nice bit of rough," as an Englishman might put it. The attraction of social opposites has fed literature and cinema since the beginning of both, and rock'n'roll is no stranger to the concept, either. Not every song deals with a love affair, of course; sometimes, it's simply the notion of the noble savage that sets the songwriter's pen a-flutter. But, for a music that always proclaimed itself to be classless, there's an awful lot of class awareness going on, isn't there?

♫ Backstreet Luv BY CURVED AIR (1971)

IN HER OWN WORDS—SONJA KRISTINA (composer, vocalist): 'Backstreet Luv' is autobiographical. When I was 15 I was skipping school repeatedly and was spending time under the spell of a volatile 24 year old man. My father was the headmaster of a borstal for teenagers and this man was a former inmate. The song is inspired by my experiences during this escapade.

♫ That's Entertainment BY THE JAM (1981)

Life in a dark and dingy suburban apartment.

♫ Lady Jane BY THE ROLLING STONES (1966)

An immaculate Andrew Loog Oldham production heightens its Elizabethan atmosphere with the use of Brian Jones' dulcimer.

♫ The Days of Pearly Spencer **BY DAVID MCWILLIAMS** (1967)

Irish songwriter McWilliams wrote his best known song about a homeless man he knew in Ballymena.

♫ Muswell Hillbillies **BY THE KINKS** (1971)

Written at a time when British society was trying to "improve" the lot of its working class families, by ripping them away from their roots and transplanting them all to anonymous "New Towns." Whether they wanted to go or not.

♫ Eastbourne Ladies **BY KEVIN COYNE** (1973)

Eastbourne, on England's south coast, is a renowned retirement area. Not, the late Coyne discovers, the best place to go to pick up women.

♫ Morning Glory **BY TIM BUCKLEY** (1967)

Buckley grew up close to a hobo camp in southern California, and wrote this song about the pride of its inhabitants.

WE'RE AN AMERICAN BAND— AND OTHER STATES OF BEING

I'm writing these words on July 4th. Need I say more?

America BY SIMON & GARFUNKEL (1968)

The song that launched a million bus rides; and still the most evocative exploration of the country that has ever been set to music.

Statesboro Blues BY THE ALLMAN BROTHERS (1971)

A Blind Willie McTell opus, immortalizing his hometown, and taken to worldwide extremes by the Allmans.

Tupelo Honey

BY VAN MORRISON (1971)

Van sings of his new found domestic bliss.

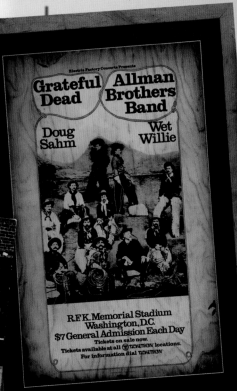

Up On Cripple Creek

BY THE BAND (1969)

Americana at its most powerfully evocative.

♫ American Girl

BY TOM PETTY & THE HEARTBREAKERS (1977)

"I wrote that in a little apartment I had in Encino," Petty explained. "It was right next to the freeway and the cars sometimes sounded like waves from the ocean, which is why there's the line about the waves crashing on the beach. The words just came tumbling out very quickly—and it was the start of writing about people who are longing for something else in life, something better than they have."

♫ Back in the USA

BY CHUCK BERRY (1959)

Both the Beach Boys and the Beatles took a musical lead from this one.

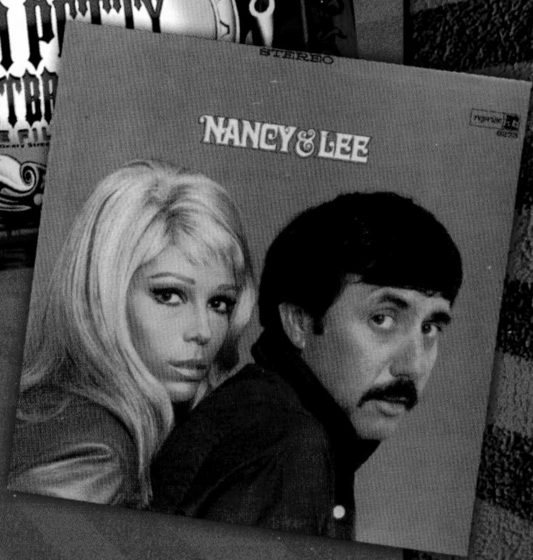

♫ Jackson **BY NANCY SINATRA AND LEE HAZLEWOOD** (1967)

Nancy Sinatra had already stepped into the world of duets when she teamed with father Frank for "Something Stupid"—a lachrymose love song that was only kinda creepy if you paused to consider their familial relationship. Two years later, she was on somewhat safer territory when she linked up with Lee Hazlewood for an album of absolute mayhem, headed off by the supremely quarrelsome "Jackson." Pop has never sounded so pointed.

♫ Stuck Inside of Mobile with the Memphis Blues Again

BY BOB DYLAN (1966)

Dylan laments his continued reputation as a folkie (Mobile, Alabama, was a center of the folk movement) when what he really wanted was to play R&B, Memphis style.

Black Water BY THE DOOBIE BROTHERS (1974)

Two songs in one, the first a slightly swampy romp through the catfish-infested Mississippi, with a gentle hook that just oozes gumbo and fiddles; the second, the seemingly random selection of a lyric that you barely noticed the first time around, elevated into one of the most compulsive chants of the age.

Massachussets (The Lights Went Out In)

BY THE BEE GEES (1967)

Originally written for fellow Australians the Seekers, Robin Gibb later admitted "We have never been [to Massachusetts], but we loved the word and there is always something magic about American place names. It only works with British names if you do it as a folk song."

We're an American Band BY GRAND FUNK (1973)

"We're an American Band" might have been the most redundant statement of the age, but it was also one of the most glorifyingly affirmative. "We're coming to your town, we'll help you party down."

Young Americans

BY DAVID BOWIE (1975)

The state of the nation, by an Englishman out of Philadelphia soul.

America BY THE NICE (1968)

Originally written for *West Side Story*, Leonard Bernstein's epic of assimilation took on a whole new meaning once the English trio wrapped Keith Emerson's organ around it, and transformed it into a brutal stab of political commentary.

Cincinatti Fatback BY ROOGALATOR (1976)

IN HIS OWN WORDS—DANNY ADLER (composer): I wrote this song in London during the summer of 1973... I remember writing part of a verse on a cigarette packet on the top deck of a bus, creeping past Streatham Common in the late afternoon traffic. I was homesick and missing American summers, but also celebrating my tribal roots—ie: King Records, James Brown, Lonnie Mack, the great Russell Givens, who taught Bootsy Collins to play funk bass, Wynonie Harris, Albert T. Washington, Freddie King, the Five Royales, Hank Ballard and "The Twist." Good rockin' tonite, Caledonia, Hillbilly twang, Jump Blues, swing, funk, rock'n'roll... Cincinnati had it all; it was Nashville before Nashville, it was Motown before Motown. The end of the song is a kind of film montage, where I salute my homies and family, and mom waves goodbye as I leave town on the old Buckeye (#67), a broken down old all-night mail train headed for California.

Sweet Home Alabama BY LYNYRD SKYNYRD (1974)

A scathing riposte to Neil Young's "Southern Man."

Twenty Four Hours from Tulsa BY GENE PITNEY (1963)

Home thoughts from a day away.

Lynyrd Skynyrd

Arizona BY ALEJANDRO ESCOVEDA (2006)

A weary journey that shows no sign of ending.

Mississippi Queen

BY MOUNTAIN (1970)

"Back in August of '69," explained Mountain's Corky Laing, "we were playing at a funky beach club called 30 Acres. It was the hottest summer ever in Nantucket, and one night the power blew [out] across the entire island! ... A buddy of mine had a girlfriend with him at the club who was visiting from Mississippi. She had on a see-through dress—I can still remember this; she was amazing! Look, there were also Dexedrine in my system, and I was on overdrive. I looked at this beautiful girl and began screaming this song, 'cause there was no power."

Tobacco Road BY THE NASHVILLE TEENS (1964)

A J.D. Loudermilk blues, rocked up and spangled with one of the most evil guitar sounds of the age. Even today, it's sometimes hard to believe that this record was made so long ago... although check the production credit, Mickey Most, and it slots in alongside "House of the Rising Sun" (101) in terms of giving your ears the surprise of their lives.

Reno, Nevada BY RICHARD AND MIMI FARINA (1965)

Johnny Cash shot a man in Reno; R.E.M. suggest going there to find fame and fortune. But it was the Farinas who truly placed it on the musical map.

TO EVERYTHING THERE IS A SEASON— A ROCK'N'ROLL ALMANAC

The Beatles sang of a day in the life; Sandy Denny asked who knows where the time goes; and the Tremoloes declared that years may come, years may go. The passage of time, and the multitudinous methods that man has developed for making it has fascinated art and artists since the beginning—and many of the songs that celebrate them are equally timeless.

♫ Stairway to Heaven BY LED ZEPPELIN (1971)

"It was a milestone for us," Robert Plant said in 1975. "Every musician wants to do something of lasting quality, something which will hold up for a long time, and I guess we did it with 'Stairway'."

A pagan love song that became the most played, and most requested song in the history of American rock radio; the ultimate youth club slow dance; the best-selling single piece of sheet music in the world; the absolute zenith of Led Zeppelin's folk rock hybrid; and an epic that was *still* as dizzying a kaleidoscope in 2007, when Zeppelin included it in their reunion repertoire, as it was when it first entered their live set, following the release of *Led Zeppelin IV* in 1970.

♫ Autumn Almanac BY THE KINKS (1967)

Kinks songwriter Ray Davies was at the peak of his powers by the late 1960s, reeling off a succession of glorious paeans to the life, traditions, and history of his native England. This evocation of a day at the end of the season opens with an eye on a passing caterpillar and just grows more pastoral from there.

♫ Josephine BY JOHN OTWAY AND WILD WILLY BARRETT (1978)

IN HIS OWN WORDS—JOHN OTWAY (composer): "I think I was still in my teens when I wrote that, I had a very romantic view of females then. It's great the way some things I created back then are still appreciated, I still play this song at nearly every show I do—far more often than something like 'Geneve.' (Though of course not as often as the Hits.)"

♫ White Winter Hymn BY THE FLEET FOXES (2008)

A gorgeous invocation of winter at her most awesome.

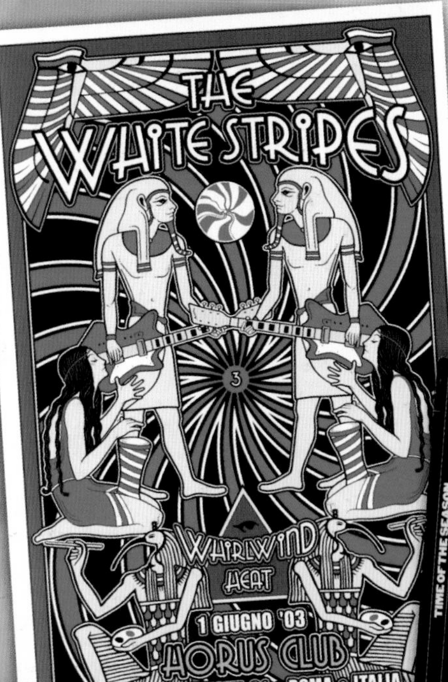

Dead Leaves And The Dirty Ground

BY WHITE STRIPES (2002)

We celebrate Autumn for her wonderful color scheme. But it's also a time of sadness and loss.

Time of the Season

BY THE ZOMBIES (1969)

The band had already broken up when this became their biggest hit in two years (since "She's Not There" - 31). Hastily reforming, they rode a few months of glory, then returned to their chosen script and gave the world Argent.

Everyday Is Halloween **BY MINISTRY** (1984)

A celebration of the Gothic lifestyle, seen through a prism of bitter irony and weary individualism—in other words, a considerably more powerful lyric than a quick listen to the chorus might let on.

Indian Summer **BY THE DOORS** (1970)

IN HIS OWN WORDS—RAY MANZAREK (organist): "Indian Summer, we found that in our bin of stuff, that is the very first day of recording of the first album, Moonlight Drive and Indian Summer, it's a simple little song to get the sound down that we found, polished it up, recorded new parts and used four years later."

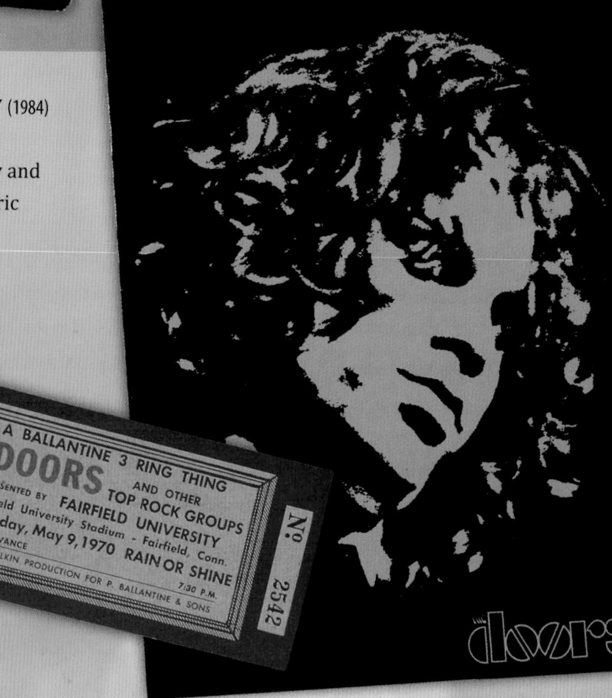

IT'S A DIRTY JOB, BUT SOMEONE'S GOT TO DO IT

HARD LABOR AND OTHER LAMENTS...

Earlier, we cast a withering glance towards all those bands who write songs about rock'n'roll, because really, who needs to hear someone singing about their job? Singing about somebody else's job, though... now, that's another matter entirely.

♫ Who Do You Love BY JUICY LUCY (1970)

Past the barbed wire fence, the ice wagon, and the human skulls, this is a song about life at the bottom of the barrel. Bo Diddley wrote and recorded the original version, but Anglo-American blues band Juicy Lucy made it their own, as vocalist Ray Owen explains. "We wanted to turn it around and make it a bit more exciting. The lyrics were pretty cool, but Bo can get pretty boring, no disrespect to him, so we wanted to make the song sound as exciting as the lyrics." Screaming slide, screeching guitars and a growl as low as the gutter saw to that, all piled together as a backdrop for lyrics that shake with rage. The guy who sings the song, continued Owen, is "somebody who's really down to earth, who's had it rough and who sees life in a very straightforward way. He cuts away all the frilly stuff. He's done a bit of traveling, he knows how to cut out the bullshit and just get on with things. The person who sings those words has done all of that."

♫ Takin' Care Of Business

BY BACHMAN TURNER OVERDRIVE (1974)

A song that started life as a pledge to simply do what needs to be done has—if not shifted its meaning, at least taken on whole new connotations, as a generation of mega corporations have adopted the term to suggest that they are somehow hip.

2968
29¢
EXCLUSIVE!
THE BEATLES
26¢
STARRING IN
A HARD DAY'S NIGHT
With a special foreword by The BEATLES themselves
THE OFFICIAL UNITED ARTISTS' PICTORIAL SOUVENIR BOOK
★ Candid cameras behind the scenes
★ Stories you won't see on the screen
THE WHOLE CRAZY MAKING-OF-THE-FILM STORY—FROM START TO FINISH
Whitman

♫ A Hard Day's Night BY THE BEATLES (1964)

One of the most wonderful Ringo-isms of them all. "We went to do a job, and we'd worked all day and we happened to work all night. I came up still thinking it was day I suppose, and I said, 'It's been a hard day...' and I looked around and saw it was dark so I said, 'Night!' So we came to 'A Hard Day's Night.'"

♫ The Weight BY THE BAND (1968)

The popular notion that "The Weight" has some kind of Biblical subtext derives from the lyric's reference to Nazareth—but that's Nazareth, Pennsylvania, as opposed to any more sacred spot, as Levon Helm explains in his autobiography, *This Wheel's on Fire.*

"We had two or three tunes, or pieces of tunes, and "The Weight" was one I would work on. Robbie had that bit about going down to Nazareth - Pennsylvania, where the Martin guitar factory is at. The song was full of our favorite characters. We recorded the song maybe four times. We weren't really sure it was going to be on the album, but people really liked it. Rick, Richard, and I would switch the verses around among us, and we all sang the chorus: Put the load right on me!"

♫ Dirty Deeds Done Dirt Cheap BY AC/DC (1976)

It's become something of an anthem for the Oz rockers, as well as an all-consuming statement of intent. But guitarist Angus Young took the title from a running gag in the 1962 cartoon series *Beanie and Cecil*; the villainous Dishonest John's business card read "Dirty Deeds Done Dirt Cheap. Holidays, Sundays, and Special Rates."

AC/DC
TV
Dirty Deeds Done Dirt Cheap

GETTING EMOTIONAL—
TEARS IN YOUR BEER AND SUNDRY SAD REMAINS

Sad

adj. sad·der, sad·dest

1. Affected or characterized by sorrow or unhappiness.

2. Expressive of sorrow or unhappiness.

***3. Causing sorrow or gloom; depressing:* a sad song, sad lyrics**

***4. Deplorable; sorry:* a very sad excuse for a song, a sad state of affairs**

5. Dark-hued; somber.

The Death Of Freddie Mercury

"It was strange, because none of us really thought he would die," May reflects. "It was unthinkable, although obviously you have the possibility in the back of your head 24 hours a day. It's the most unreal thing to go through with somebody you've been that close with for that long. And having 'The Show Must Go On' out as a single at that time, it was very bizarre, because the way the song came about in the first place was strange.

"For some reason, John and Freddie and Roger had been playing around with things in the studio and I heard one of the sequences they had come up with, and I could just hear the whole thing descending from the skies... almost in the form, soundwise, that it ended up. It's something that came as a gift from heaven, I suppose. I did some demos, chopped things up, did some singing demos, and some guitar and got it to a point where I could play it to the guys, and they all thought it was something worth pursuing.

"Then Freddie and I sat down, and I got out my scribblings and said 'what do you think of all this?' It was a very strange and memorable moment really, because what I'd done was come up with something which I thought was the world viewed through his eyes. We didn't talk about it as such, we talked about in terms of the story... it was very poignant at the time, but strangely, not precious in any sense, it was just a song and we just loved the idea of it. I was very pleased with the way it came out, especially the way Freddie pushed his voice to ridiculous heights. Some of that stuff I mapped out in falsetto for him, and I remember saying 'I really don't know if this is asking way too much...' and he went, 'oh darling, not a problem. I'll have a couple of vodkas then go ahead and do it.' And he did."

Bridge Over Troubled Waters

BY SIMON & GARFUNKEL (1970)

One of the most oft-covered songs of all time, and one of the few to have topped both U.S. and U.K. charts simultaneously, "Bridge Over Troubled Waters" started life, said composer Paul Simon, as a gospel song, and it retains that spirit.

Let It Be **BY THE BEATLES** (1970)

A simple tribute to his mother, written by McCartney following a dream.

Privilege **BY THE PATTI SMITH GROUP** (1978)

Originally composed for the movie of the same name, starring Manfred Mann frontman Paul Jones, "Privilege" became a touchstone in the Patti Smith Group's early live repertoire, before being recorded for her third album, *Easter*—and sparking controversy via her insertion of sundry blasphemies into the lyric.

♫ Cryin' BY AEROSMITH (1973)

The song has been described by some as, possibly, a metaphor for drug use. But it works equally well as a lament for a rollercoaster relationship that has a lot more downs than ups.

♫ The Show Must Go On BY QUEEN (1991)

Vocalist Freddie Mercury was near death when he wrote and recorded this, for release on what would become the original Queen's final album; anthemic and stirring, it is a song of hope-against-hope, defiance and a solid refusal to bow down to the inevitable. But tinged with such regret that, had "My Way" never been written, this could have stepped into its shoes.

♫ 96 Tears BY QUESTION MARK AND THE MYSTERIONS (1966)

Originally titled "Too Many Teardrops," the song became "69 Tears" before concerns were raised about its suitability for airplay. Finally they reached the magic number 96, and the mysterious Mysterions sent garage rock soaring to the top of the chart.

♫ Glory Box BY PORTISHEAD (1995)

The despairing calm before the storm of commitment.

♫ Hurt BY NINE INCH NAILS (1994)

Deeply personal and darkly revelatory, Trent Reznor's personal favorite of all his own songs gained a new lease on life after Johnny Cash caught it for a cover, towards the end of his life.

Lost Cause BY BECK (2002)

The father of Nineties low-fi returns with what might well be the cruelest kiss off ever sent to music.

Pack Up Your Sorrows BY RICHARD AND MIMI FARINA (1965)

A Richard Farina song that has been covered so often that it's now a folk standard, "Pack Up Your Sorrows" lines up the same theme of redemption as "Bridge Over Troubled Waters" (30), "Wrap You Troubles in Dreams" and even "Pack Up Your Troubles in Your Old Kit Bag," but with an intriguing twist—"you would lose them, I know how to use them, give them all to me."

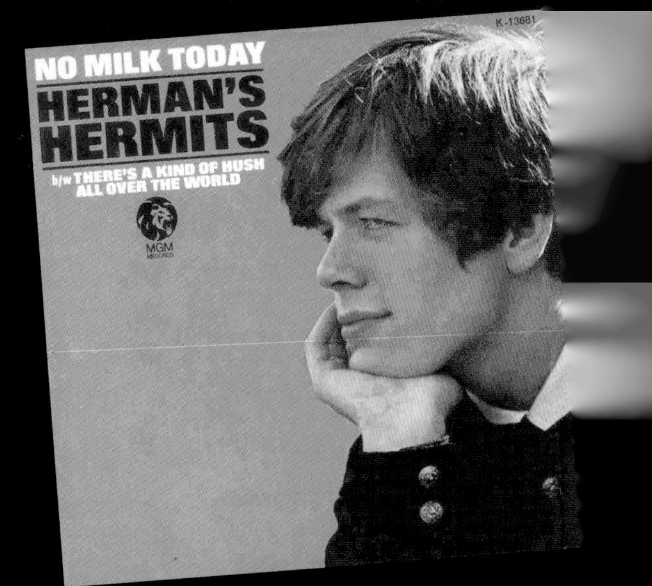

Second Skin BY THE GITS (1991)

Seattle punk mavens the Gits entered rock history following the murder of their lead singer, Mia Zapata, in 1993. They deserved so much more than that—songs released on ether side of the tragedy revealed Zapata to be one of the most thoughtfully gifted, and dramatically honest songwriters ever to grace that genre, and this plea for a harder shell to protect her from her own feelings captures Zapata at her best.

No Milk Today BY HERMAN'S HERMITS (1967

That's right, tell the delivery boy your problems..

DO ROCK STARS DREAM OF ELECTRIC GUITARS?—

SONGS WHEN YOU'RE SLEEPING

Some of the greatest songs, their composers have said, came to them in a dream. Even "Satisfaction" was delivered to Keith Richard while he slept, and Paul McCartney caught "Let It Be" in the same way. But songs about sleep and dreams themselves seem unanimously to have been written during the waking hours. Which is sort of odd, when you think about it, isn't it?

♫ Dream On BY AEROSMITH (1973)

They should have recorded it with a full choir, and they should have told Steve Tyler to put a bit more oomph into his vocal. But if you have a cigarette lighter handy, you're already waving it in the air.

♫ Daydream Believer BY THE MONKEES (1967)

Composed by the late John Stewart, author, also, of "Gold" (477).

#9 Dream BY JOHN LENNON (1975)

Despite (or maybe because) its chorus line, "Ah bowakawa, posse, posse"," being meaningless, "#9 Dream" recounts a dream Lennon had about himself and then-lover May Pang, tied to the number nine because it was one that pursued Lennon throughout his songwriting.

Lady Rachel BY KEVIN AYERS (1969)

"Lady Rachel" rides a lyrical narrative that itself is as disconnected as any dream could be, before resolving into a chorus that is as irresistible as it is portentous.

Journey From Eden

BY THE STEVE MILLER BAND (1972)

The melody itself is a dream, to which the breathily gentle lyrics simply add new layers of imagery.

UTOPIA

A NICE PLACE TO VISIT BUT WOULD YOU REALLY WANT TO LIVE THERE?

It was Thomas More, chancellor to the English King Henry VIII, who coined the term "utopia," intending it as a pun that combined both the concept of a "good place" and "no place." Discovered on a voyage to the newly-discovered Americas, Utopia was a land bereft of crime, evil, or any of the other sins that benighted 16th century England, ruled according to what can best be described as a system of benevolent Communism. Both a political and a philosophical ideal, Utopia has since come to mean any place that has shrugged off the problems of the modern world, an earthly paradise where the pursuit of individual pleasure is the only reason for living. Yeah, right....

John Lennon and Yoko Ono

♫ Imagine BY JOHN LENNON (1971)

Remove everything that divides people from one another… religion, politics, nationality, favorite sports teams, the lot… and it would probably be a pretty boring planet. But it's a nice idea, and sufficient people agree with that sentiment that there's a small army of cover versions out there.

♫ Running Up That Hill

BY KATE BUSH (1985)

Bush's original draft of this song was "Deal With God"—a title that her label, EMI, asked her to change because radio has never been big on songs that take the Lord's name in vain. Unhappily, she agreed, but the song's sentiment, of bargaining with the supreme power to get a better role in life, remains to convey her initial intention.

♫ Woodstock

BY JONI MITCHELL (1970)

"Woodstock" reminds us of precisely how quickly the legend became engrained in the popular psyche. And how pernicious it remains. If we rely upon history, memory and, perhaps, way too many drugs, a four-day festival in a muddy field in upstate New York, at the height of the final summer of the Sixties, was the peak of all the peace and love and flowers that the previous few years had been building up to. And maybe, for the half million or so kids who sat through the music, it was, although out in the real world, life carried on as normal. The number one single in the week of the Woodstock festival was the Archies' "Sugar Sugar," while the headlines were still consumed by the as-yet unsolved Manson murders. A bunch of kids getting high to Hendrix and Santana seemed insignificant by comparison.

♫ Big Yellow Taxi **BY JONI MITCHELL** (1970)

Like the song says, they paved paradise, put in a parking lot. Which has since been demolished and turned into a multiplex theater, a strip mall, an office building and, the last I heard, they're building a super church there.

"I wrote 'Big Yellow Taxi' on my first trip to Hawaii," Mitchell later revealed. "I took a taxi to the hotel and when I woke up the next morning, I threw back the curtains and saw these beautiful green mountains in the distance. Then, I looked down and there was a parking lot as far as the eye could see, and it broke my heart... this blight on paradise. That's when I sat down and wrote the song."

Celebrate with:
JOAN BAEZ
CROSBY, STILLS, NASH & YOUNG
JONI MITCHELL
JOHN SEBASTIAN
And Introducing
DOROTHY MORRISON
Everyone did it... for the sheer love of it.
CELEBRATION AT BIG SUR
...it happened one weekend by the sea.
Ted Mann Productions presents a film by Baird Bryant & Johanna Demetrakas
Produced by Carl Gottlieb Released by 20th Century-Fox COLOR by DE LUXE
GP

WHITHER SHALL I WANDER?

"It takes much longer to get up north the slow way"—Ian Dury

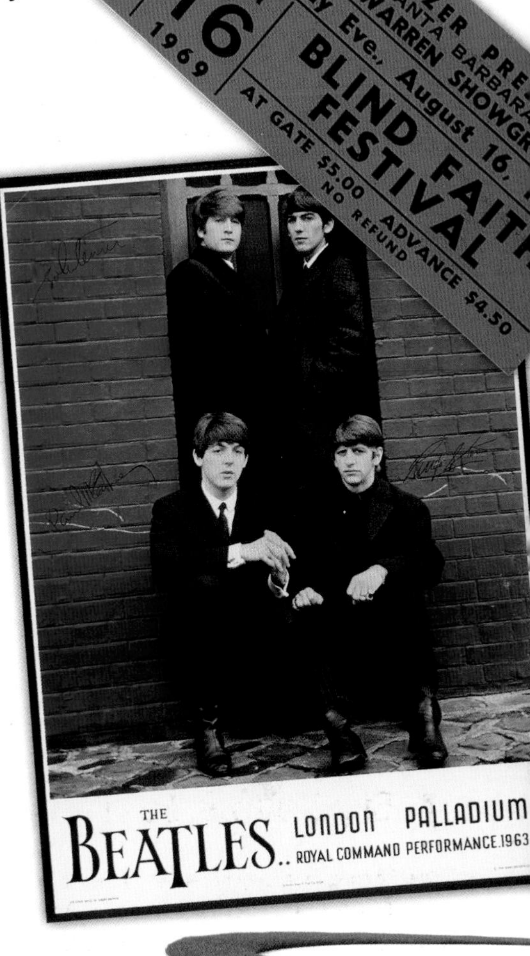

♫ Can't Find My Way Home **BY BLIND FAITH** (1969)

The Blind Faith supergroup was an attempt, by both Eric Clapton and Steve Winwood, to escape the lengthening shadows of their earlier careers—Winwood as the teenaged prodigy who led the Spencer Davis Group and Traffic, Clapton as a guitar playing god. It was only a partial success, but this searching, acoustically-based ballad allowed both to at least put their quests into song.

♫ Across the Universe **BY THE BEATLES** (1970)

"I was a bit… artsy-fartsy there," John Lennon admitted in 1980. "I was lying next to my first wife in bed, and I was irritated. She must have been going on and on about something and she'd gone to sleep—and I kept hearing these words over and over, flowing like an endless stream. I went downstairs and it turned into a sort of cosmic song rather than an irritated song—rather than 'Why are you always mouthing off at me?' or whatever, right? ...and I've sat down and looked at it and said, 'Can I write another one with this meter?' It's so interesting. 'Words are flowing out like endless rain into a paper cup / They slither while they pass, they slip away across the universe.'

"Such an extraordinary meter and I can never repeat it! It's not a matter of craftsmanship—it wrote itself. It drove me out of bed. I didn't want to write it... and I couldn't get to sleep until I put it on paper... It's like being possessed—like a psychic or a medium. The thing has to go down. It won't let you sleep, so you have to get up, make it into something, and then you're allowed to sleep. That's always in the middle of the night when you're half-awake or tired and your critical facilities are switched off."

♫ These Days **BY JACKSON BROWNE** (1973)

Written by Browne at the age of sixteen, "These Days" had already been cut by Nico and Greg Allman, before the composer recorded his definitive version for his *For Everyman* album. It was the latter that most influenced Browne. "When [Allman] did it I thought that he really unlocked a power in that song that I sort of then emulated in my version. I started playing the piano. I wasn't trying to sing it like Gregg; I couldn't possibly. I took the cue, playin' this slow walk. But it was written very sort of, kind of—[strums opening to 'These Days']—a little more flatpicking."

♫ On the Road Again BY CANNED HEAT (1968)

The loneliness of the long distance jam band!

♫ Walk This Way BY AEROSMITH (1975)

It's not really about walking, of course. Not unless you consider being led through your first sexual experience by a promiscuous cheerleader to be a stroll in the park....

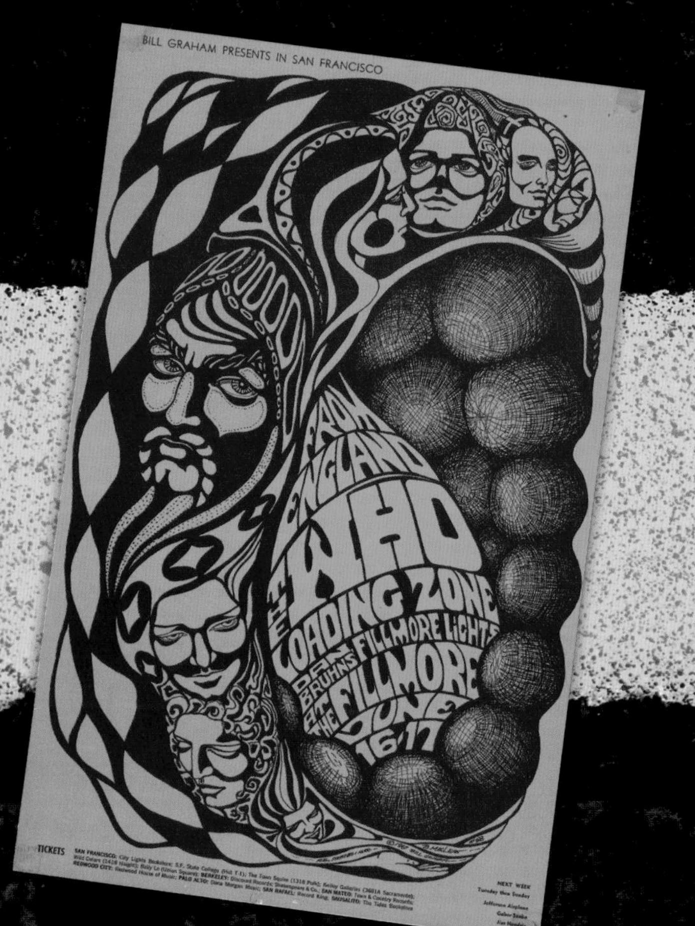

♫ Magic Bus BY THE WHO (1968)

IN HIS OWN WORDS—JOHN ENTWISTLE (bassist): I wish I'd had my sampler echo then. I could have played the first ba-ba-ba, gone offstage for a cup of tea, then come back for the bit that went ba-biddy-ba-biddy."

♫ Truckin' BY THE GRATEFUL DEAD (1970)

According to Bob Weir, "There was a romance about being a young man on the road in America, and you had to do it! It was a rite of passage. And at the same time, it was the material that you drew from to write about. We were starting to become real guys, and really enjoying the hell out of it. We toured more or less four to six months out of the year. It was our bread and butter—we weren't selling that many records. And we had a lot of fun out on the road, got into a lot of trouble... We left some smoking craters of some Holiday Inns, I'll say that, and there were a lot of places that wouldn't have us back. All of this is absolutely autobiographical, all the stuff in 'Truckin'.'"

The Grateful Dead

♫ Ramblin' Man BY THE ALLMAN BROTHERS (1973)

The Allmans' first Top 10 hit was rooted around an old Hank Williams number, about traveling the world and taking life as it comes.

♫ Starting Over BY JOHN LENNON (1980)

Less a physical journey than an emotional one, Lennon's last big hit before his murder was inevitably redefined by the events of December 1980. At its heart, however, it remains a song of undying love, seen through the prism of life's long journey—with a rock'n'rolling rhythm that takes the listener back to the days when John himself was just starting out.

♫ I Get Around BY THE BEACH BOYS (1964)

Another of the Beach Boys' ultimate teenaged anthems, a celebration of life on the sunny side of the strip, with a car that can't be beat and the girls lining up for a ride.

♫ Me and Bobby McGee BY JANIS JOPLIN (1971)

According to composer Kris Kristofferson, it was his music publisher, Fred Foster, who came up with the song title, then left it to Kris to come up with the words. "I was trying to write that song all the time I was flying around Baton Rouge and New Orleans. I had the rhythm of a Mickey Newbury song going in the back of my mind, 'Why You Been Gone So Long,' and I developed this story of these guys who went around the country kind of like Anthony Quinn and Giuletta Masina in [Fellini's] *La Strada*. At one point, like he did, he drove off and left her there. That was 'Somewhere near Salinas, I let her slip away.' Later in the film he hears a woman hanging out her clothes, singing the melody she [Masina] used to play on the trombone, and she told him, 'Oh, she died.' So he goes out, gets drunk, gets into a fight in a bar and ends up on the beach, howling at the stars. And that was where 'Freedom's just another word for nothing left to lose' came from, because he was free from her, and I guess he would have traded all his tomorrows for another day with her."

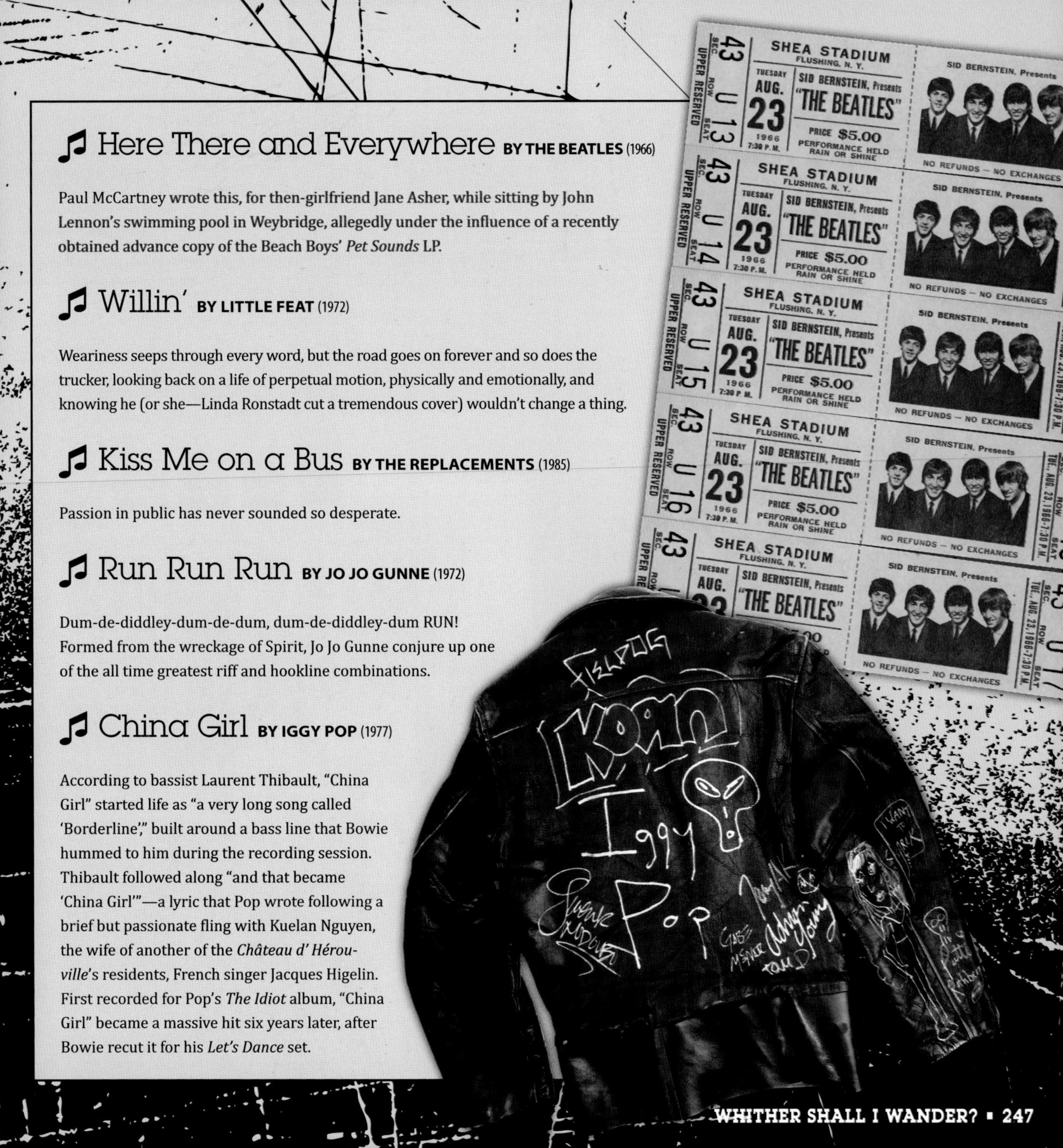

♫ Here There and Everywhere **BY THE BEATLES** (1966)

Paul McCartney wrote this, for then-girlfriend Jane Asher, while sitting by John Lennon's swimming pool in Weybridge, allegedly under the influence of a recently obtained advance copy of the Beach Boys' *Pet Sounds* LP.

♫ Willin' **BY LITTLE FEAT** (1972)

Weariness seeps through every word, but the road goes on forever and so does the trucker, looking back on a life of perpetual motion, physically and emotionally, and knowing he (or she—Linda Ronstadt cut a tremendous cover) wouldn't change a thing.

♫ Kiss Me on a Bus **BY THE REPLACEMENTS** (1985)

Passion in public has never sounded so desperate.

♫ Run Run Run **BY JO JO GUNNE** (1972)

Dum-de-diddley-dum-de-dum, dum-de-diddley-dum RUN! Formed from the wreckage of Spirit, Jo Jo Gunne conjure up one of the all time greatest riff and hookline combinations.

♫ China Girl **BY IGGY POP** (1977)

According to bassist Laurent Thibault, "China Girl" started life as "a very long song called 'Borderline'," built around a bass line that Bowie hummed to him during the recording session. Thibault followed along "and that became 'China Girl'"—a lyric that Pop wrote following a brief but passionate fling with Kuelan Nguyen, the wife of another of the *Château d' Hérouville*'s residents, French singer Jacques Higelin. First recorded for Pop's *The Idiot* album, "China Girl" became a massive hit six years later, after Bowie recut it for his *Let's Dance* set.

♫ To Bring You My Love

BY P.J. HARVEY (1995)

Everybody has their own ideas of what the blues should sound like, but this cracked and broken croak through the desert makes even Robert Johnson sound lighthearted.

♫ Going Up the Country

BY CANNED HEAT (1969)

Bluesman Henry Thomas' "Bull Doze Blues," transported forty years to a field in upstate New York. One of *the* anthems of Woodstock.

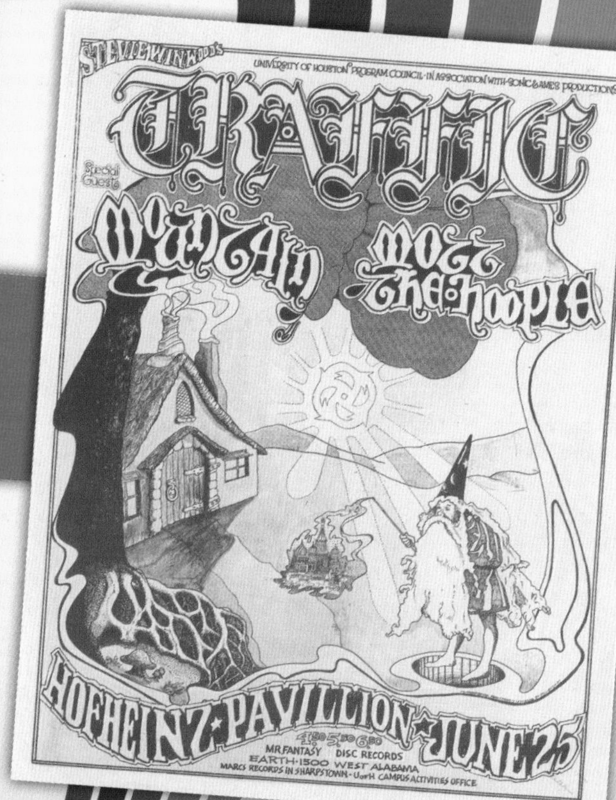

♫ Hole in My Shoe **BY TRAFFIC** (1967)

The young Steve Winwood sings us through a psychedelic dream… with wet feet.

♫ Far Far Away **BY SLADE** (1974)

By 1974, Slade were moving far, far away from the fist punching stomp of their earlier hits, and turning out more thoughtful opuses. And these "home thoughts from abroad," tracing the band's travels and travails, are as visual as anything they ever recorded.

SITTING IN THE MIDDAY SUN —SONGS FOR A SUNNY AFTERNOON

Yes, it's time to talk about the weather again.

Rising Sun BY MEDICINE HEAD (1973)

IN HIS OWN WORDS—JOHN FIDDLER (composer): "A constant glimpse of something you find to be truly beautiful, or uplifting is what I'm to say in this song. To describe someone as a 'constant glimpse of the rising sun,' ever-never changing, the same but not the same, stationary, but written in movement. To suggest newness and poetic awareness is so important in this song—never to 'underestimate what you mean to me'; to see that 'you're open like a child's first book'; that 'when you speak, it's just like a symphony'; and 'your fingers touch me with poetry'; and then to say that 'you're like a constant glimpse, of the rising sun.'

"Peter [bandmate Hope Evans] and I welded our Spirit-Ancient Mouth Bows and Vibrato Guitars to Tony Ashton's Symphoniser, and his rinky dink drum machine, and maybe, just maybe, this was/is, embryonic 'Soul Technology'."

Waiting for the Sun BY THE DOORS (1970)

IN HIS OWN WORDS—RAY MANZAREK (organist): "Waiting for the Sun was a song we had two years before but it wasn't ready, it hadn't come out of the oven yet, and I'm glad we waited because it came out a stunning piece of music. But we loved the title so much that we called the album *Waiting for the Sun,* the artwork was done but the song wasn't ready, but no-one will know there's a song called 'Waiting for the Sun,' so when it finally came out, people went—wait a sec!"

Summer Breeze BY SEALS AND CROFT (1972)

Soft, warm, gentle... which is exactly what it sounds like. The Isley Brothers recorded this same song exquisitely, but the original makes you feel great too.

Sunny Afternoon BY THE KINKS (1966)

It doesn't matter what the world throws at you, or what it takes from you either. So long as you've got a sunny afternoon, all is right with the universe.

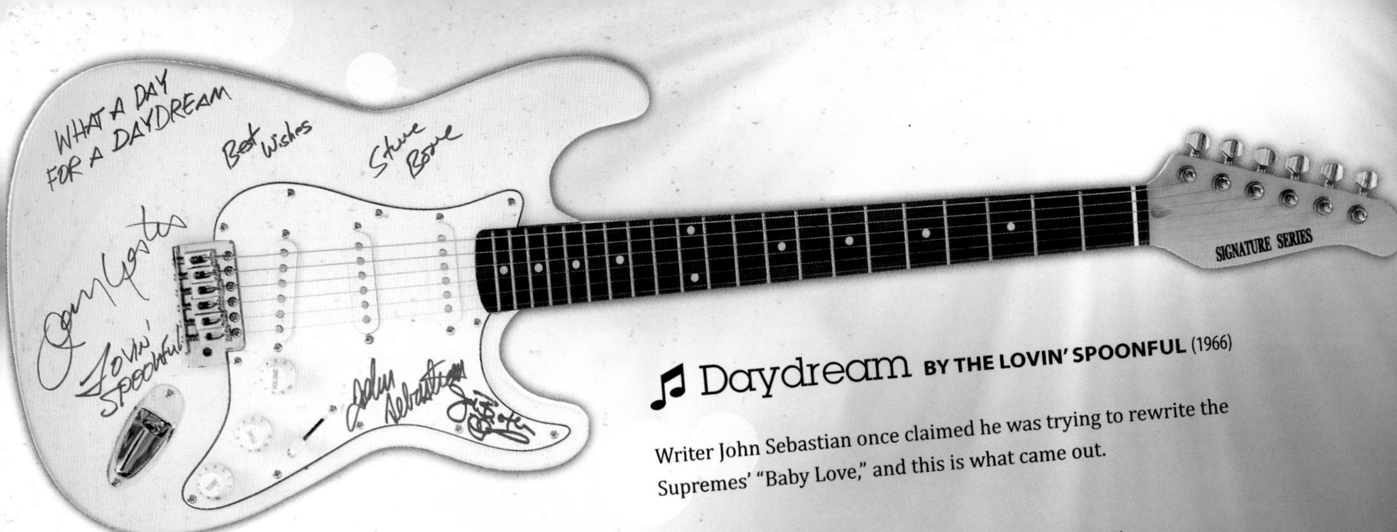

Daydream BY THE LOVIN' SPOONFUL (1966)

Writer John Sebastian once claimed he was trying to rewrite the Supremes' "Baby Love," and this is what came out.

Perfect Day BY LOU REED (1972)

Picnics in the park, a visit to the zoo, all those silly things that add up to one of the best days of your life.

Sunburn BY MUSE (2000)

Written in the studio, "Sunburn" was always a band favorite; it just seemed too weak a song to be used. But, said Matthew Bellamy, "I wanted to make it sound good. So that was when John Leckie, our producer, had this idea to work out the guitar part on the piano. That was the first time I played piano in years it seems, and I had to spend two or three days just practicing 'Sunburn,' which is a pretty simple part."

July Flame BY LAURA VEIRS (2010)

A July Flame, explains Veirs, is a type of peach. "I just saw it at the market and I was like, 'Oh, that's a cool name for a peach, I'll write a song about that.'"

July Morning BY URIAH HEEP (1971)

IN HIS OWN WORDS—KEN HENSLEY (composer): "I wrote July Morning during [Uriah Heep's] U.K. tour with Sha Na Na. We were waiting around on the bus and I just took my acoustic and began scribbling the first verse. It was a July morning but the rest of the song is just imagination. By the time I got it to the rehearsal room, it was basically an acoustic ballad so you can see/hear how great the band´s influence was in those days. It´s one of David [Byron]´s best vocals in my opinion and I still love to play it because it stuck with audiences everywhere and they go crazy at the intro and sing all the words with (or, in some cases, instead of) me! It has also become a kind of a national anthem in Bulgaria where people go to the beach on July 1st and sing it as the sun comes up. I am looking forward to being there for this again this year! Who knew?""

In the Summertime BY MUNGO JERRY (1970)

With that playful jugband punch, one of those songs that makes the sunshine no matter what the weatherman reckons.

IS THERE ANYBODY OUT THERE? IN SPACE, NO-ONE CAN HEAR YOU SOLO

I warned you there were a lot of sci-fi songs, didn't I?

Iron Man BY BLACK SABBATH (1970)

IN HIS OWN WORDS—OZZY OSBOURNE (vocalist): "If I couldn't create a great vocal melody, I would just sing along in unison to the riff, like on 'Iron Man.' It was the easiest solution—I wanted to get the fucking thing done."

Hello Spaceboy BY DAVID BOWIE (1995)

From the 1995 *1: Outside* album, a hard riffing, sharply lyrical slice of space age savagery, transformed into a hit single by a superlative Pet Shop Boys remix.

Starman BY DAVID BOWIE (1972)

"We never thought of 'Starman' as a single," admitted guitarist Mick Ronson. "It just seemed to happen that way. It was never a song which worked well live, and there were far stronger songs on the album. I thought so, anyway." Bowie himself quickly admitted that the song was based in part on "Somewhere Over the Rainbow," from *The Wizard of Oz*, and even delighted in singing a few lines from that song during concert performances of this gentle, acoustic rocker.

Yet it was "Starman" which, in June, 1972, gave Bowie and his Spiders from Mars the British Top Ten hit that six months of delirious media attention insisted they land; and "Starman" that unleashed the future legend of Ziggy. But it wasn't this little song about a spaceman that sparked the Glam Rock revolution that the openly bisexual Bowie was about to launch; it wasn't Bowie's hair, nor bassist Trevor Bolder's spray-painted silver sideburns. It was the moment, on British television's *Top of the Pops*, when Bowie's arm flopped languorously round Ronson's shoulders, and Love and Rockets' Daniel Ash speaks for an entire generation of 40-somethings when he recalls, "I couldn't believe his eyes. I went into town the next day, and I was shaking when I went to buy that record. Because I knew it was going to change my life, and I didn't know if I wanted to have my life changed."

David Bowie

♫ Flash BY QUEEN (1980)

IN HIS OWN WORDS—BRIAN MAY (guitarist): "Really there had never been a rock soundtrack to a movie that wasn't about rock music before; up to that point, it was considered impossible. Even Mr. De Laurentis said it'd never work. It was Mike Hodges, the producer, who brought us in to the project, and I think there was a fundamental gap between his view of the film, and Mr. De Laurentis'; Mike Hodges really made it into a cult film by being very self-consciously kitsch, whereas Dino regarded it as an epic, and not to be messed with. I'll never forget, he came to the studio, sat down and listened to our first demos, and said 'I think it's quite good, but the theme will not work in my movie, it is not right.' And Mike walked over and said "a chat with you, Dino. You don't understand where this film is going to be pitched....' But I had a really nasty moment there, 'oh no, he hates my "Flash"... aaaahh-aaaaaahhh,' and it's going to go on the cutting room floor."

♫ Are Friends Electric BY TUBEWAY ARMY (1979)

The song that launched the synthipop movement of the late 1970s, that in turn fired the New Romantic explosion that ignited MTV, Gary Numan and Tubeway Army crossed earthly alienation with the dreams of Philip K. Dick and created a record that even icicles could fall in love to.

♫ Master of the Universe BY HAWKWIND (1971)

IN HIS OWN WORDS—NIK TURNER (composer): I wrote the lyric as a poem about my crazy mixed up introspective take on enlightenment, influenced by the psychedelic and alternative reality/society/culture of the day. When working in the studio recording the album *In Search of Space*, there was need for a lyric to a riff which I seem to remember both Dave Anderson and Dave Brock claimed to have written. [Dave Anderson said he'd written it when in Amon Duul in Germany].

"It seemed to magically fit, so I naturally sang it, having already become the band's singer by default, as no-one else seemed especially keen on being the front person in the band, and because I seemed to have had a natural aptitude to perform, and to be able to communicate with an audience, without any self-consciousness or stage-fright, from the first gig we had performed, gate-crashing the legendary concert at the Notting Hill All-Saints Hall, as 'Group X.' I think this was due to my theatrical family background, my grandfather made films and ran concert party/theatre groups, involving most of my family.

"The song then seemed to become the band's anthem. I remember being at the Stonehenge festival one year, and everywhere I went, it was being played, I was completely blown away. similarly when we toured U.S.A. it was being given airplay all over. I think it's a timeless song [even though I do say so, and I co-wrote it], and the sentiment and feel are still current. It is still Hawkwind's most popular song, and the one of which there are most recordings by the band."

CRIME AND PUNISHMENT

If you really think about it, there's probably not many topics** less **suitable for song than a riot in a high security prison. The convicts are there for a reason, after all, and the idea of them taking control of the armory, caging a few of their warders, and then making a break for it is** not **the kind of scenario guaranteed to help you sleep at night. In other words—yes, it's precisely the kind of thing that reprobate rockers should be singing about.

♫ Ball and Chain

BY BIG BROTHER AND THE HOLDING COMPANY (1968)

The song—or, rather, the performance—that made a superstar of Janis Joplin, footage of her performing it at the Monterey Pop festival in 1967 remains one of the era's most indelible images.

♫ Jailbreak **BY THIN LIZZY** (1976)

Sirens wail, engines rev and the guitars smash down the prison bars—and the moment when singer Phil Lynott cries "breakout" is one of the most exhilarating moments in all rock'n'roll.

♫ Riot in Cell Block #9 **BY JOHNNY WINTER** (1974)

A Lieber-Stoller classic from 1954, when it became the first single by the Robins (the early Coasters), the riot has since been played out across the rock spectrum. And, every time you hear it, you hope that Scarface Jones will get away.

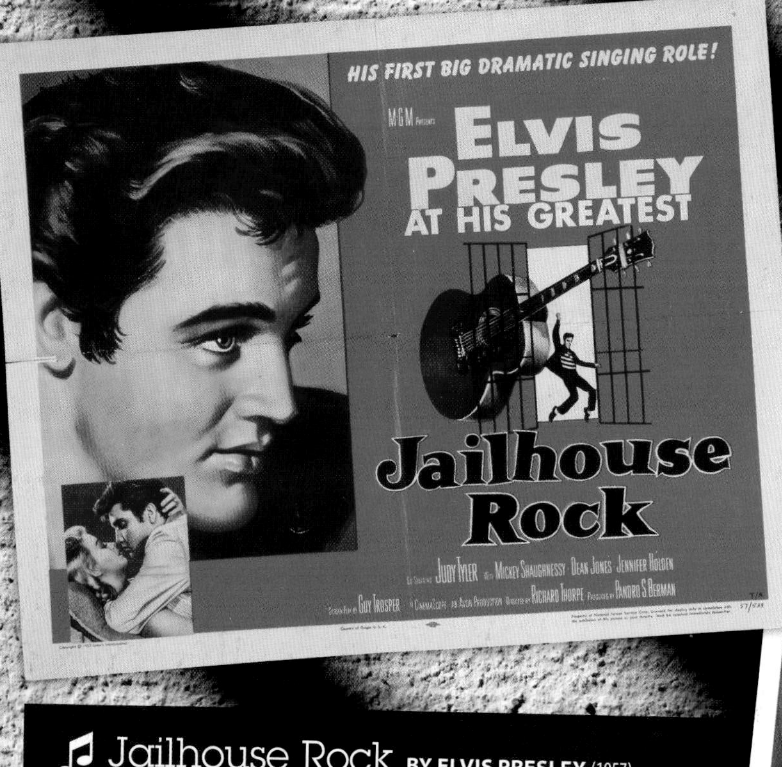

Jailhouse Rock BY ELVIS PRESLEY (1957)

The hot rocking theme to the movie of the same name, cell block number nine throws a party and even the prison governor is invited.

We've Got to Get Out of This Place BY THE ANIMALS (1965)

According to Adrian Cronauer, on whose life the movie *Good Morning Vietnam* was based, this Barry Mann/Cynthia Weill song was Armed Forces radio's single most requested song during his tour of duty. It might also be noted that the U.S. hit version of the song was, in fact, an out-take that the band had discarded, only for their British label to inadvertently ship the wrong tape to America.

Rubber Bullets BY 10CC (1973)

IN HIS OWN WORDS—KEVIN GODLEY (co-writer, drummer): "Apparently a big street anthem in Northern Ireland at the time of the troubles even though the narrative was more akin to a James Cagney prison movie than political rhetoric. Love those speeded up guitars. The only song appropriate to conclude our live shows."

♫ Band on the Run BY PAUL MCCARTNEY AND WINGS (1974)

McCartney combined two different songs to create this masterpiece, building its theme around an offhand remark that George Harrison once made, during a lengthy meeting with the accountants. "If I ever get out of this house…" The band on the run imagery was furthered by the accompanying album's cover photograph, of the band and friends caught up in a police spotlight.

♫ Back on the Chaingang BY THE PRETENDERS (1982)

Despite both titular and lyrical nods towards Sam Cooke's "Chain Gang," "Back on the Chain Gang" was in fact written in tribute to Pretenders guitarist James Honeyman-Scott, following his death in 1982, and bassist Pete Farndon, who passed away ten months later.

♫ Whipping Post BY THE ALLMAN BROTHERS (1969)

An in concert epic (the protracted live version still receives more airplay than the concise studio take ever could), "Whipping Post" equates the appalling behavior of the protagonist's girlfriend to being tied down and beaten. Greg Allman wrote the original lyric on an ironing board cover. "It came so fast. I didn't even have a chance to get the paper out. That's the way the good songs come—they just hit you like a ton of bricks."

LADIES OF THE NIGHT— DOLLARS FOR DAMES IN THE DARKNESS

The House of the Rising Sun

Considering that it's the best known bordello in the world, it seems strange that we don't even know whether the House of the Rising Sun actually existed. There's a few places that have claimed to be the original, but if you actually follow the lyric, we're not even certain what the house was. It might have been a bordello. But it could as easily have been a jailhouse, a hospital, a tavern, a plantation house, or even a slave pen. We just assume, and then we purvey the historical record in search of something to back our assumptions up.

In the early 1820s, a Rising Sun hotel stood on Conti Street, in New Orleans' French Quarter, before burning down in 1822. The site was excavated archaeologically in 2005 and the diggers not only discovered a vast quantity of rouge and cosmetics, there was also an advertisement whose language was a masterpiece of euphemism for anybody seeking a good time girl.

Another Rising Sun grew up on the riverfront in the same city's Carrollton neighborhood towards the end of that same century, a social club that appears to have been above suspicion, but that wasn't saying much in an age where corruption was officialdom's middle name. A third flourished between 1862 and 1874 at 1614 Esplanade Avenue, again in New Orleans, and this one was purportedly titled for the woman who ran it, a Madam Marianne LeSoleil

Levant, whose name itself means "rising sun." A fourth, for which some sources confusingly relate the exact same story, was placed (by the guidebook Offbeat New Orleans) at 826-830 St. Louis St, and again we are reminded that archaeologists did uncover the remains of a brothel on this very site in 2005.

A fifth, a more modern construction that was named for, rather than as, the original establishment can be found at 333 Bourbon Street. There's a House of the Rising Sun B&B in Historic Algiers Point, across the Mississippi River from the French Quarter. And there's probably a whole bunch more. It's a little like traveling up and down the American east coast. Wherever you go, George Washington spent the night there and, if he didn't, then Paul Revere did. One can only imagine what would have happened had they both demanded a bed the same night.

So yes, the House of the Rising Sun could have stood upon almost any of these sites. Or it may not have stood on any of them, and it might not have existed at all.

But it doesn't matter, because it came to life anyway.

The earliest recorded version of the song called "The House of the Rising Sun" was made around 1933 by the one-eyed Appalachian fiddler Clarence "Tom" Ashley and singer Gwen Foster. But when folklorist Alan Lomax commenced his travels around the country later that decade, he discovered versions playing throughout Kentucky. In Pineville in September 1937, Lomax and his wife Elizabeth heard (and recorded) the song being sung by one Tilman Cadle. Later that month in Middlesboro, Kentucky, they taped another performance by sixteen-year-old Georgia Turner, the daughter of a local miner, and were so impressed by her rendering that, four years later, in his songbook Our Singing Country, Lomax credited Turner with having written the lyric in the first place. The fact that she would have been just twelve years old when Ashley first recorded it clearly escaped his notice.

Other versions by fellow eastern Kentuckians Bert Martin and Daw Henson followed, but by that time, the first commercially successful recording had been made by Roy Acuff—who probably learned it from Tom Ashley, with whom he occasionally performed. And now the floodgates of appreciation opened. Woody Guthrie, Josh White, Leadbelly, Pete Seeger and the Weavers, Glenn Yarborough, Frankie Laine, Joan Baez, Miriam Makebe, Dave Van Ronk, Bob Dylan, and finally the Animals… in whose hands it became a classic.

But we still don't know where the house is.

♫ The House of the Rising Sun BY THE ANIMALS (1964)

IN HIS OWN WORDS—MICKIE MOST (producer): "The beauty of that song was that a lot of people already knew it because of the Dylan version, but his version was a drag, it was just him playing his guitar and singing the words. There was no intent or emotion in his voice, he could have been singing his laundry list, which was a problem with a lot of early Dylan, I thought.

Eric [Burdon] put himself into the song, and it didn't matter that nobody outside Newcastle had really heard of him or the Animals at that time. They heard Eric's voice and they knew he wasn't messing them around. His mother *was* a tailor, his father *was* a gambler, and every word he sang was gospel truth autobiography. There wasn't another singer in the world who could have put that much soul into that song, and that's what made the record so great for me. A lot of people talk about Alan [Price]'s organ part, or Hilton's guitar, but they would have been meaningless if Eric hadn't put so much feeling into the lyrics."

♫ Killer Queen BY QUEEN (1974)

"It's about a high class call girl," Freddie Mercury explained. "I'm trying to say that classy people can be whores as well. That's what the song is about, though I'd prefer people to put their interpretation upon it—to read into it what they like."

♫ Plaistow Patricia

BY IAN DURY AND THE BLOCKHEADS (1977)

Preluded by one of the most violent explosions of Anglo-Saxon oathery every unleashed in an innocent piece of vinyl, "Plaistow Patricia" tells the tale of an east London lady of the loosest morality imaginable. Play it when your parents are out.

♫ Roxette

BY DR FEELGOOD (1974)

The titular tart may not have charged money for her services, but her boyfriend, the song's protagonist, doesn't trust her an inch regardless.

♫ When the Sun Goes Down

BY THE ARCTIC MONKEYS (2006)

The Monkeys' second U.K. number-one hit is set in the Neepsend district of their hometown Sheffield—an area renowned for its red light district.

♫ (She Sells) Sanctuary **BY THE CULT** (1985)

Well, that's one word for it!

♫ Angeline **BY FAITHLESS** (1997)

"Out on the tiles, winning the smiles of men of low persuasion." That first line says it all, doesn't it?

♫ Strange Kind of Woman

BY DEEP PURPLE (1971)

"Her name was Nancy, her face was nothing fancy"... but it wasn't her face that the men were paying for.

♫ La Grange

BY ZZ TOP (1973)

ZZ Top intended immortalizing the oldest whorehouse in Texas, "The Chicken Ranch," or Miss Edna's Boarding house in La Grange. Instead, the publicity that surrounded the song apparently got the place closed down!

♫ Lalena **BY DONOVAN** (1969)

"I was fascinated with *The Threepenny Opera* as a socially conscious musical," Donovan explains. "So when I saw the movie version with Lotte Lenya I thought, OK, she's a streetwalker, but in the history of the world, in all nations women have taken on various roles from priestess to whore to mother to maiden to wife. This guise of sexual power is very prominent, and therein I saw the plight of the character: 'That's your lot in life, Lalena/Can't blame ya, Lalena.' Women have roles thrust upon them and make the best they can out of them, so I'm describing the character Lotte Lenya is playing and a few other women I've seen during my life, but it's a composite character of women who are outcasts on the edge of society: Bohemia."

WHAT'S IN A NAME? THE GIRLS

The boys have already had their turn.

♫ Rosalita (Come Out Tonight)

BY BRUCE SPRINGSTEEN (1973)

The Boss comes howling into town, to rescue Rosie from her mom.

♫ Sweet Jane

BY THE VELVET UNDERGROUND (1970)

From an LP that Lou Reed titled *Loaded* because it was "loaded with hits," "Sweet Jane" rides one of the all-time classic rock riffs.

♫ Eloise **BY BARRY RYAN** (1968)

Subsequently covered as far apart as ex-punks the Damned, and ex-Roller Ian Mitchell, passion and a great rhyme too—"Eloise-er! I'd love to please her!"

♫ Sara **BY FLEETWOOD MAC** (1979)

Stevie Nicks in excelsis. Incredibly, the first CD release of the *Tusk* album featured an edited version of the song, in order to fit all the music onto one disc. The fans were not impressed.

♫ Maybelline **BY CHUCK BERRY** (1955)

From that moment when everything Chuck touched turned to gold.

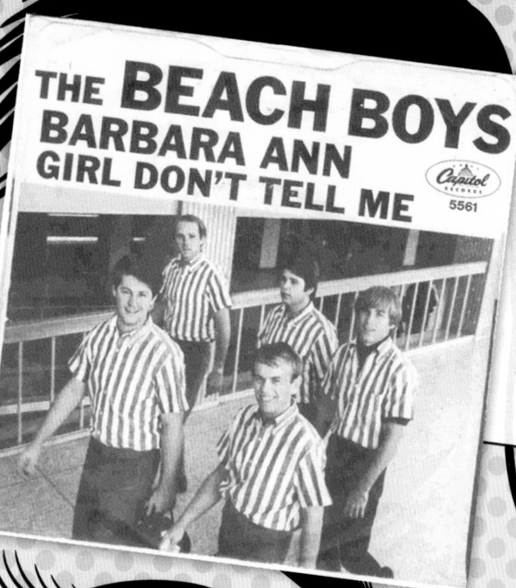

THE BEACH BOYS
BARBARA ANN
GIRL DON'T TELL ME
Capitol
5561

♫ Marie and Joe BY THE DOCTORS OF MADNESS (1976)

Vocalist Richard Strange once compared himself to Dylan and Lennon and, on this evidence, he wasn't far wrong.

♫ Barbara Ann BY THE BEACH BOYS (1966)

A knockabout melody that can't be whipped.

♫ Lady Eleanor BY LINDISFARNE (1971)

Remembering songwriter Alan Hull's time working as an orderly at a mental hospital.

♫ Madame George BY VAN MORRISON (1974)

Van Morrison has denied it, but a lot of people still like journalist Lester Bangs' insistence that "Madame George" was written about a Belfast transvestite. Well, it worked for the Kinks!

♫ Angie
BY THE ROLLING STONES (1973)

May or may not have been about David Bowie's wife, but the gossip clung beautifully to this classic Stones ballad.

♫ Ruby **BY THE KAISER CHIEFS** (2007)

Proof that great rock'n'roll didn't die sometime around your twenty-second birthday.

♫ Carol **BY CHUCK BERRY** (1958)

See "Maybelline" (145)!!!

♫ Mona **BY THE QUICKSILVER MESSENGER SERVICE** (1969)

A riff, a rhythm, and a heartfelt chant. Classic Bo Diddley, blasted by the best.

♫ Sara Smile BY HALL & OATES (1975)

All the nice boys love an air stewardess. From the days when that was what they were called.

♫ Suzanne BY LEONARD COHEN (1968)

So many covers, so many interpretations, but laughing boy's remains the definitive version.

♫ Rita Mae BY BOB DYLAN (1975)

Incredibly, Dylan kept this song back for a B-side, but play it within his *Desire* song cycle and its magnificence cannot be denied.

♫ Elenore BY THE TURTLES (1968)

For rhyming "think you're groovy" with "let's go to the movies," the Turtles can do no wrong.

♫ Veronika BY TRICKY (2008)

Duet for voice and percussion, and one of the most dislocating love songs you never wanted directed your way.

Hall & Oates

♫ Melissa **BY THE ALLMAN BROTHERS** (1972)

Gregg Allman wrote "Melissa" in 1967, "in a place called the Evergreen Hotel in Pensacola, Florida. By that time I got so sick of playing other people's material that I just sat down and said, 'OK, here we go. One, two, three—we're going to try to write songs.' And about 200 songs later—much garbage to take out—I wrote this song called 'Melissa.' And I had everything but the title. I thought (referring to lyrics): 'But back home, we always run... to sweet Barbara'—no. Diane...? We always run... to sweet Bertha.' No, so I just kind of put it away for a while. So one night I was in the grocery store—it was my turn to go get the tea, the coffee, the sugar and all that other s--t... and there was this Spanish lady there and she had this little toddler with her—this little girl. And I'm sitting there, getting a few things and what have you. And this little girl takes off, running down the aisle. And the lady yells, Oh, Melissa! Melissa, come back, Melissa!' And I went, 'Oh—that's it.' I forgot about half the stuff I went for, I went back home and, man, it was finished."

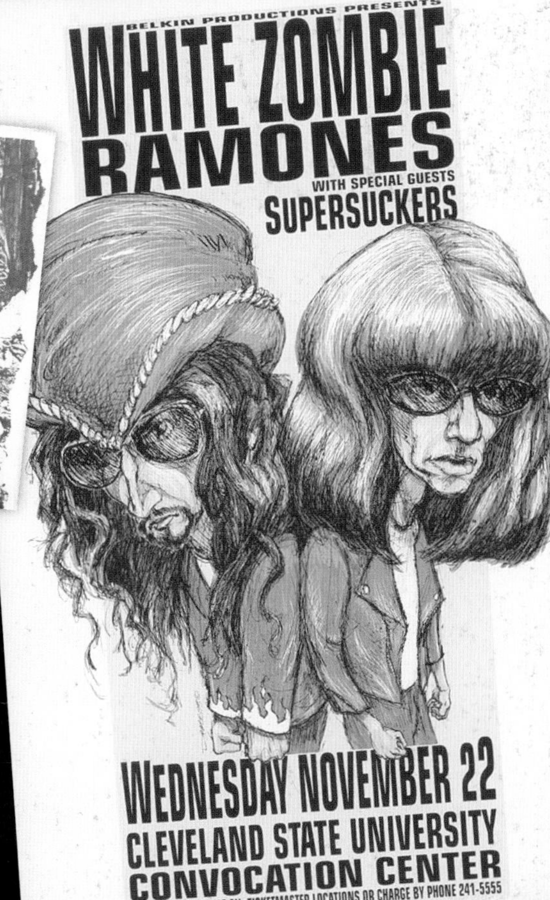

BELKIN PRODUCTIONS PRESENTS
WHITE ZOMBIE
RAMONES
WITH SPECIAL GUESTS
SUPERSUCKERS
WEDNESDAY NOVEMBER 22
CLEVELAND STATE UNIVERSITY
CONVOCATION CENTER
TICKETS AVAILABLE AT ALL TICKETMASTER LOCATIONS OR CHARGE BY PHONE 241-5555

♫ Sheena Is a Punk Rocker

BY THE RAMONES (1977)

Like the Beach Boys armed with chainsaws, the Ramones carved through the summer of Punk with simplicity, melody, and balls.

♫ Jane Says

BY JANE'S ADDICTION (1988)

"Around 1984," says Jane's frontman Perry Farrell, "I rented a big house on Wilton, near Hancock Park, right in the heart of everything good in Hollywood, but the whole neighborhood seemed deteriorated. I deceived the landlord into thinking I was a gay interior decorator rather than a Punk rocker, and one of my housemates was Jane, this strangely beautiful, well-to-do girl who got caught up in the drug scene and fell in love with a dealer named Sergio. Jane was an intellectual and knew how to act aristocratic, even with a needle and a spoon on the table."

♫ Carrie **BY CLIFF RICHARD** (1980)

Looking for a lost love, but she left no forwarding address.

NO MATTER WHO YOU VOTE FOR, THE GOVERNMENT ALWAYS GETS IN

With the possible exception of sport, politics is the most divisive topic we have to talk about. Even the title of this section will probably set somebody steaming (so don't blame me—I borrowed it from an old Bonzo Dog Band 45). But before you get too hot beneath the collar, load this selection onto your iPod, and see how you feel about things after that. The garden might not seem too rosy after all.

♫ Desolation Row BY BOB DYLAN (1965)

A succession of increasingly apocalyptic images builds up to create what was, at the time, Dylan's longest and most visual composition yet.

♫ London Calling BY THE CLASH (1979)

The end of the world in a dozen easy scenarios.

♫ Gimme Some Truth BY JOHN LENNON (1971)

The Beatle's most overtly political song yet, railing at the hypocrisy, bullshit, and downright dishonesty that now comprised mainstream western government. The Tricky Dicky in the opening line is the later-impeached President Richard Nixon.

♫ Rocking in the Free World BY NEIL YOUNG (1989)

Quickly adopted as an anthem as Eastern Europe stepped away from Communism, "Rocking in the Free World" was inspired by, and reflected, the political changes being introduced by the recently elected President George Bush (father, not son... he would receive his own damning diatribes).

♫ Out Demons Out BY THE EDGAR BROUGHTON BAND (1970)

In 1967, at the height of the Vietnam War protests in the United States, a march through Washington, D.C., paused outside the Pentagon, the heart of the nation's military complex. Up to 150,000 people, representing the combined might of some 150 different protest groups, then joined hands and encircled the building to stage an exorcism, while the cops and the National Guard looked on in bewilderment.

What happened? According to the official reports, nothing. Led by Ed Sanders, the lead singer of the Fugs, the crowd chanted "Out, demons out" until it grew bored, and then the march continued. According to the organizers, however, the Pentagon rose thirty feet into the air, turned orange, and vibrated. "Out Demons Out" is *that* kind of song.

♫ Ghost Town BY THE SPECIALS (1981)

A nightmare vision of a broken society, drawn from the headlines of early 1980s Britain.

♫ Oliver's Army BY ELVIS COSTELLO AND THE ATTRACTIONS (1978)

Written following Costello's first visit to Northern Ireland, at the height of the so-called Irish Troubles. The image of British soldiers on the streets contrasted sharply with the military's then apparently carefree recruitment advertisements.

♫ The Only Living Boy in New Cross

BY CARTER THE UNSTOPPABLE SEX MACHINE (1992)

A sobering examination of the legislation being thrown into the U.K. arena in the late 1980s, all of which seemed to be aimed at further treading down the already disenfranchised.

♫ Metal Postcard

BY SIOUXSIE AND THE BANSHEES (1978)

A dramatic piece of boiling percussion and stentorian vocal, inspired by the work of the Nazi-era German anti-fascist artist John Heartfield.

♫ Political World

BY BOB DYLAN (1989)

Maybe not his most powerful lyric, but like Neil Young's "Rocking in the Free World" (260), a sobering look at the creeping malaise of late Eighties America.

♫ Shipbuilding

BY ROBERT WYATT (1982)

An Elvis Costello composition, damning the incumbent British government's systematic destruction of the country's industrial and manufacturing infrastructure.

I HATE MYSELF AND I WANT TO DIE

Beck

♫ Loser BY BECK (1994)

The song that introduced the singularly named Beck to the world, "Loser" was inspired by a friend's nickname for Beck himself. Other friends, however, were more encouraging, including one who introduced the would-be performer to "this guy who does hip-hop beats and stuff. I said, 'Oh yeah, well sometimes I rap between songs and get people from the audience to do the beat-box thing into the mike.' So we went to this guy's house and I played him a few of my folk songs. He seemed pretty all-around unimpressed. Then I started playing this slide guitar part and he started taping it. He put a drum track to it and it was, you know, the 'Loser' riff. I started writing these lyrics to the verse part. When he played it back, I thought, 'Man, I'm the worst rapper in the world—I'm just a loser.' So I started singing, 'I'm a loser baby, so why don't you kill me.' I'm always kinda putting myself down like that."

♫ Someone Saved My Life Tonight BY ELTON JOHN (1975)

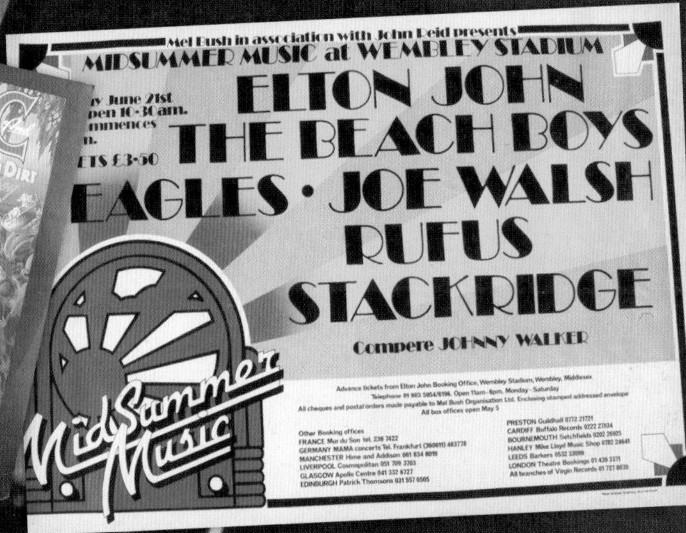

Faced with the prospect of marrying a woman he didn't love, but not wanting to end the relationship, the then-unknown Elton John decided to end his life instead. His long-time lyricist Bernie Taupin returned to their shared apartment to find Elton lying on the floor by the open, hissing gas oven—and the windows wide open.

Help! BY THE BEATLES (1965)

According to those who read meaning into everything, the first John Lennon song to truly comment upon his state of mind at the height of Beatlemania.

Longview BY GREEN DAY (1994)

"I was just in a creative rut," Billie Joe Armstrong said about writing this song. "I was in-between houses sleeping on people's couches. It's a song about trying not to feel pathetic and lonely. I was coming from a lonely guy's perspective: No girlfriend, no life, complete loser."

Everybody Hurts BY REM (1993)

Yes, they probably do. Winner of this book's Most Over-Played, Over-Analyzed and Downright Annoying Video award, by the way.

Paranoid BY BLACK SABBATH (1970)

"We'd finished recording [our second album, *Paranoid*] already when we wrote 'Paranoid'," recalled Ozzy Osbourne. "That song came about when our producer told us to jam for four minutes. I came up with the vocal line, Tony came up with the riff, and Geezer came up with the lyric. It was done within an hour."

The State That I Am In BY BELLE AND SEBASTIAN (1996)

If any single song can be considered the Scottish combo's mission statement, this litany of personal hang-ups, horrors, and embarrassments is it.

Boys and Girls BY BRYAN FERRY (1985)

The title track from Ferry's mid-1980s peak, and a highlight of his Live Aid performance, too. Death, sings Bryan, is the friend I've yet to meet. Cheery chap, isn't he?

Crystallized BY XX (2009)

The debut single by one of the hottest bands of the late 2000s, a chillingly spectral ballad poising love on the edge of a precipice.

TEENAGE WASTELAND

It's a natural part of growing up. Fight your parents, fight the system, overthrow capitalism, and home in time to go to the movies with your friends. Ah, good times....

I'm Eighteen BY ALICE COOPER (1971)

IN HIS OWN WORDS—NEAL SMITH (cowriter, drummer): "After our first two albums on Frank Zappa's Straight Record label failed to launch us into Rock Stardom, we desperately needed a hit single. The summer of 1970 all five members of Alice Cooper were writing brand new songs in a much more commercial vein. Michael Bruce came up with the original idea for a new song called 'I'm Eighteen.' A song celebrating the awkward teenage transformation from adolescence to adulthood. Over the summer into the fall, we all worked and reworked an eight minute arrangement of this song for stage. In late 1970 we recorded 'I'm Eighteen' at RCA Studios in Chicago. That shorter single version off of our *Love It to Death* album, was arranged and produced by Canadian Studio Masters & Hit Makers Jack Richardson and Bob Ezrin. Finally after three record albums we got our first Alice Cooper hit single blistering the top 40 radio airwaves."

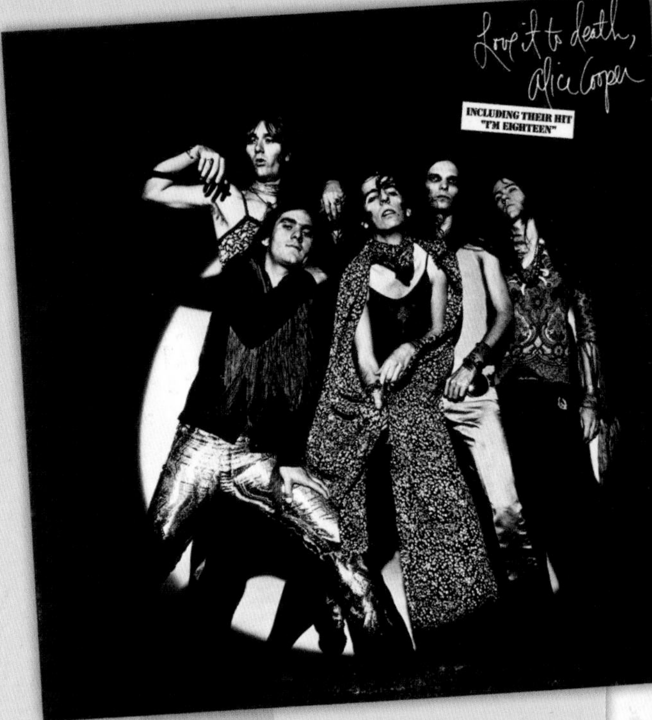

Bored Teenagers BY THE ADVERTS (1977)

Both the National and the Notional Anthem of U.K. Punk, 1977.

All the Young Dudes BY MOTT THE HOOPLE (1972)

Mott were on the brink of splitting up when David Bowie handed them the ultimate Glam Rock rallying cry. They did such a good job of it that it would be twenty-plus years before his own version was finally released.

Baba O'Riley BY THE WHO (1971)

Partly named for a guru who had taken a vow of silence, "Baba O'Riley" is a bitter remonstration towards a society that seemed hell-bent on hanging an entire generation of kids out to rot. The fevered whiplash of synth and guitar also ushered in one of Pete Townshend's most potent slogans. "It's Only Teenaged Wasteland."

My Generation BY THE WHO (1965)

Unrestrained violence, an unrepentant stutter… "My Generation" was the ultimate teen anthem in 1965, and it still holds that spot today.

Come Out and Play BY THE OFFSPRING (1994)

Gang warfare, mid-1990s LA style.

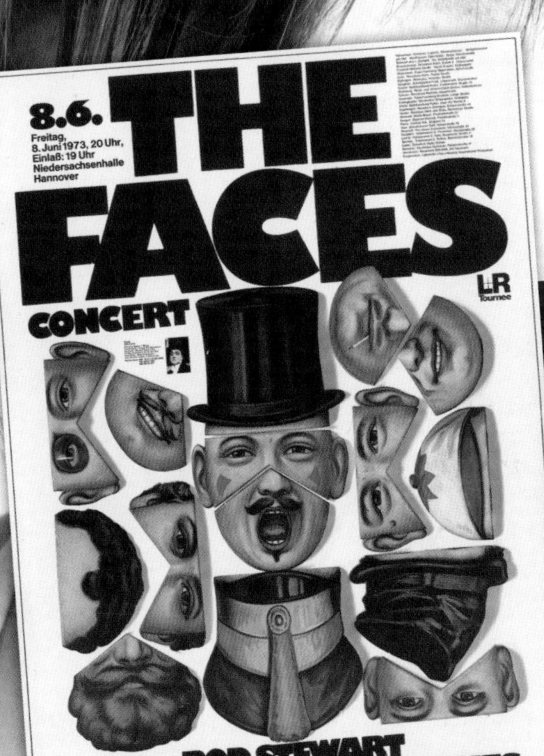

White Punks on Dope BY THE TUBES (1975)

Young, rich, and bored out of your brains? There is a remedy.

Young Turks BY ROD STEWART (1981)

Teenaged runaways updating any number of old Shangri-Las songs—only with a happy ending.

Search and Destroy BY THE STOOGES (1973)

The song that both christened and confirmed Iggy Pop as "the world's forgotten boy."

♫ Sonic Reducer BY THE DEAD BOYS (1977)

Nihilism is the new self-sufficiency!

♫ No Fun BY THE STOOGES (1969)

Chilling ennui set to one of the most compulsively hamfisted riffs in history.

♫ Cherry Bomb BY THE RUNAWAYS (1976)

The all-teenaged girl rock band's debut single was written at vocalist Cherie Currie's audition, to give her something to try out with. Guitarist Joan Jett and manager Kim Fowley "wrote 'Cherry Bomb' in 20 minutes," an astonished Currie reported. "Done. Joan sings it to me while Kim shows [the others] the song. We did the song and then they all walked out of the room. They were gone for like fifteen minutes. I was sweating bullets, thinking there was no way I would get into this band. When they walked back in, Joan walks up to me and says, 'Welcome to the Runaways!' It was the happiest day of my childhood."

♫ Carry On Wayward Son BY KANSAS (1976)

Any number of interpretations have been piled upon this prog rock classic, but composer Kerry Livgren recommends that you take the words at face value.

Kansas

♫ Kick Out the Jams BY THE MC5 (1969)

Late Sixties Detroit blazes with righteous rage.

♫ Blank Generation BY RICHARD HELL (1976)

And a decade later, New York catches the same bitter chill.

PRODUCED (AND OTHER THINGS) BY ANDREW LOOG OLDHAM

Bittersweet Symphony **BY THE VERVE** (1997)

"You're a slave to money, then you die." A scathing look at modern life, seen through a genuinely captivating sample, lifted from the Andrew Loog Oldham Orchestra's version of the Rolling Stones' "The Last Time."

Down in the Boondocks **BY GREGORY PHILIPS** (1965)

Originally cut by Billy Joe Royal, but revisited by Oldham for an Immediate label single, a young man laments his love for his boss' daughter.

Play with Fire **BY THE ROLLING STONES** (1965)

"Your mother," sneers Jagger, is "an heiress." But it won't do you any good.

Back Street Girl **BY THE ROLLING STONES** (1966)

Class consciousness was a constant theme in Mick Jagger and Keith Richard's early songwriting, but usually (332, 714) it was the woman who was raised up the social scale. Not this time.

As Tears Go By **BY MARIANNE FAITHFULL** (1964)

In 1964, the Rolling Stones were still little more than a covers act, with a nice line in blues riffs… much like every other band on the block. So one day, manager Andrew Loog Oldham locked two of them, singer Mick Jagger and guitarist Keith Richards, in the kitchen and told them they couldn't come out until they'd written a song. This, the lament of an older woman reflecting on the passing of time, was *not* the first thing they came up with. But it was certainly the best of their earliest attempts, and Oldham never needed to hide the kitchen key again.

GHOSTIES AND GHOULIES AND LONG LEGGED BEASTIES (AND THINGS THAT ROCK OUT IN THE NIGHT)

John Cale once declared that fear is a man's best friend, and to judge by the success of so many horror books and movies, he's right. Screaming Jay Hawkins was the first rock'n'roller to set out to terrify his audience; Black Sabbath and Alice Cooper refined it into an art form; and Heavy Metal, in particular, has been banging on about demons and wizards, dismemberment and monsters, ever since. And you have to admit, it's a lot of fun.

♫ I Walk on Gilded Splinters BY DR. JOHN (1968)

The backing vocals are Creole curses, the lyrics themselves a brutal invocation, and the music is as intense as it is hypnotic. Other artists had touched upon the bayou's sinister underside in the past—Beausoleil's "Zydeco Gris-Gris," for example. But "Walk on Gilded Splinters" felt like the real thing because, in a lot of ways, it was the real thing. Maybe, if you're really serious about your folklore and religion, it was little more than a B-Movie, grabbing mass-market superstitions by the scruff of the neck, and sending reality scuttling even further from view. But there's your reality, there's my reality and there's reality itself, and "I Walk on Gilded Splinters," all jerking ropes and clouds of smoke, charnal chants and crazy-eye staring, takes a little piece of all three, to create a fourth of its own.

♫ Black Sabbath BY BLACK SABBATH (1970)

IN HIS OWN WORDS—OZZY OSBOURNE (vocalist): "I remember when the first Black Sabbath album came out I thought, "Great, I can show my dad." We put it on the old radiogram and I remember him looking at mum with this really confused look on his face and turning to me and saying, 'Son, are you sure you're just drinking the occasional beer?'"

♫ Big Bad Moon BY JOE SATRIANI (1989)

The God of American guitar virtuosity gets down and dirty with a blues that could have stepped (or swept!) out of the Bo Diddley catalog.

♫ Lullaby BY THE CURE (1989)

Drawn from 1989's landmark *Disintegration* album, and accompanied by one of the creepiest videos of the age, the Cure look back on their early reputation as a Gothic band and rewrite it as a horror movie. Arachnophobia comes round for a sleep over.

Faith Healer BY THE SENSATIONAL ALEX HARVEY BAND (1972)

SAHB's traditional set opener, oozing shamanic medicine and a wicked riff.

One of These Nights

BY THE EAGLES (1975)

That burbling bass into is so laid back that it could be horizontal. But Don Felder's multi-tracked guitar won't let it relax and, though you suspect the rock is too soft, there's just enough of a frantic edge to keep things moving.

I Walked with a Zombie

BY ROKY ERICKSON (1981)

Titled for Jacques Tourneur's 1943 horror film of the same name, and subsequently covered by R.E.M.

Green Manalishi BY FLEETWOOD MAC (1970)

The manalishi, Green explained, was money, but the song was inspired by a nightmare he had, about a mysterious dog. "It scared me because I knew the dog had been dead a long time. It was a stray and I was looking after it. But I was dead and had to fight to get back into my body, which I eventually did. When I woke up, the room was really black and I found myself writing the song."

Roland the Headless Thompson Gunner BY WARREN ZEVON (1978)

The revenge of a murdered mercenary.

Magic Man BY HEART (1976)

The Zeppelin comparisons ran like rain when Heart first emerged, but they meant absolutely nothing when confronted with this, lascivious, slippery, and sultry as hell, and all underpinned by that impossibly fluid guitar.

Race with the Devil BY GENE VINCENT (1956)

It was a race that Gene would ultimately lose.

I GOT DEM OL' "SONG ABOUT THE BLUES" BLUES AGAIN MOMMA

To tell the story of the blues would take a lifetime. To live it would take even longer.

♫ Subterranean Homesick Blues

BY BOB DYLAN (1965)

The importance of thinking for yourself, laid out in the clearest possible tones.

♫ Blind Willie McTell **BY BOB DYLAN** (1983)

Originally recorded in 1983, but left unreleased until1991,"Blind Willie McTell" takes its melody from "St James Infirmary" and its title from the legendary bluesman. Nobody sang the blues like him! "I started playing it live because I heard the Band doing it," Dylan said of the original version. "Most likely it was a demo, probably showing the musicians how it should go. It was never developed fully, I never got around to completing it. There wouldn't have been any other reason for leaving it off the record."

♫ It Don't Come Easy

BY RINGO STARR (1971)

With the Beatles having crumbled and the future an unknown palette, Ringo turned in one of the best solo Fab 45s ever.

♫ Story of the Blues (Parts One and Two) **BY WAH!** (1982)

Dramatic, uplifting, and magnificently inspiring, Pete Wylie grasps the defiance of the original music, and translates it into the landscape of the early 1980s post-punk potpourri.

♫ I Guess That's Why They Call It the Blues

BY ELTON JOHN (1983)

From 1983's *Too Low For Zero* album, his best new LP in years, Elton describes the blues as a state of mind.

I'M GETTING MARRIED IN THE MORNING

One in the eye for those critics (and there were many) who claimed that pop songs were all about immorality, free love, and promiscuous living.

Wedding Bell Blues **BY LAURA NYRO** (1966)

Nyro's cousin, songwriter Alan Merrill, recalls, "I watched Laura write her first songs, and was in the room as a sounding board more or less. Every day after school I'd go around, have a tuna sandwich and listen to Laura's new tunes and make a commentary." A number one for Fifth Dimension, "Wedding Bell Blues" was "written about my mum [Nyro's aunt]'s relationship with b-film actor Bill Carter. Laura was capturing a real situation. Bill was married. It was an affair going nowhere."

Chapel of Love **BY THE DIXIE CUPS** (1964)

The simplest love song of them all—we're going to the chapel and we're going to get married. What else is there to say?

Bachelor Boy **BY CLIFF RICHARD** (1962)

Has there been a more self-fulfilling prophecy than this? Single in 1963, when he recorded it for the *Summer Holiday* movie soundtrack, Richard remains stubbornly unmarried almost half a century later.

Happy Together **BY THE TURTLES** (1967)

The future Flo and Eddie chime the ultimate romance.

The Ballad of John And Yoko

BY THE BEATLES (1969)

Banned in Australia, where the use of the word "Christ" apparently upset delicate sensitivities, John and Paul alone chart the rocky path of the Lennons' love.

STEREO

the DIXIE CUPS riding high

...last BLUSH (in GREECE)

AMERICAN INTERNATIONAL presents

"SUMMER HOLIDAY"

...and the fabulous summer affair! in TECHNICOLOR and CINEMASCOPE

starring the nation's hottest new swinger... singing "Les Girls"... "Summer Affair"... "Bachelor Boy"... and many more...

CLIFF RICHARD

That Hobbs girl is on the loose again...

LAURIE PETERS

DAVID KOSSOFF · RON MOODY · THE SHADOWS · PETER MYERS and RONALD CASS

KENNETH HARPER · PETER YATES · HERBERT ROSS

MADNESS

AND OTHER PASSING FANCIES

It is said that a true madman doesn't actually realize that he (or she) is mad.

Psychotic Reaction BY THE COUNT FIVE (1966)

A bristling saber toothed tiger of a single," Psychotic Reaction" is one of the songs people are talking about when they start going on about Garage Rock. And it's true – it does fit all the criteria; the sound of a mid-sixties teenaged rock band, punking it up in the car port. But it also transcends almost all that it *ought* to be, to emerge a song so brutal that one can only imagine... if the Count Five had been as big as the Beatles, would the sixties have stayed peace and love?

Come Together BY THE BEATLES (1969)

Forget the lift from "You Can't Catch Me" that set Chuck Berry's music publisher salivating, Lennon looks at life outside the goldfish bowl, knowing he will never be able to live there.

Basket Case BY GREEN DAY (1994)

"Doctor, doctor, I think I'm falling to pieces."

"Just pull yourself together, man."

Crazy On You BY HEART (1976)

Hmm, well, there's crazy and there's *crazy*...

Nineteenth Nervous Breakdown BY THE ROLLING STONES (1966)

After that many, who's still counting?

I Wanna Be Sedated BY THE RAMONES (1978)

The sheer craziness of life on the road, and one way of getting away from it.

♫ The Killing Moon **BY ECHO AND THE BUNNYMEN** (1984)

Liverpool, England, was responsible for a lot of great band in the early 1980s,and the intriguingly named Bunnymen were one of the best. Fronted by the loquaciously quote-able Ian McCulloch, the band released three stellar albums before going off the boil, and a string of stellar singles, too. But this one chilled as it charmed and the beautiful emptiness that played out in its wake simply reflected the theme of the lyric. Quite simply, it's a song about death.

♫ Madman Across the Water **BY ELTON JOHN** (1971)

Forget the LP of the same name, what you really need to hear is the alternate version cut a short while before, with guitarists Mick Ronson and Michael Chapman helping Elton out.

♫ The Girl Can't Help It **BY LITTLE RICHARD** (1957)

Lionizing the kind of beauty that could drive you insane.
"When she winks an eye, bread turns to toast."

♫ Walking On Thin Ice **BY YOKO ONO** (1981)

The last song John Lennon recorded before his murder was, he can be heard saying at the start of the session, Yoko's "first number one." He died still holding the final mix in one hand. Listening to the song after it was released as a single, with all the hindsight that the tragedy layered onto it, well that *could* drive you crazy.

♫ Crazy **BY GNARLS BARKLEY** (2008)

The first record ever to top the U.K. chart on the strength of downloads only was, perhaps ironically, a rumination on the fact that ... unlike a file of mp3s... life cannot be kept in a succession of orderly boxes. And, if you try too hard to keep it that way, you'll go crazy.

♫ Megalomania **BY BLACK SABBATH** (1975)

A schizophrenic at war with himself.

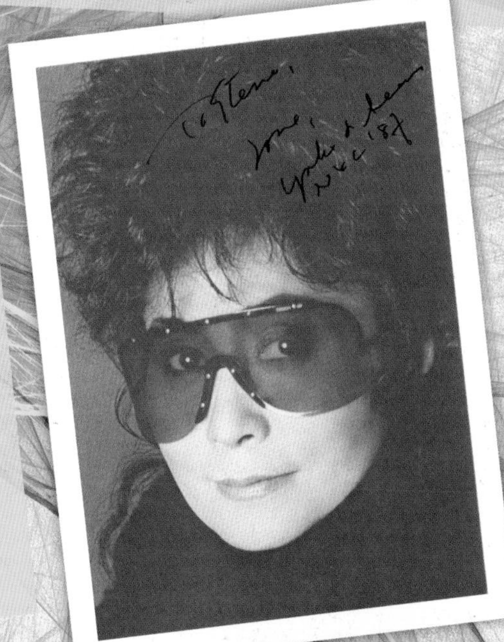

TROUBLE ON THE DANCEFLOOR

Sweet Gene Vincent

"Blue jean baby..."

It was Ian Dury, himself the creator of some of the greatest records of his era, who hit the nail on the head, in one of the greatest tribute records of all time: "Sweet Gene Vincent," from his New Boots and Panties album, in 1977.

"White face, black shirt, white socks, black shoes, black hair, white Strat, bled white, dyed black...."

"It took about six weeks to write it," Dury said at the time. "I wanted to make every phrase into something that reflected... sort of poetry, but you can't write poetry if you're a rock'n'roller because you've got to fit it into a format. But there had to be a bit of poetry, so there's a pretty bit at the beginning, which is really over the top. I knew when I'd done it [that] it was a tribute, but it was a very sad story because the geezer's golden era was about 18 months long, and then he was down the tubes."

And successive generations have been wrestling with his specter ever since. In June, 1998, just six months after Vincent was inducted into the Rock and Roll Hall of Fame, a Q magazine reader wrote in asking whether there were any decent Vincent compilations around, because "...his albums [are] dreadful, and nothing like I'd imagined."

The magazine's response was not encouraging. "It's almost impossible to recommend specific albums.... He was never very good at picking his material, and was recording in the early days of rock'n'roll when a version of, say, 'Over the Rainbow' was considerably perfectly suitable."

But still Vincent's reputation lives on. Ian Dury, after all, was not his only vocal admirer: Jim Morrison, John Lennon, and Mick Farren all adored him, and there's a tantalizing rumor that David Bowie was so blown away when he met Vincent in L.A. in February 1971, that he dragged him into the studio on the spot, to record a version of "Hang Onto Yourself." And maybe that, should it ever see the light of day, is the performance which 40 years of posthumous devotion has been waiting for, the high octane cross between the MC5 and Mott the Hoople (with a touch of Motorhead thrown in for luck) which Vincent's style and story demanded.

Or maybe that's what he was all along, and it's modern tastes that have gone astray, while Vincent's music remains the same as it ever was, a snarling, spitting ball of defiance that wrapped itself around the musical manners of the time... and tore them to bloody shreds. For at his peak, and for another decade thereafter, Gene Vincent was rebellion personified. And rebellion, of course, is what great rock'n'roll is all about.

At the Hop BY DANNY AND THE JUNIORS (1958)

One of the all time great slabs of rock'n'rolling exuberance, a reminder that you can almost anything at the hop…

I Bet You Look Good on the Dancefloor BY THE ARCTIC MONKEYS (2005)

"Dancing to electro-pop like a robot from 1984"! How time flies…

Blitzkrieg Bop BY THE RAMONES (1976)

Hey ho, let's go. The chant that launched a million soundalikes.

Zoom Club BY BUDGIE (1974)

The Welsh Metal wizards celebrate the live concert circuit.

John, I'm Only Dancing BY DAVID BOWIE (1972)

The follow-up to the 1972 breakthrough hit "Starman," "John I'm Only Dancing," said Bowie, was written for a boyfriend who got upset when he saw him dancing with a girl. In other words, relax and stop getting so jealous.

Death Disco BY PUBLIC IMAGE LTD (1979)

Built around a recurring motif from Swan Lake, inspired by the death of frontman John Lydon's mother, and powered by the heaviest bass riff *ever*, PiL pushed the concept of rock music to its limit here, and still scored a hit single.

The Ramones

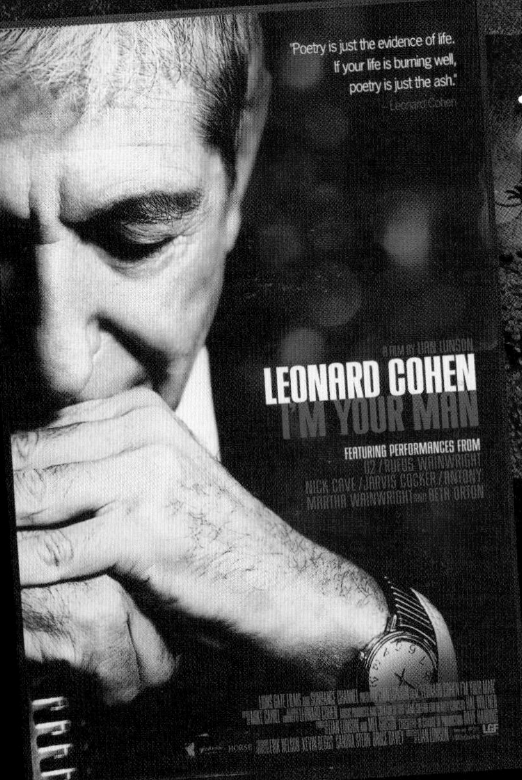

"Poetry is just the evidence of life.
If your life is burning well,
poetry is just the ash."
—Leonard Cohen
A FILM BY LIAN LUNSON
LEONARD COHEN
I'M YOUR MAN
FEATURING PERFORMANCES FROM
U2 / RUFUS WAINWRIGHT
NICK CAVE / JARVIS COCKER / ANTONY
MARTHA WAINWRIGHT AND BETH ORTON

♫ Dance Me to the End of Love

BY LEONARD COHEN (1985)

"It's curious how songs begin," Cohen explained. "Because the origin of the song, every song, has a kind of grain or seed that somebody hands you or the world hands you and that's why the process is so mysterious about writing a song. But that came from just hearing or reading or knowing that in the death camps beside the crematoria, in certain of the death camps, a string quartet was pressed into performance while this horror was going on, those were the people whose fate was this horror also. And they would be playing classical music while their fellow prisoners were being killed and burnt. So, that music, "Dance me to your beauty with a burning violin," meaning the beauty there of being the consummation of life, the end of this existence and of the passionate element in that consummation. But, it is the same language that we use for surrender to the beloved, so that the song—it's not important that anybody knows the genesis of it, because if the language comes from that passionate resource, it will be able to embrace all passionate activity."

♫ Blue Jean Bop **BY GENE VINCENT** (1956)

Vincent's third single is a masterstroke of innuendo.

♫ Dancing Barefoot **BY THE PATTI SMITH GROUP** (1979)

The highlight of the Smith group's fourth and final album, "Dancing Barefoot," didn't even exist until the recording was almost over, and producer Todd Rundgren demanded more songs. Guitarist Ivan Kral produced a cassette tape of song ideas that he carried round with them; Rundgren listened, then came back to say which one he wanted them to work up. And so it was that the last song Kral wrote for the Patti Smith Group was one of the first he had ever written—the riff for "Dancing Barefoot" was first written when he was thirteen or fourteen years old.

♫ The Ballroom Blitz **BY THE SWEET** (1973)

IN THEIR OWN WORDS—ANDY SCOTT (guitarist) "We thought 'Ballroom Blitz' was going to take the place apart. But, by the time we came to release it [in America], the copy of 'Ballroom Blitz' that was a big hit in Europe, 'Radar Love' (881), was number one in America and everybody thought we were imitating Golden Earring. Great record, 'Radar Love,' but people were saying 'Sweet are doing a Golden Earring here' and we were galled because we thought that could have been our best shot in America."

Alone Again Or BY LOVE (1968)

Love guitarist Bryan MacLean wrote this as a tribute to his mother, who was a Flamenco dancer.

Do the Strand BY ROXY MUSIC (1973)

A fictional dance, and a who's who of the real-life people who, apparently, did it.

Willie and the Hand Jive BY ERIC CLAPTON (1974)

Johnny Otis cut the song while the dance itself was still hot (1958), but Slowhand brought it back from *461 Ocean Boulevard*, and period live versions almost get you learning the movements all over again.

Wrecking Ball BY EMMYLOU HARRIS (1995)

A Neil Young number, brought added weary resonance by Emmylou's darkest vocal.

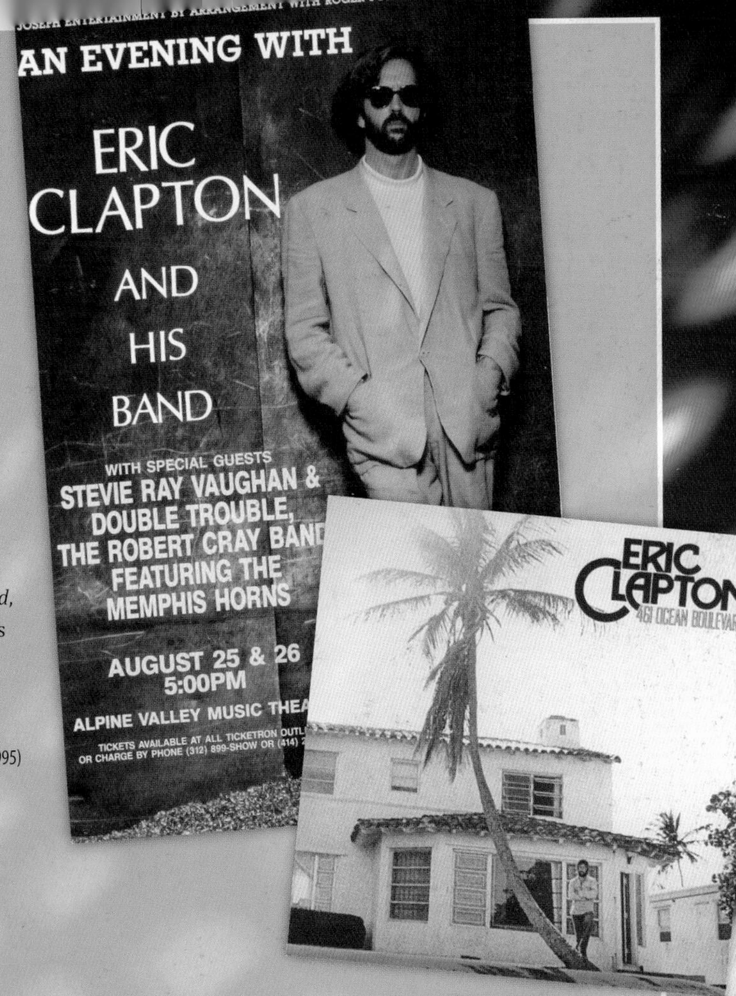

AN EVENING WITH
ERIC CLAPTON
AND HIS BAND
WITH SPECIAL GUESTS
STEVIE RAY VAUGHAN &
DOUBLE TROUBLE,
THE ROBERT CRAY BAND
FEATURING THE
MEMPHIS HORNS
AUGUST 25 & 26
5:00PM
ALPINE VALLEY MUSIC THEA
ERIC CLAPTON
461 OCEAN BOULEVARD

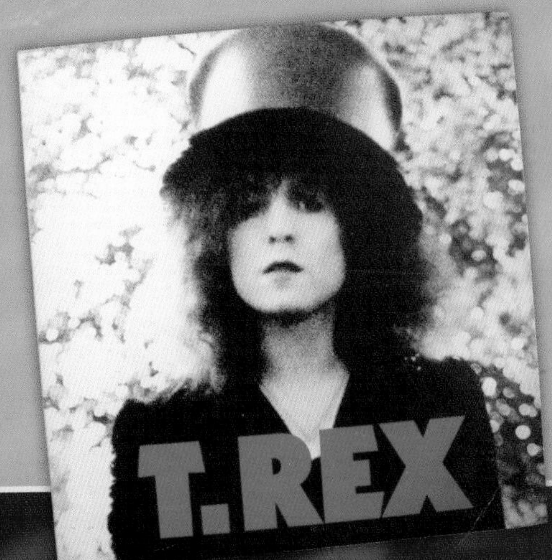

Ballrooms of Mars BY T REX (1972)

A lustrous lyric, a lush melody, and the promise of an interstellar boogie.

Dance to the Bop BY GENE VINCENT (1957)

A frenzied rocker tinged by country-fied guitars, Vincent's final classic 45.

EN DOWN SO LONG THAT THE GUTTER LOOKS LIKE UP—
ONGS OF DEPRESSION AND USELESSNESS

In a Broken Dream BY PYTHON LEE JACKSON (1972)

With his regular gig aboard the Jeff Beck Group at a standstill, and his first solo album still awaiting release, Rod Stewart was happy to pick up work wherever he could find it. So when D.J. John Peel called, asking if he'd fancy laying down some guide vocals for a band called Python Lee Jackson, Stewart was happy to oblige. He even agreed to be paid in carpeting for his car. But he wasn't so sanguine three years later. The best of the three songs he recorded with the band, "In A Broken Dream," was riding high up both the British and American charts, buoyant on the brilliance of the most recognizable voice in contemporary rock—and Stewart wasn't owed a penny in royalties. He'd long got shot of the carpeting, as well. "I was conned," he snarled.

Ballad of a Thin Man

BY BOB DYLAN (1965)

Ever the friendly neighborhood paranoiac, Rolling Stone Brian Jones was convinced that Dylan wrote this song about him.

Take Me Out

BY FRANZ FERDINAND (2004)

"This song is about the tensions between two people, in a sexual sense," says composer Alex Kapranos. "That situation when two people are in love with each other but neither will admit it, as if they'd take rejection over acceptance just to end the tension in the situation."

Bob Dylan

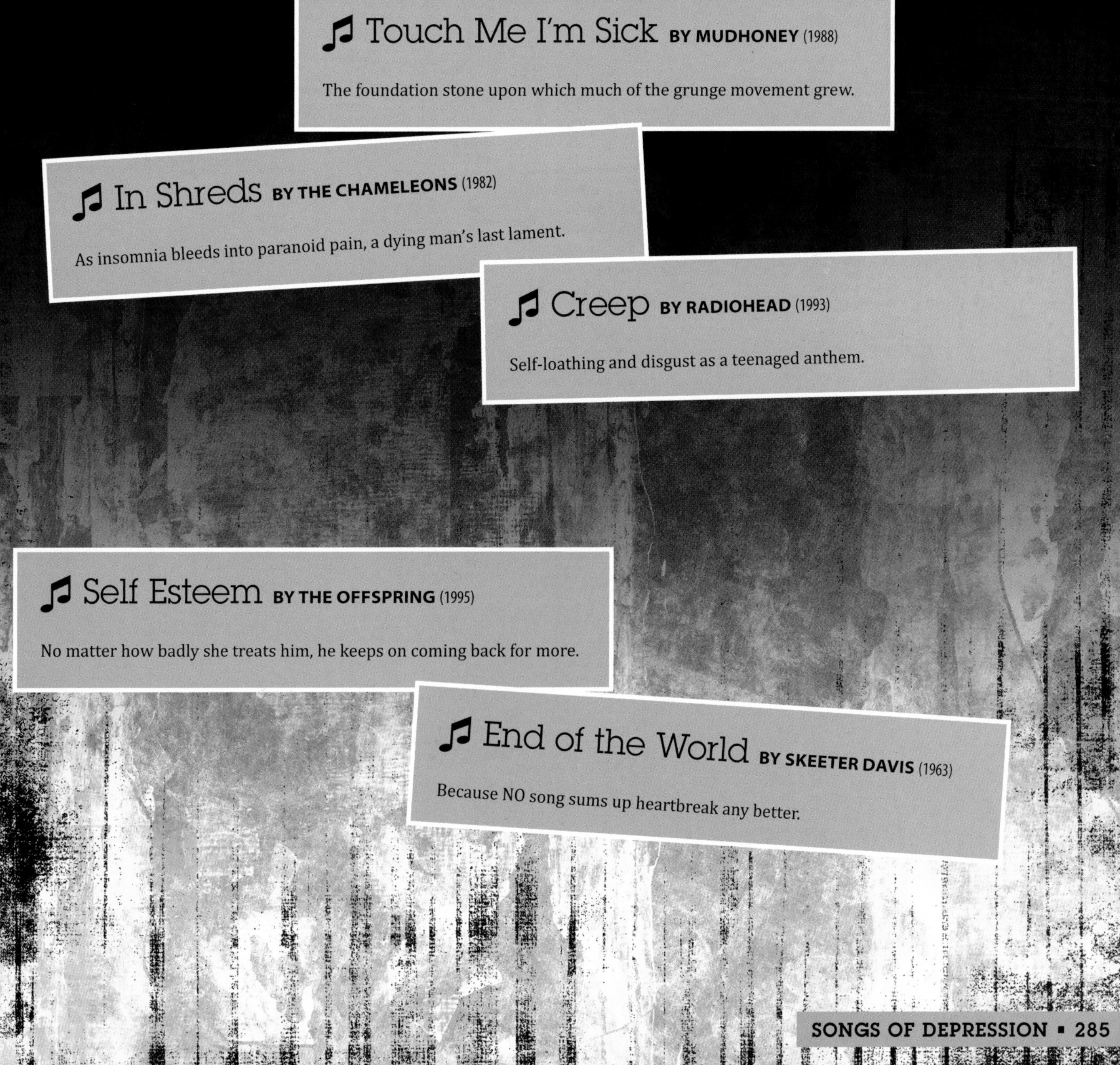

♫ Touch Me I'm Sick **BY MUDHONEY** (1988)

The foundation stone upon which much of the grunge movement grew.

♫ In Shreds **BY THE CHAMELEONS** (1982)

As insomnia bleeds into paranoid pain, a dying man's last lament.

♫ Creep **BY RADIOHEAD** (1993)

Self-loathing and disgust as a teenaged anthem.

♫ Self Esteem **BY THE OFFSPRING** (1995)

No matter how badly she treats him, he keeps on coming back for more.

♫ End of the World **BY SKEETER DAVIS** (1963)

Because NO song sums up heartbreak any better.

DEAL ME ANOTHER ONE

Gambling is usually considered a country song staple, but the old demon cards have been dealt a few times in rock as well.

♫ Ace of Spades **BY MOTORHEAD** (1980)

Be careful who you play with!

♫ The Jack **BY AC/DC** (1975)

It's about a card game. It's about masturbation. It's about a disease. You choose, but please don't pick the scabs. The song's original title, incidentally, was "The Clap." It's about applause. It's about thunder. It's....

The lyrics make it seem so innocent. She's got the Jack, he's got the King... and then the band's vocalist, the late Bon Scott, explained what "the jack" really means. It's Australian slang for an STD. "We were living with this houseful of ladies who were all very friendly, and everyone in the band had got the jack. So we wrote this song and, the first time we did it on stage, they were all in the front row with no idea what was goin' to happen. When it came to repeatin' 'She's got the jack,' I pointed at them one after another."

♫ Deuce **BY KISS** (1974)

Gene Simmons wrote the song while riding a bus. "I heard the lick, the riff, the melody, the whole thing. 'Deuce' was written on a bass. It was a very linear song. As soon as the riff came, the first verse came, then I wrote the bridge, and then I wrote the chorus. We arranged it right on the spot and knew that it would be a staple for years. In fact, when we first went on tour with our first record, it was the opening song of the show and we would come back for encores and not have any songs left and do 'Deuce' again. Then if we got a second encore we would do 'Deuce' again. Lyrically, I had no idea what I was talking about. Sometimes stuff means a lot, sometimes it means nothing."

Kiss

The Joker BY THE STEVE MILLER BAND (1974)

IN HIS OWN WORDS—STEVE MILLER (Vocalist, Composer, Guitarist): "I knew every vaudeville hall in the United States, and was playing each one of them three times a year. Then *The Joker* happened, we had just finished a 60-city tour and were just starting another one—that's the way we booked them. 'The Joker' was the #1 record in the country, and we were playing 3,000 seat halls."

Deal BY THE GRATEFUL DEAD (1981)

Just another great gambling anthem by the Dead.

DAVID BOWIE—PIN UPS

In 1973, looking to gain the upper hand during a contract dispute with his music publisher, David Bowie headed off to France to record a new album—and didn't write a note of new music in the process. Instead, he recorded an LP's worth of his favorite Sixties oldies and, whether you enjoy Bowie's music or not, you have to admit that he had very good taste. For anybody keeping score, just two songs from the Bowie LP didn't make the 1,000—the Who's "Anyway Anyhow Anywhere" and the Merseys' "Sorrow."

♫ See Emily Play BY PINK FLOYD (1967)

Pink Floyd's first major hit single was written by Syd Barrett, following what may or may not have been a psychedelic experience. "I was sleeping in the woods one night, after a gig somewhere, when I saw this girl appear before me. That girl is Emily."

Indeed she was. According to Floydian apocryphia, the 16-year-old Honorable Emily Kennet was a familiar sight around the club circuit, where regulars at the U.F.O. Club nicknamed her "the Psychedelic Schoolgirl." Unfortunately, it is equally likely that this charming tale is as fanciful as so many of the others surrounding Syd Barrett's time with the Floyd.

FREDERICK BANNISTER PRESENTS PINK FLOYD THE STEVE MILLER BAND CAPTAIN BEEFHEART ROY HARPER AND LINDA LEWIS AT KNEBWORTH JULY 5th 1975
ALL ROADS LEAD TO KNEBWORTH · PINK FLOYD · 1975
04 HeritageCoin.com

Mick Farren, vocalist with those other U.F.O. regulars, the Deviants, explains, "when not playing, I used to oversee the door and run the security at U.F.O., and I never heard of the Hon. Emily, who I would absolutely have noticed since she would have been a bust waiting to happen. The cops would have liked nothing better that to nail the organizers for contributing to the delinquency, etc, etc. She could have been a Syd schoolgirl groupie, but she never hung out at the club."

In truth, of course, it doesn't matter whether Emily really did play or not. The show for which she was invoked, a major London event titled Games for May, was arguably the single most important show Pink Floyd had played, the moment which blew them out of the last lingering confines of their underground cult, and into the mainstream-at-large. "See Emily Play" only narrowly missed out on a Top 5 placing; the band had been "discovered" by the serious newspaper critics; they even received the blessing of the Beatles, as the two bands dropped in on each other's sessions, to see how things were progressing.

Pink Floyd

♫ Shape of Things BY THE YARDBIRDS (1966)

One of the most significant records of the sixties, by one of the most significant bands. "As far as the Yardbirds go, my musical utopia was back in early '66, before all the hang-ups," recalls guitarist Jeff Beck. "We were all on the threshold of this new thing. The Yardbirds were the very first psychedelic band really, just an experimental psychedelic crazy bunch of loonies from England. That's the strongest thing we had, this underground thing. You couldn't buy it in the shops, you couldn't go and see it on TV. You had to be there."

♫ Everything's Alright BY THE MOJOS (1964)

History recalls the Mojos as one of the Liverpool-based bands that didn't follow the Beatles to glory. But their one hit was worth as much as any period Fab waxing.

♫ Don't Bring Me Down BY THE PRETTY THINGS (1964)

The second U.K. hit for the band that out-Stoned the Stones when it came to titillating the tabloids… but, incredibly, an American miss. Bet you all feel very silly about that now.

♫ Rosalyn BY THE PRETTY THINGS (1964)

Another explosion of dirty-ass R&B from the filthiest band of them all.

♫ Friday on My Mind BY THE EASYBEATS (1966)

The lone U.S. hit for the Australian Invaders.

♫ Here Comes the Night BY THEM (1965)

Van Morrison has never sounded so impassioned or mean, while Them became the standard bearers for a host of future garage bands.

STEREO PAS 71005
THEM
featuring
HERE COMES THE NIGHT

I Can't Explain BY THE WHO (1965)

"I really like my first few songs because they were an incredible surprise," Pete Townshend later stated. "Through writing I discovered how to free my subconscious. I discovered that I had this ability to just sit down and scribble things out and think that I was writing consciously. But the real meaning was coming from somewhere else that I had absolutely no control over. Like odd things would give me a complete surprise. I suppose I was surprised by how obviously observant I was without ever really being conscious of it."

When he completed "I Can't Explain," he says, "I thought it was about a boy who can't explain to a girl that he's falling in love with her. But two weeks later, I looked at the lyrics and they meant something completely different. I began to see just what an outpouring that song was. Then I realized that's why Bob Dylan doesn't know what to say when people ask him about one of his songs—because he doesn't fucking know what it's all about. I know, because I'm on the outside reacting to it, and whatever it means to me is it. But he doesn't. How could he? All he did was write it."

Where Have All the Good Times Gone? BY THE KINKS (1965)

Back when you were a kid, you probably got sick of hearing your parents quote this doughty refrain. Now that you're *not* a kid, you know exactly what they were on about.

London Boys BY DAVID BOWIE (1967)

Often described as little more than a rewrite of the Kinks' "Big Black Smoke" (853), but a lot darker and more personal, too. Bowie was five years away from stardom when he wrote this, but he came close to rerecording it in 1973, as a recurrent link between the covers elsewhere on *Pin Ups*; and revisited it again in 2000 for the unreleased *Toy* album.

I Wish You Would BY THE YARDBIRDS (1965)

A wiry cover of the Billy Boy Arnold blues number, and an early showcase for the young Eric Clapton.

READ ALL ABOUT IT—
ROCK GOES TO THE LIBRARY
Literature into lyrics.

♫ Sympathy for the Devil **BY THE ROLLING STONES** (1968)

Written after Jagger read Soviet author Mikhail Bulgakov's *The Master and Margarita*, many people prefer to view "Sympathy for the Devil" as unadorned autobiography. Even today, as many legends and myths adhere to this feast of percussion and yelping as to the rest of the Stones' output combined.

♫ Beautiful Day **BY U2** (2000)

Bono and co dig into James Joyce's *Ulysses*.

♫ The Ghost of Tom Joad **BY BRUCE SPRINGSTEEN** (1995)

Tom Joad is a character from Steinbeck's *The Grapes of Wrath*; his ghost has also been summoned by Woody Guthrie.

♫ We Are the Dead **BY DAVID BOWIE** (1974)

David Bowie was planning a musical version of George Orwell's *1984* when he wrote this song, only to be stymied by Orwell's estate—"why would anyone want to set that book to music?" asked his widow, Sonia. Several of the scheduled songs, including "We Are the Dead," "1984," and "Big Brother," were salvaged for Bowie's next LP, *Diamond Dogs*.

♫ Starless BY KING CRIMSON (1974)

A doomladen instrumental titled from the opening g lines of Dylan Thomas' *Under Milk Wood*—"Starless and bible Black."

♫ 1984 BY SPIRIT (1970)

Orwell that ends well... A lot of songs have been written about George Orwell's year to end all years, and in the decades leading up to it, there was a certain amount of trepidation as well. But then 1984 came and went, the same as any other year, and we wonder what all the fuss was about. "1984" helps to remind us.

♫ The Jean Genie BY DAVID BOWIE (1972)

A play on the name of playwright Jean Genet, the song may also have been written about Marc Bolan or Iggy Pop, depending upon which rumor you prefer. Bowie himself insisted it was a straightforward rocker that he wrote for actress Cyrinde Foxe while they were hanging out in her apartment one day, and she challenged him to write a song. So he did, a pounding riff-rider dedicated to "a white-trash kind of trailer park kid... the closet intellectual who wouldn't want the world to know that he reads."

♫ Oxford Comma BY VAMPIRE WEEKEND (2008)

The Oxford comma is the name for any comma employed prior to a grammatical conjunction (and, or, not) that precedes the final item in a list of three or more items—as in, and, or, or not, in fact.

♫ Here's Where the Story Ends BY THE SUNDAYS (1990)

One of the most promising young bands of the early 1990s, their first single celebrated the final page.

LIVING ON THE EDGE—

MAKING THE BEST OF A LOUSY ADDRESS

BILL GRAHAM AND BARRY FEY PRESENT
THE ROLLING STONES
JANUARY 21 & 22
HONOLULU INTERNATIONAL CENTER

It was Joe Walsh, in his stardom-scathing "Life's Been Good," who painted the archetypal portrait of a rock star and his mansions. He has one, it's huge, and his people tell him it's nice. He hasn't had the chance yet to see it for himself.

But not everybody is as fortunate (or wealthy) as Joe, so let's hear it for the folk who make the most of the homes that don't make it into song....

♫ Gimme Shelter BY THE ROLLING STONES (1969)

Foreboding, forbidding, and chilling, even before you heard the lyrics, "Gimme Shelter" looked around at the state of America in the last years of the '60s, and emerged pregnant instead with all the menace that seemed to be gathering round the Stones. Two years after, "Gimme Shelter" would be lifted for the title of the Stones' Altamont movie, and that has colored its reputation even further. Even before that, it was uneasy listening.

♫ Refugees BY VAN DER GRAAF GENERATOR (1971)

Peter Hammill's most timeless melody, heartbreaking and hopeful hand in hand, and home a distant point on an unknown horizon.

♫ Heartbreak Hotel BY ELVIS PRESLEY (1956)

Presley's first single for RCA was written by Tommy Durden and Mae Boren Axton, after they read of a young suicide whose farewell note included the line "I walk a lonely street."

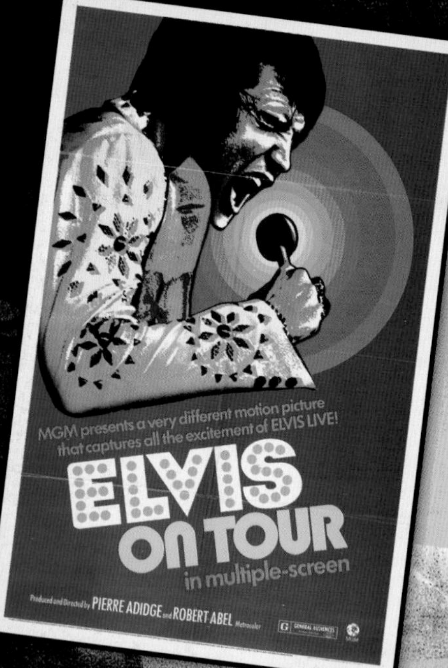

MGM presents a very different motion picture that captures all the excitement of ELVIS LIVE!
ELVIS ON TOUR
in multiple-screen
Produced and Directed by PIERRE ADIDGE and ROBERT ABEL

♫ Badlands BY BRUCE SPRINGSTEEN (1978)

Kicking off the Boss' *Darkness on the Edge of Town* album with a look inside the darkest edges of all.

♫ In the Ghetto BY ELVIS PRESLEY (1969)

After too many years making lousy, bland records, Mac Davis' "In the Ghetto"—a social protest number originally titled "Vicious Circle"—was the song that suggested Elvis was on his way back.

♫ Debris BY THE FACES (1971)

A Ronnie Lane jewel, and a bittersweet slice of lost London life.

♫ Bedsitter Images BY AL STEWART (1967)

Bedsitters are a peculiarly English institution, cut-price one-room housing that makes even the average studio apartment look luxurious. But they were also the staple of teenaged student life for decades, and there's more secrets engrained in their wallpaper than in homes a hundred times their size.

♫ Pleasant Valley Sunday BY THE MONKEES (1967)

Sunny on the surface, but there's also something very Stepford Wives-like lurking under the surface.

The Monkees

Dead End Street BY THE KINKS (1965)

A celebration of English working class life and attitudes, made all the more poignant by the oncoming rush of "improvements" that would eventually destroy an entire way of life.

Memory Motel BY THE ROLLING STONES (1976)

Heartbreak Hotel is where you go when your lover leaves you. Memory Motel is the place to remember the good times.

Living Next Door to Alice BY SMOKEY (1976)

Written by British tunesmiths Nicky Chinn and Mike Chapman, alongside 502, 641 and 674, and originally recorded by New Zealand's New World, the answer to that perennial question of what to do when the girl next door moves away. You fall in love with her friend, of course.

Hell Is Round the Corner BY TRICKY (1995)

An unforgettable warning from one of the founding fathers of the Trip-Hop storm.

Lake of Fire BY MEAT PUPPETS (1984)

An apocalyptic reminder of where bad folk go to live when they die. Nirvana later covered the song during their MTV *Unplugged* broadcast.

The Dark End of the Street BY LINDA RONSTADT (1974)

A Muscle Shoals soul classic, deliciously reignited by Ronstadt, the dialogue between an adulterer and his lover has never been captured so vividly.

Stoney End BY LAURA NYRO (1966)

Best known for Barbra Streisand's hit version (it also titled her 1971 LP), Nyro's fragile original chills with its simplicity.

THE LOOK OF LOVE

(PART THREE) WHY CAN'T YOU PEOPLE SING ABOUT SOMETHING ELSE FOR A CHANGE?

Indeed!

♫ Suite: Judy Blue Eyes BY CROSBY STILLS & NASH (1969)

Steven Stills' dedication to then-girlfriend Judy Collins. "It started out as a long narrative poem about my relationship with Judy.... It poured out of me over many months and filled several notebooks. I had a hell of a time getting the music to fit. I was left with all these pieces of song and I said, 'Let's sing them together and call it a suite,' because they were all about the same thing and they led up to the same point."

♫ New Rose BY THE DAMNED (1977)

Beating out the Sex Pistols by mere weeks, the first ever Punk Rock single.

♫ Sunshine of Your Love BY CREAM (1967)

According to Eric Clapton, what became the foundation for "Sunshine of Your Love" was "strictly a dedication to Jimi"—a wheel that turned full circle when, following Cream's decision to split, Hendrix took to featuring the song in his own set, as a tribute to the trio.

♫ Good Vibrations BY THE BEACH BOYS (1966)

"My mother used to tell me about vibrations," Brian Wilson once explained. "I didn't really understand too much of what she meant when I was a boy. It scared me, the word 'vibrations'—to think that invisible feelings existed. She also told me about dogs that would bark at some people, but wouldn't bark at others, and so it came to pass that we talked about good vibrations."

♫ Sad Eyed Lady of the Lowlands **BY BOB DYLAN** (1966)

Upon release in 1966, the closing track from Dylan's epochal *Blonde by Blonde* was, at over thirteen minutes, the longest single song ever released by a so-called rock or pop artist.

♫ Devoted To You **BY THE EVERLY BROTHERS** (1958)

The sound of summer, for 1958 and every year since then.

♫ Make Me Smile (Come Up and See Me) **BY STEVE HARLEY AND COCKNEY REBEL** (1975)

Cockney Rebel never meant much to American audiences, but this song knows no borders.

♫ Hello I Love You **BY THE DOORS** (1968)

Riding a riff that the early Kinks could have conjured, the Doors rock like a garage band.

♫ Three Steps to Heaven **BY EDDIE COCHRAN** (1959)

Amazingly, this Cochran classic failed to make the American chart!

♫ Since I've Been Loving You **BY LED ZEPPELIN** (1970)

A bluesy classic that was originally intended for Zeppelin's second album—but was dropped in favor of "Whole Lotta Love." It made it onto their third, instead.

♫ For You BY JUDY TZUKE (1979)

So simple, but so multi-faceted, brought to the world by Elton John's Rocket label.

♫ Sweet Child of Mine BY GUNS N' ROSES (1987)

Written by Axl Rose for his soon-to-be wife Erin Everly—daughter of Don.

♫ A Lover's Concerto BY THE TOYS (1965)

Recognize the melody? Yeah, it's Bach's "Minuet in G"—only Bach didn't really write it. The real composer was Christian Petzold.

♫ Close Watch BY JOHN CALE (1975)

The former Velvet Undergrounder has recorded this tender jewel twice, for his *Helen of Troy* album in 1975, and half a decade later for *Music for a New Society*.

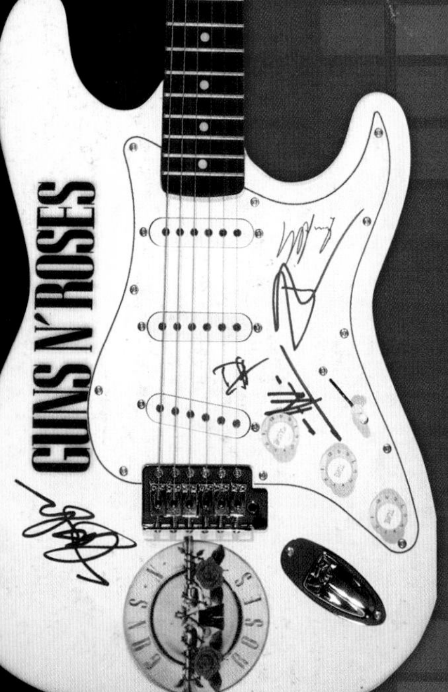

♫ Maybe I'm Amazed BY PAUL MCCARTNEY (1970)

From a debut album packed with snatches, ideas, and songs that the Beatles rejected, Macca's first bona fide solo classic.

AND FINALLY…
WHERE DO WE GO FROM HERE?

Rock'n'roll used to be a kid's game, the province of the young, loud, and snotty. The idea of anybody continuing to rock past thirty was something we'd snigger about behind raised palms, if we could even conceive of such a concept. But even the first stars of the 1980s have passed that watershed now and... well, yes, some of them do look very funny indeed.

A lot of them are still going strong as well, though, and Bob Dylan in his seventies remains as electrifying as he was... ooh, way back in his forties, at least.

♫ Johnny Mekon BY RADIO STARS (1977)

IN HIS OWN WORDS—MARTIN GORDON (composer): "'Johnny Mekon' began life as a two chord jam to assess the abilities of would-be guitarists. Then I added some other musical bits, and some random words. After hearing Brian Eno's *Taking Tiger Mountain by Strategy* album, I thought I would also try the random cut-up approach to words, and recorded one such version. But the appeal quickly palled (the following day) and so the tragic tale of a onetime rock star living on his former glories emerged. I finalized the details… satchels, school gates… while associating with glamour models perhaps there was something in the air. Osmosis, that sort of thing. People seemed to like it, I stuck a Heavy Metal pastiche on the end, and they liked it even more, even though it unbalanced the song a bit. Johnny is still trundled out at functions and the occasional Radio Stars 32nd anniversary gig."

♫ Old Wild Men BY 10CC (1974)

"Comical little geezer, you'll look funny when you're 50," Mick Jagger was warned during his movie debut *Performance*, in 1968, and Jagger no doubt agreed with that assessment. So did 10cc, when they cut "Old Wild Men," and envisioned nursing homes packed with aged popsters, strumming their oldies on withered strings and cracked skin drums.

♫ Garden Party BY RICK NELSON (1972)

Former 50s pop idol Nelson was on the comeback trail when he hit Madison Square Garden in 1971, performing a new breed of fine country rock… except the audience didn't think it was so fine. They still wanted to hear the oldies, and Nelson was booed offstage. He, however, was not deterred. Writing "Garden Party" in the aftermath, he concluded it with a lyric that all old rockers should have tattooed to their private parts. "If memories are all I sing, I'd rather drive a truck."

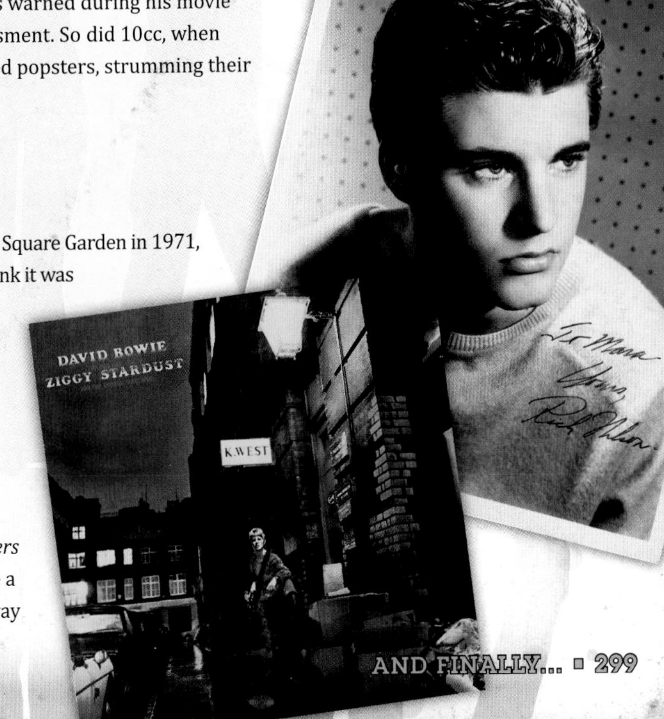

♫ Rock'n'Roll Suicide BY DAVID BOWIE (1972)

From the breakthrough The Rise and Fall of *Ziggy Stardust and the Spiders From Mars* LP, a reminder that, if all else fails… live fast, die young, leave a beautiful corpse. Although judging by the looks of some of people, it's way too late for that….

PHOTO CREDITS

Heritage Auctions (www.ha.com): 20, 21, 25, 32, 35, 37, 41, 43, 46, 47, 48, 52, 54, 57, 60, 63, 66, 69, 74, 75, 77, 82, 83, 86, 87, 88, 95, 96, 97, 98, 99, 101, 102, 104, 105, 109, 110, 112, 113, 115, 117, 118, 119, 121, 124, 125, 127, 129, 131, 134, 136, 137, 138, 139, 140, 143, 144, 145, 147, 149, 150, 151, 152, 153, 154, 155, 156, 157, 159, 162, 163, 164, 165, 166, 167, 168, 169, 170, 171, 172, 174, 176, 177, 180, 181, 189, 190, 191, 194, 196, 198, 199, 200, 202, 204, 205, 207, 210, 211, 212, 214, 215, 216, 217, 218, 223, 226, 227, 228, 232, 234, 236, 237, 238, 239, 240, 241, 242, 243, 244, 245, 246, 247, 248, 249, 250, 251, 254, 255, 260, 261, 262, 263, 265, 266, 268, 269, 270, 271, 272, 273, 274, 275, 276, 277, 278, 279, 281, 283, 284, 286, 287, 288, 289, 290, 291, 294, 296, 297, 298, 299

Getty Images (www.gettyimages.com): 28 (Ebet Roberts/Redferns); 31 (GAB Archive/Redferns); 32 (Michael Ochs Archives/Stringer); 33 (Naki/Redferns); 34 (Paul Natkin/WireImage); 41 (Michael Ochs Archives/Stringer); 42 (Kevin Cummins/Premium Archive); 44 (Michael Ochs Archives/Stringer); 46 (Lorne Resnick/Redferns); 47 (Richard E. Aaron/Redferns); 55 (Terry O'Neil); 59 (Tim Mosenfelder/Getty Images Entertainment); 62 (Peter Still/Referns); 68 (David Montgomery/Hulton Archive); 78 (Hutton Archive/Stringer); 79 (Bertrand Guay/Staff/AFP); 90 (Keystone/Stringer/Hutton Archive); 91 (Jorgen Angel/Redferns); 93 (Richard E. Aaron/Redferns); 103 (Marc Hauser Photography Ltd/Hutton Archive); 104 (K & K Ulf Kruger OHG/Redferns); 114 (Chris Walter/WireImage); 116 (Kevin Cummins/Premium Archive); 124 (Michael Ochs Archives/Stringer); 126 (Petra Niemeier – K&K/Redferns); 128 (Jan Persson/Redferns); 131 (Mick Hutson/Redferns); 133 (Jan Persson/Redferns); 140 (David Redfern/Redferns); 149 (Michael Ochs Archives/Stringer); 150 (Bob King/Redferns); 157 (Estate of Keith Morris/Redferns); 161 (Michael Putland/Hulton Archive); 164 (Ron Howard/Redferns); 167 (Paul Ryan/Michael Ochs Archives); 171 (Kevin Cummins/Premium Archive); 173 (Jim Steinfeldt/Michael Ochs Archives), 176 (Waring Abbott/Premium Archive); 180 (Fin Costello/Redferns); 185 (Anna Krajec/Michael Ochs Archives); 188 (Hulton Archive/Stringer), 190 (Kevin Cummins/Premium Archive), 199 (Jeffrey Mayer/WireImage); 201 (Richard E. Aaron/Redferns); 202 (Michael Ochs/Michael Ochs Archives); 202 (GAB Archive/Redferns); 203 (Terry Lott/Sony Music Archive); 205 (Beth Gwinn/Redferns); 213 (Bob King/Redferns), 222 (Keystone/Stringer/Hulton Archive); 224 (David Redfern/Redferns); 229 (Richard E. Aaron/Redferns); 233 (David Redfern/Redferns); 234 (Michael Ochs Archives/Stringer), 239 (Jeffrey Mayer/WireImage); 241 (Bob Thomas/Bob Thomas Sports Photography); 245 (Larry Hulst/Michael Ochs Archives); 251 (Archive Photos); 264 (Gijsbert Hanekroot/Redferns); 268 (Jim Steinfeldt/Michael Ochs Archives); 272 (Jon Sievert/Premium Archive); 281 (Roberta Bayley/Redferns); 284 (Sony BMG Music Entertainment); 286 (Fin Costello/Redferns); 288 (Andrew Whittuck/Redferns); 294 (Michael Ochs Archives); 295 (David Redferns/Redferns)

TOP 1,000 BY ARTIST

C

D

E

F

G

H

I

J

K

L

M

N

O

P

Q

R

S

T

U

V

W

X

Y

Z

TOP 1,000 BY YEAR

1955 - Bill Haley & the Comets – Rock Around the Clock, 189
1955 - Bo Diddley – Bo Diddley, 156
1955 - Bo Diddley – I'm a Man, 86
1955 - Chuck Berry – Maybelline, 261
1956 - Buddy Holly – That'll Be the Day, 191
1956 - Elvis Presley – Heartbreak Hotel, 293
1956 - Elvis Presley – Hound Dog, 75
1956 - Elvis Presley – I Want You, I Need You, I Love You, 181
1956 - Elvis Presley – Love Me Tender, 166
1956 - Frankie Lymon & The Teenagers – Why Do Fools Fall in Love, 77
1956 - Gene Vincent & His Blue Caps – Be Bop a Lula, 181
1956 - Gene Vincent & His Blue Caps – Blue Jean Bop, 282
1956 - Gene Vincent & His Blue Caps – Race with the Devil, 275
1957 - Buddy Holly – Everyday, 191
1957 - Buddy Holly – Not Fade Away, 191
1957 - Buddy Holly – Oh Boy, 191
1957 - Buddy Holly – Peggy Sue, 191
1957 - Chas McDevitt Skiffle Group (Featuring Nancy Whiskey) – Freight Train, 172
1957 - Chuck Berry – Rock and Roll Music, 147
1957 - Elvis Presley – All Shook Up, 87
1957 - Elvis Presley – Jailhouse Rock, 254
1957 - Everly Brothers – Wake Up Little Susie, 110
1957 - Gene Vincent & His Blue Caps – Dance to the Bop, 283
1957 - Jerry Lee Lewis – Great Balls of Fire, 96
1957 - Jerry Lee Lewis – Whole Lotta Shakin' Goin' On, 87
1957 - Little Richard – Lucille, 166
1957 - Little Richard – The Girl Can't Help It, 279
1957 - Little Richard – Tutti Frutti, 88
1958 - Buddy Holly – Maybe Baby, 181
1958 - Buddy Holly – Rave On, 191
1958 - Chantels – Maybe, 218
1958 - Chuck Berry – Carol, 263
1958 - Chuck Berry – Johnny B Goode, 166
1958 - Chuck Berry – Sweet Little Rock'n'Roller, 147
1958 - Cliff Richard – Move It, 148
1958 - Danny and the Juniors – At the Hop, 281
1958 - Eddie Cochran – 20 Flight Rock, 181
1958 - Eddie Cochran – Summertime Blues, 75
1958 - Everly Brothers – All I Have to Do Is Dream, 205
1958 - Everly Brothers – Devoted To You, 297
1958 - Poni Tails – Born Too Late, 190
1958 - Teddy Bears – To Know Him Is to Love Him, 206
1958 - Vince Taylor – Brand New Cadillac, 84
1959 - Buddy Holly – It Doesn't Matter Anymore, 191
1959 - Buddy Holly – It's So Easy, 191
1959 - Chuck Berry – Back in the USA, 227
1959 - Chuck Berry – Little Queenie, 116
1959 - Chuck Berry – Memphis, Tennessee, 211
1959 - Eddie Cochran – Something Else, 83
1959 - Eddie Cochran – Three Stars, 194
1959 - Eddie Cochran – Three Steps to Heaven, 297
1959 - Fats Domino – I'm Ready, 181
1959 - Ray Charles – What'd I Say?, 88
1960 - Bo Diddley – Roadrunner, 83
1960 - Chuck Berry – Bye Bye Johnny, 99
1960 - Everly Brothers – Cathy's Clown, 214
1960 - Everly Brothers – When Will I Be Loved, 77
1960 - Hollywood Argyles – Alley Oop, 138
1960 - Ricky Valance – Tell Laura I Love Her, 55
1960 - Shadows – Apache, 170
1960 - Ventures – Walk Don't Run, 170
1961 - Everly Brothers – Ebony Eyes, 167
1961 - John Lennon – Stand By Me, 207
1961 - John Leyton – Johnny Remember Me, 53
1961 - Johnny Kidd & The Pirates – Shaking All Over, 87
1962 - Carole King – It Might As Well Rain Until September, 139
1962 - Cliff Richard – Bachelor Boy, 277
1962 - Cliff Richard – The Next Time, 47
1962 - Everly Brothers – Crying in the Rain, 140
1962 - Tornadoes – Telstar, 40
1963 - Beach Boys – Little Deuce Coupe, 84
1963 - Bob Dylan – A Hard Rain's A-Gonna Fall, 171
1963 - Bob Dylan – Blowing in the Wind, 74
1963 - Bob Dylan – Don't Think Twice, It's Alright, 57
1963 - Chantays – Pipeline, 170
1963 - Crystals – Da Doo Ron Ron, 64
1963 - Crystals – Then He Kissed Me, 75
1963 - Dave Clark 5 – Glad All Over, 101
1963 - Gene Pitney – 24 Hours from Tulsa, 229
1963 - Jan and Dean – Surf City, 187
1963 - Lesley Gore – It's My Party, 49
1963 - Skeeter Davis – End of the World, 285
1963 - Swinging Blue Jeans – Hippy Hippy Shake, 87
1964 - Animals – House of the Rising Sun, 258
1964 - Beach Boys – Fun Fun Fun, 85
1964 - Beach Boys – I Get Around, 246
1964 - Beatles – A Hard Day's Night, 234
1964 - Beatles – I Feel Fine, 156
1964 - Cilla Black – Anyone Who Had a Heart, 101
1964 - Dixie Cups – Chapel of Love, 277
1964 - Gerry & the Pacemakers – Ferry Cross the Mersey, 102
1964 - Jan and Dean – Dead Man's Curve, 84
1964 - Johnny Allen – Promised Land, 162
1964 - Kingsmen – Louie Louie, 72
1964 - Kinks – All Day and All of the Night, 155
1964 - Kinks – You Really Got Me, 100
1964 - Manfred Mann – Do Wah Diddy Diddy, 64
1964 - Marianne Faithfull – As Tears Go By, 273
1964 - Mojos – Everything's Alright, 289
1964 - Moody Blues – Go Now, 100
1964 - Nashville Teens – Tobacco Road, 230
1964 - Phil Ochs – Talking Airplane Disaster Blues, 168
1964 - Pretty Things – Don't Bring Me Down, 289
1964 - Pretty Things – Rosalyn, 289
1964 - Rolling Stones – I Just Wanna Make Love to You, 166
1964 - Sandy Shaw – Girl Don't Come, 49
1964 - Searchers – Needles and Pins, 102
1964 - Shangri-Las – Leader of the Pack, 43
1964 - Shangri-Las – Remember Walking in the Sand, 187
1964 - Twinkle – Terry, 54